J. Ranade IBM Series

VSE/ESA

Performance Management and Fine Tuning

Bill Merrow

Foreword by Pete Clark

McGraw-Hill, Inc.

New York San Francisco Washington, D.C. Auckland
Bogotá Caracas Lisbon London Madrid Mexico City
Milan Montreal New Delhi San Juan
Singapore Sydney Tokyo Toronto

Library of Congress Cataloging-in-Publication Data

Merrow, Bill.
    VSE/ESA : performance management and fine tuning / Bill Merrow;
foreword by Pete Clark.
    Includes index.
    ISBN 0-07-041753-9
    1. Operating systems (Computers) 2. DOS/VSE. I. Title.
QA76.76.063M46 1993
005.4'429—dc20   92-33251
                                        CIP

1 2 3 4 5 6 7 8 9 0 DOC/DOC 9 8 7 6 5 4 3 2

ISBN   0-07-041753-9

*The sponsoring editor for this book was Jerry Papke, the editing
supervisor was Jim Halston, and the production supervisor was
Suzanne W. Babeuf.*

Printed and bound by R. R. Donnelley & Sons Company.

Contents

Foreword

It started in 1964 and was intended to be an interim operating system, while certain strategic "situations" with a somewhat more complex operating system could be remedied. It was initially called DOS, for Disk Operating System, and, although it was temporary, it grew to become VSE, one of the most successful mainframe operating systems in the world.
So much for business planning and strategic decision making.

But why did VSE, from such humble beginnings, become a mainframe legend? Well, probably because it was in the right place at the right time, presenting cost-effective business solutions. But most likely, VSE was successful because of the people that insisted that it survive. It continued to evolve because of dedicated users, developers, planners, and support personnel whose involvement went beyond what was expected, and occasionally ventured beyond what might be considered prudent. To these pioneers goes the credit for VSE's survival and success.

How does one measure success in today's mainframe environment? There are currently 20,000 to 25,000 VSE installed systems with as many software licenses. But VSE's success can be measured in other ways as well. There is little doubt that VSE has the best return on investment of the three mainframe operating systems, primarily because of its relatively small and efficient development process, and the large number of product licenses. VSE is the only system that continues year after year to add new users, new software licenses, and new hardware platforms.

Why does VSE continue to attract new users to the mainframe computing environment? Because it possesses the ability to support a large "seamless" growth path for an expanding data processing environment. VSE can run on the smallest mainframe in single system mode, or on the largest mainframe under PRSM or VM.

Ultimately, the continued viability of mainframe systems may rest with VSE. VSE is easy to install, easy to operate, and is reasonably priced. It is an attractive and cost effective entry point for new mainframe users, with extraordinary capacity and growth options.

How far can you take VSE performance? With inventive, committed users, a host of intelligent software suppliers, and a strong, committed VSE development group, there may be no performance end for VSE.

VSE users are progressive, highly motivated people, unencumbered by a large business mentality. They have an "attitude" in the truest sense of the word. They know no limits, and are unwilling to accept limits imposed by others. This devilish need to smash through lines that have been defined makes for successful performance tuning. Most of the world categorizes performance issues as easy, difficult, or impossible. The only difference from the VSE perspective is that "impossible" takes a little longer and costs a little more.

There are many different opinions concerning potential VSE performance levels. Don't accept any of them. No one has reached the ultimate performance level, but many have expanded the performance envelope, and continue to do so.

VSE performance and tuning tasks can range from the simple to the complex. Performance and tuning techniques that produce excellent results on simpler systems work very well on complex systems, and visa versa. Tuning any VSE system will substantially improve throughput and responsiveness, regardless of hardware size or system complexity. A careful performance evaluation and implementation will maximize hardware and software resource usage.

All VSE users should periodically undertake a performance review of installed VSE systems. Why? Because application and system loads change. New features offer better ways of processing. Performance priorities require adjustments. And performance trade-offs made yesterday may not be appropriate today. Performance tuning means taking advantage of excess resources in one area to offset a resource shortage in another. As new applications and new releases are implemented, excess resources tend to disappear, and new trade-offs must be considered.

What kind of performance can one really expect from VSE? With a properly configured system, a CPU can run at 100% while maintaining excellent CICS response time. Users have been consistently able to go beyond VSE's performance limits because they have employed user extensions and third party vendor products. Selection of appropriate vendor software is an important consideration when tuning VSE.

The VSE software capabilities delivered with VSE/ESA versions 1.1, 1.2, and 1.3 offer the VSE user an opportunity to deliver performance levels that were difficult, if not totally unattainable, under previous releases. The "performance and tuning game" of VSE has been positively impacted by the delivery of VSE/ESA. Now is the time to focus on performance tuning.

One can never have too much performance related information. One can never consider too many inputs. Performance measurement and tuning means gathering as much information and ideas as possible, and making rational and logical decisions and implementations that have a positive effect on the system.

In many cases it has been the work of the users that has provided the creative ideas and demonstrated the progress in VSE tuning and capacity planning. Contained within this book are numerous references and examples straight "from the mouth of the user"-- real world experience by real world users.

Over the last many years a host of users, IBMers, vendors, and developers have participated in very frank discussions relative to VSE performance. The results of these discussions have had a profound effect on performance capabilities in many VSE installations. I hope that this book is just the beginning of a series of VSE information books that will relate that information to the VSE populace.

Reading this book once is not enough. So much valuable material is contained within this book that it will become a standard reference for all VSE users. I am certain that a copy will always be available in my reference library at home and at work.

May your VSE partitions never go RUR, may your CICS never encounter an LTA wait, may your real pages always be available, and may your first born boldly enter the world of VSE performance measurement and tuning.

Pete Clark
Chattanooga, TN.

Preface

Who is this book for?

The title of this book is *VSE/ESA: Performance Management and Fine Tuning*. It is designed to provide VSE systems programmers with the methods and data needed to analyze the performance of their systems, and to identify possible actions to rectify problems.

Most of the problems that are described, and the methods of correction apply to VSE/SP Version 2 and subsequent releases. Special emphasis is placed on tuning considerations that apply to VSE/ESA throughout the book. Also, the new VSE/ESA features and some of the VSE/SP to VSE/ESA conversion issues are discussed in a separate chapter (refer to chapter 4). Please note that we have been informal when referring to operating system components. Thus, the term POWER is used herein for the VSE/POWER component, and likewise the common usage CICS for VSE/CICS, and VTAM for ACF/VTAM. This is done because the short forms are the more familiar ones, and with all due respect for the formal names which are introduced where appropriate, included in the glossary, and also in the list of trademarks.

It is assumed that the reader is familiar with the basic objectives of the performance measurement and tuning process, and the parameters used to install and tailor their VSE system.

An overview of the philosophy and methodology utilized in this book is included to assist the reader in the performance management task. A detailed discussion of the control files, parameters, and commands used to manage typical VSE systems is provided to aid new VSE systems programmers in using this book. Sample *ASI* procedures are presented to illustrate performance benefits. This book addresses the VSE/SP and VSE/ESA operating systems. It covers the Systems Control Program (SCP), POWER, the VSE Librarian, and hardware aspects of tuning in detail.

Basic material on the tuning of VSAM, CICS, and VTAM is also included. Advanced information on VSAM concepts and tuning may be found in J. Ranade's book *VSAM: Performance, Design, and Fine Tuning.* Additional information on CICS may be found in S. Piggott's book *CICS: A Practical Guide to System Fine Tuning.*

General Performance Methodology and Philosophy

In general, performance tuning involves both *minimizing resource consumption* and *trading off one resource for another.* Tuning is often guided by data center policy to ensure that critical tasks get preferential treatment, deadlines are met, and that minimal service levels are not violated.

You meet the objective to minimize resource consumption by selecting system parameters and options that optimize resource usage for your hardware and software configuration. This book covers many resource management options related to tuning. Resource management objectives are also a factor in selecting hardware for upgrades, migrating to new releases of VSE, and in determining how new applications will be best run. Your knowledge of your hardware and software environment is the primary input to system tuning.

Resource tradeoffs are a factor in the daily operations in every data center. Whenever you hold one job in order to complete another, or alter task priorities from standard values, or change the number of available partitions or their classes, you are performing resource tradeoffs. An understanding of policy is critical to this part of the tuning process. As used here, the term *policy* refers to the formalized or the informal (and often implicit) needs of the data center.

However, policy is often described in nebulous terms; *favor CICS over batch, ensure payroll runs by the end of first shift, prioritize POWER printers* (so that this slow/expensive I/O gear is kept busy), or even *keep Joe happy.* Policy can be imprecise. It is the responsibility of the systems professional to translate corporate needs into the parameters required by the VSE system to accomplish these objectives. Chapter two provides some tools for establishing a performance methodology.

The Structure of this book

This book is comprised of *training* and *tuning* chapters. The purpose of a training chapter is to give you the background needed to tune your system. The mission of a tuning chapter is to describe a specific performance problem area and to provide specific tuning techniques to correct that area.

A *training chapter* serves to define an aspect of the operating system which we need to understand before we can begin to tune it. The training chapters introduce a subject then expand on it with coverage in depth. The basic structure of each training chapter is:

- An overview of the chapter's contents.
- Technical information in depth.
- Examples (where applicable).

A *tuning chapter* is concerned with the performance measurement and tuning of a component of a VSE/ESA system. Each tuning chapter contains both cookbook answers and information in depth. The basic structure of each tuning chapter is:

- An overview of the chapter's contents.
- Cookbook section (quick fixes for common problems).
- In depth information.
- Examples (where applicable).

The *cookbook section* provided with each tuning chapter lists the important rules or tuning tips covered in that chapter. The items listed are all covered in detail in the remainder of the chapter. Any new terms found in a cookbook item will be explained within the body of the chapter.

A *glossary* is provided to define all technical terms used in this book. In addition, each new term is defined within the text when it is first used. The critical definitions are all pinpointed within the index with a secondary "defined" entry under the name of the technical term.

A detailed *index* is provided. If you encounter a technical term and need more information than what is provided in the glossary, the index will direct you to additional information. Where many entries occur for a subject, a subentry is provided to help locate where the term is Defined, or where Tuning information can be found, or to describe an associated Wait state. A lot of effort has gone into producing the index and the author is very interested in suggestions and corrections.

About the Figures

Figures are used extensively to illustrate the VSE system, document command formats, and to show the output of commands. A list of all figures is provided after the table of contents.

The figures in this book that depict storage layouts have the lowest addresses at the bottom and the highest addresses at the top of the diagram (this is consistent with most of the IBM VSE documentation). The space shown in each figure for a specific area of storage is not intended to be strictly proportional to its allocation. Instead, the figures are intended to illustrate the relationships of storage areas. Storage is indicated for a SHARED=LOW environment (this is the only layout supported by VSE/ESA 1.3).

Every effort has been made to keep figures close to the associated text. However; an occasional reference to a figure in another part of the book is necessary to avoid excessive duplication.

Conventions, Typesetting and Others

Commands used with the operating system are shown using boldface, such as COMMAND operands. Optional operands are shown surrounded by braces, as in CMD op1 { , op2 } (where op1 is a required parameter and op2 is an optional parameter).

Italics are used to introduce new terms, such as *paging subsystem*, or to set off the title of a book referenced in the text, such as *VSE/ESA Performance Management and Tuning*.

Unless otherwise stated, all numbers used in this book are decimal. Numeric values expressed as "nKB" refer to "n" blocks of 1024 bytes. Thus, 256KB is actually 262144 bytes. Numeric values expressed as "nMB" refer to "n" megabytes of storage. A megabyte is 1024KB. Finally, "2GB" refers to two gigabytes of storage (a gigabyte is 1024MB).

Acknowledgements

I would like to thank all of the people who have helped me grow during my last 25 years with DOS as it grew into VSE/ESA. I owe special thanks for technical assistance with this book to Thurman O. Pylant who taught me the scientific method of tuning, and without whom countless flaws would not have been uncovered. Thurman contributed enormously through several indepth reviews with his detailed criticisms and suggestions. All remaining problems are solely mine. Pete Clark brought me back to reality when I forgot what real performance problems were all about, and he provided a number of examples of good and bad performance. Bob Rudolph provided his configuration for analysis and use in examples.

Jeff Barnard contributed his wealth of performance experience to the VTAM and CICS chapters. Mike McFarlane provided both his wit and his SQL/DS expertise. Dave Martin did much original work for a class from which the VSAM chapter grew. Smitty Brewster is the Grand VSAM who was the fount of knowledge for answers to questions like "How many buffers is enough?" and "Why did IDCAMS change my DEFINE?". Susan McFarland proofed the entire book and contributed technical suggestions, especially in the SQL/DS chapter. Neal Ater gained approval for the book from Goal Systems, and also contributed to it's overall technical accuracy.

Wolfgang Kraemer of the Boeblingen lab provided much technical information in his *VSE/ESA Performance Considerations* document and reviewed large portions of this book. Many other IBM staff in the US, France, and Germany also contributed materials, time, information, guidance, and support to the development of this book. The IBM GUIDE user group provided channels of communication with these and other contributors.

My wife Pat tirelessly edited and proofed the entire document several times, and rewrote chapter two when it could not be fixed with editing alone. Throughout this process she remained my best friend, and strongest supporter.

Jay Ranade at McGraw Hill asked for this book to be written. Jim Halston was the Editing Supervisor and Suzanne W. Babeuf the Production Supervisor for this project. I wish to thank all the staff at McGraw Hill who made this book better than it would have otherwise been and who helped bring it to reality.

I am sure that I have missed others in this hurried list, and wish to credit them for what is good in this effort. None of them are responsible for what is incorrect or unclear.

Bill Merrow
Columbus, Ohio

Copyrights and Trademarks

This section is provided to give credit to the copyright and trademark holders whose products are mentioned throughout this book, and I apologize for any that have been inadvertently omitted from this list.

The IBM Corporation holds trademarks for many terms used herein including IBM™, VSE™, VSE/ESA™, VM/XA™, VM/ESA™, PR/SM™, Processor Resource/Systems Manager™, Enterprise Systems Architecture/370™, Enterprise Systems Architecture/390™, CICS/VSE™, ACF/VTAM™, ES/9000™, ESA/370™, ESA/390™, 370-XA™, SQL/DS™, DB2™, MVS/XA™, and MVS/ESA™.

Various commercial software packages mentioned within the text are also trademarked including Landmark's TMON, Goal Systems Explore, the Syncsort product, Computer Associate's CASORT, and possibly others. If any trademark is not properly identified, the omission is unintended.

Chapter

1

DOS to ESA –
A Brief History of VSE

This chapter presents a brief history of VSE/ESA, and its predecessors. Those concentrating solely on VSE performance may wish to skip it. However, origins of various VSE features are presented, including those key features that define the current VSE environment. This background information may prove helpful to a fuller understanding of VSE tuning elements. Many of the acronyms encountered in modern VSE systems are also defined in this chapter, and are used within the context of other operating system components. The IBM manual *VSE/ESA: Evolution and Support of ESA/390* (GC33-6502) briefly reviews the history of VSE. The figure below lists the various DOS releases.

DOS	1965	
DOS/VS	1973	
DOS/VSE	1979	
VSE/SP	1984	
VSE/ESA	1990	Major Enhancement

Figure 1.1 Summary of DOS Releases

The first version of VSE was called simply DOS (for Disk Operating System). This alone was a step forward. Most operating systems before DOS were card or tape based. In fact, many earlier operating systems were designed only for single job systems, and did not even stay in the machine while a job was running.

DOS was delivered by IBM in 1965 to support the System/360 (S/360) machines, when the early OS/360 could not be delivered on time, and after it was determined that OS/360 would not fit in the smallest S/360 machines. This original DOS was planned as a stopgap piece of software, and was not intended to survive more than a few years after the delivery of OS.

DOS Releases 1 through 27 were delivered from 1965 through 1972. DOS started as a basic operating system that would support only a single job executing at a time in a single partition. The original system did not require a system programmer, and all software was shipped on a single tape.

DOS Release 3 added multiprogramming support (a total of three partitions) and BTAM. The early releases of DOS came out fairly quickly, to react to customer requirements and to correct design issues.

DOS Release 13 added support for private libraries. Prior to this release all programs had to be catalogued into a single library. Private libraries were important because they made it possible to maintain a test version of a program, a production version, and even a backup of the old production version. They also simplified the installation and support of new operating system releases.

Release 16 added support for batch job foreground multiprogramming. Before this release, the operator had to manually start the foreground partitions.

OS did not replace the *temporary* DOS operating system for a number of reasons. The original OS was too large for the smallest 360 machines. As OS grew and functionality was added to it, it only got larger. This left a widening gap at the bottom end of IBM hardware that DOS continued to fill. Also, the original OS was complex to administer, and this complexity only increased over time. An OS environment required an expensive full time staff of systems programmers, while DOS started out needing only occasional attention and never required significantly more. Lastly, a conversion from DOS to OS was not trivial and only got harder the longer a customer stayed on DOS.

DOS had many growth inhibitors that were identified over its lifetime. It lacked a relocating loader, did not support online processing, and only supported three partitions. Only the BG partition of those three could be used for all tasks. DOS lacked storage management, only supported device dependent I/O, and did not even include a spooler as part of the operating system.

Although a movement existed among some IBMers to eliminate DOS and force a migration of its customers to OS, the loyal DOS user base resisted the change. Finally, common sense won out and IBM decided to continue to invest in this young operating system's future.

DOS/VS

DOS/VS (Disk Operating System/Virtual Storage) replaced DOS in 1973. It was the version of DOS for the new System/370 machines. DOS/VS added virtual storage support to DOS. Up to 16 million bytes of virtual storage was supported by DOS/VS. This was a major feature, especially when you consider that machines often had less than 512KB of real memory.

DOS/VS supported a total of five partitions in that virtual storage. All of the DOS/VS partitions were equally usable. In the older DOS system, only BG was fully functional, and the foreground partitions were started and operated differently than BG.

POWER became the spooling package for DOS/VS. Near the end of the life of DOS, POWER had become available as a type III program. *POWER* is an acronym for Priority Output Writers, Execution processors, and input Readers (honest!). The support of a robust spooler in DOS/VS greatly enhanced the usability of the operating system and won it many more fans.

The online system CICS and the database DL/I were added to DOS/VS which grew into a robust transaction processing and database management environment. Of course, the addition of online systems and data base support to DOS/VS assigned a whole new dimension to performance management.

A new linkage editor and a relocating loader were also important new components of DOS/VS. The early DOS system did not support relocatable programs. All programs either had to be written to be self relocating, or the user was required to linkedit three copies of each program, one copy for each of the three partitions. The new relocating loader allowed a single copy of a program to be executed in any of the five partitions.

The initial DOS/VS release also added support for VSAM. The Virtual Storage Access Method was intended to solve all of the problems of ISAM, and provided ISAM compatibility at the same time. VSAM was delivered with the promise of consistent performance even as records were inserted into a file, with good sequential and random performance characteristics, and with efficient use of DASD space. VSAM did ultimately meet most of these objectives, but was a real challenge for some early customers. VSAM tuning was initially a dirty word, later an art, and only now can it be described as somewhat of a science.

ETSS was added late in the life of DOS/VS as an interactive system. ETSS became known as ICCF later, and this is the name we are most familiar with. DOS/VS releases 28 through 34 were delivered from 1973 through 1979. DOS Release 34 Advanced Functions added support for seven partitions near the end of the life of DOS.

By 1979 DOS was already 15 years old and again was feeling some growing pains. The most commonly encountered growth inhibitors were the primitive I/O scheduler that only supported a single path to a string of DASD, the limited number of partitions, an error prone IPL process, and difficulty in the application of maintenance.

DOS/VSE

DOS/VSE (Disk Operating System/Virtual Storage Extended) was delivered in 1979. Release one increased the standard number of partitions from five to seven. Support was added to DOS for the 4300 processors and for FBA DASD. This release also added support for the infamous MSHP. MSHP is still pronounced "Mishap" by many VSE system programmers because it can cause some problems if not used with care. The MSHP acronym is also sometimes expanded to mean *More Sweat, Heartache, and Pain* by its fans.

The startup of DOS/VSE was automated via the addition of the *ASI* (Automatic System Initialization) procedures. Prior to this time, the operator had to manually start the system components. ASI permitted system startup commands to be catalogued to special procedure library members, that were automatically read and executed at IPL time.

Release one added support for DASD device channel switching. Previous releases had supported a single path to a device, and I/O to one device while that path was busy had to wait. Channel switching allowed for two paths to a device, and improved DASD throughput was realized by many customers. The old DOS/VS ETSS time share system was re-engineered and renamed to ICCF.

Early VSE customers will always remember April 11, 1980 – the day that VSE stood still. At 8:00 GMT on April 11 of 1980, the Time Of Day (TOD) clock high-order bit turned over and all applications using timers stopped running. Since this list of applications included CICS, essentially everyone was affected by this bug. The author was lucky, a friendly IBMer in Endicott called just after the system hung and gave us the fix. The only really good news from this story is that the clock will not turn over again until late in the night of September 17, 2042. Mark your calendars.

DOS/VSE Release 2 increased the number of partitions to twelve in 1980. DASD sharing support was also added. DASD sharing was initially a configuration nightmare, because data was destroyed if you implemented it wrong as so many did. It also introduced a whole new class of performance issues to VSE. In fact, tuning of current VSE shared DASD environments is one of the major challenges addressed by this book!

This release of DOS/VSE also eliminated the need to assemble a new supervisor each time a device was added, changed, or even removed from the system. Instead, device ADD statements were supported as part of the IPL procedure.

DOS/VSE Release 3 simplified the supervisor generation process, and added the missing interrupt handler (MIH). The MIH made recovery from lost interrupts possible, and provided a mechanism to inform the operator of missing interrupts in a timely fashion. Before the introduction of the MIH, operators would identify a problem only after users complained, and would then have to run around the computer room pressing reset/ready or attention buttons on every device until the system resumed running.

The year 1983 brought the introduction of VSE/SP Version 1 (Virtual Storage Extended/System Package). This was basically a repackaging of DOS/VSE. Some extensions that were part of the release were support for 16 megabytes of real storage, support for Start I/O Fast, support for large uniprocessors such as the 3033 model S, and new peripheral device support.

Just as the original DOS had a list of known growth constraints at the end of its life that drove the development of DOS/VSE, so did

DOS/VSE become encumbered with a list of deficiencies. One major problem was that the 16 megabytes of virtual storage that seemed so large when first delivered had become filled by giant CICS systems, POWER, and even a few batch user applications. Another problem was the VSE librarian. Designed when storage was more important than performance, it used absurdly small block sizes which wasted as much as 85 percent of every track of a 3380 DASD unit. For core image (program) libraries the original librarian even used disk records with hardware keys! And, DOS/VSE users were having trouble maintaining their operating systems or implementing any kind of effective change management with the original system and private library scheme.

Virtual Storage Extended/System Package

VSE/SP Version 2 was announced in 1984. It added support for up to three address spaces to VSE via its Virtual Addressability Extensions (VAE) support. This meant that VSE could finally define more than 16MB virtual memory. Each virtual address space could be 16 megabytes. The total virtual area supported was 40 megabytes. VSE/SP replaced the old cumbersome DOS library structure with a new librarian that no longer used wasteful and slow key fields in directories and did not have to be manually condensed. It also allowed all member types to be stored in the same directory, dynamically allocated different directories from a single pool of disk space, and could be defined (and automatically extended) within VSAM space.

This was the first release to be called VSE/SP. The additional virtual storage made ICCF truly usable for all VSE customers. The Interactive User Interface (IUI) was added with a set of panels to assist in the system generation and management tasks.

VSE/SP added support for workstations (PCs) for the first time. VSE VSAM data could be transferred to a PC as ASCII data. PC files could be transmitted to the mainframe and translated to EBCDIC. This initial upload/download support was well received by the VSE user community.

Conditional JCL was also added in the release. This support included parameterized procedures, procedure nesting, and support for parameter comparison and branching within procedures. These features enabled users to eliminate manual steps in the running of many jobstreams, and also helped reduce the number of different variations of the same job from which operators had to select the right one.

VSE/SP Version 2 is the first version of VSE that this book addresses. Except where otherwise noted, all tuning methods discussed in this book apply to VSE/SP Version 2 through VSE/ESA. Let us now look at the later VSE/SP releases which are still used in some VSE shops.

VSE/SP Version 3 and Version 4

Released in 1986, Version 3 of VSE expanded the number of address spaces to 9 and increased the maximum page data set virtual size. The initial 9370 processor models were supported, as were intelligent workstations. The IUI was also enhanced by this version of VSE.

Version 4 soon followed to add support for more 9370 models, and unattended VSE systems. It was finally possible to have a VSE system locked in a closet, with no operator in sight, and all operations automated.

By this time (late 1989), VSE had reached its design limits just as the original DOS, DOS/VS, and DOS/VSE before it. A major problem faced by large VSE users was the ever present 16 megabyte limit. This became more and more critical as the size of POWER and VTAM and the SVA grew, forcing applications into smaller and smaller partitions. The twelve partitions of VSE/SP were also completely filled in many shops. Some customers were even having trouble with the 254 device limit of VSE/SP. And, VSE customers had continued to avoid the expensive conversion to MVS. They demanded constraint relief in VSE. IBM listened and responded with VSE/ESA.

VSE/ESA

VSE/ESA Version 1 was shipped late in 1990. VSE/ESA means Virtual Storage Extended/Enterprise System Architecture. VSE/ESA Version 1 Release 1 increased the number of partitions from 12 to about 200. The XA I/O subsystem was also supported (XA means Extended Architecture). This allowed for much higher I/O throughput and provided more tuning options for VSE. The maximum real storage and virtual storage support was also increased by over an order of magnitude (real storage support went from 16MB to 384MB while total virtual storage increased to 256MB). New subsystems included CICS V2, POWER V5, and enhanced VTAM support. VSE/ESA took DOS the rest of the way from the 60s to the 90s as we see below.

DOS..DOS/VS..DOS/VSE..VSE/SP..VSE/ESA

1965 ——————————————➤ 1992

Figure 1.2 DOS to VSE/ESA

VSE/ESA offered more growth constraint relief than any single prior release in the history of DOS. The performance related features of VSE/ESA are extensively discussed in Chapter 4.

VSE/ESA Release 2 was issued early in 1991 to add to this functionality. Maintenance to Release 2 later increased the number of devices supported from 254 to 1024. In addition, a future VSE/ESA release was committed to support 31-bit addressing, and thus increase the maximum size of a partition from under 16MB to 2 gigabytes. A gigabyte is a billion bytes.

VSE/ESA 1.3 was announced in June of 1992 for delivery in the first quarter of 1993. This release implements the promised 31 bit addressing. It also adds support for data spaces, virtual disks, and additional real memory up to the hardware maximum. With VSE/ESA 1.3, essentially all VSE growth inhibitors have been eliminated.

This book is oriented towards tuning VSE/ESA and VSE/SP operating systems. Chapter 4 covers the VSE/ESA additional function, the unique performance characteristics of this release, and tuning advice for users converting from VSE/SP to VSE/ESA. The other chapters contain tuning advice for both systems. The term VSE is used to refer generically to VSE/SP and VSE/ESA. The term VSE/ESA is used when the tuning techniques apply only to users of the VSE/ESA system.

VSE/ESA provides support for System/370, 370-XA, ESA/370, and ESA/390 processors. The user selects the supervisor mode used by VSE/ESA. The full capabilities of VSE/ESA are only available when a MODE=ESA supervisor is used.

The VM modes (MODE=VM and MODE=VMESA) support the new components, but since they only support a single address space, most new functions are not available with these supervisor modes.

For MODE=370, the following new support is provided:

- Support for VTAM in a private address space without requiring that the VTAM applications reside within the same address space.

- Support for up to 200 new partitions.

- Support for the new languages (COBOL-II and C/370) in both batch and online.

A MODE=ESA supervisor can be IPLed on a 370-XA processor and provides the following additional functions over MODE=370:

- Support for up to 384MB of real storage.

- Support for the dynamic channel subsystem including up to 256 channels, four paths to each device, dynamic path selection, and dynamic path reconnection. These new terms are defined in Chapter 4.

A MODE=ESA supervisor running on an ESA/370 or ESA/390 processor provides the complete function of VSE/ESA. In addition to the MODE=370 functions described above, the following support is provided:

- Support for the ESA Access Registers which provide for efficient cross-address space communication.

- Support for VSE/POWER running within a private address space. This increases the size of a private area partition by at least 1MB.

- Improved ACF/VTAM performance due to use of Access Registers for application communication.

- ESCON channel support on ESA/390 processors.

2

Performance Tuning
Methodology

A sound methodology for performance tuning is as important to a system professional as the skills needed for implementation. System tuning is an ongoing process requiring accurate measurements and controlled changes. Like a scientific discipline, data must be gathered and analyzed. Quantitative judgements must be made about relationships and performance. The success of every judgement will relate directly to the quality of the data available, and the thought processes employed.

This chapter will discuss the reasons for a formal process of performance measurement and tuning. Since much tuning work is done as a reaction to problems, we will explore two distinct methodologies for problem solving: the Reactive approach, and the Proactive approach. Both approaches are examples of formal performance tuning methodologies.

2.1 Why Use a Formal Tuning Methodology?

Most successful system professionals already use a performance tuning methodology. Through experience and education, we pick up skills and techniques that we employ every time we tackle a problem. The concept of applying a method to solve a problem is not new to any of us.

Most of us don't like the word "formal." We tend to associate the word with systems that add considerable administrative overhead to the work process. This, however, need not be the case. Use of a formal performance tuning methodology simply means applying a *systematic thought process* to analysis and problem solving. A good formal performance tuning methodology usually has two basic characteristics: it is *consistent*, and it is *transferrable*.

Consistency means that the same methods will be used each time you approach a tuning effort. The method is reliable enough to use in a wide variety of situations. *Transferrable* means that the skill set used is understandable by other persons, and can be used by them. The process is repeatable, often with predictable results. We can see, therefore, that a formal methodology can facilitate problem solving by establishing rules for the process. It creates a framework that allows people to work together. And it enables the systems professional to expect certain predictable results in what is often a chaotic process. Adding controls to the process leads directly to significant time savings and better problem identification. A formal methodology also establishes an audit trail, which can be a helpful road map out of a complex situation.

Of course, a key element for proper analysis is accurate, timely data. The first step in establishing a formal performance tuning methodology is the identification of reporting elements needed for analysis, and the periodic creation and review of performance data. This book will help you determine the reporting you need based on the particular requirements of your unique system environment. There are many advantages to establishing these reporting structures apart from the area of system tuning. Structured reporting is integral for capacity planning and long term resource management. Disaster Preparedness programs and data processing audit processes are aided by structured reporting and analysis. Chances are good your shop already produces the basic data needed to form a sound performance tuning methodology.

2.2 Reactive Problem Solving

The *Reactive Problem Solving* method is used whenever poor system performance is noted. The objective of the process is simply to fix the problem. Problems can vary in size and complexity, as can the amount of time needed to fix them. Regardless of problem type, a formal approach to resolving performance problems can aid in analyzing the cause and implementing a solution.

The Reactive Problem Solving Methodology suggested here is similar in approach to the Scientific Method. In Figure 2.1 we list the six basic steps:

---

1. IDENTIFY the problem
2. GATHER DATA about the problem
3. DETERMINE a solution
4. IMPLEMENT the solution
5. MEASURE the effect of the solution
6. REPEAT the process if the problem is not solved

Figure 2.1 Reactive Tuning Steps

Let us now analyze each of these basic steps to better understand their meaning:

1. Identify the Problem

The most valuable time spent in reactive problem solving is in problem identification. If a wrong assessment is made at step one, much time is wasted throughout the rest of the process. Some very basic questions should be asked in the problem reporting phase:

- Is there really a problem? Too often problem reporting becomes a subjective process. Particularly when a crisis is perceived, observations can be hasty and confused. Look at all reporting carefully to determine the true nature of the situation reported.

- Is this a performance problem? With the complexity of systems and integration, the symptoms are sometimes reported as the problem. Look closely at evidence to determine (if possible) areas of functional responsibility.

- What is the scope of the problem? Understanding how many users and/or systems are effected is a great help in determining the immediacy and method of resolution.

Most performance problems are WAIT problems. Your task is to determine "who" is waiting, for "how long" and for "what." Target the largest items first. Look for any I/O wait in excess of 20 percent, and any page wait in excess of 2 percent elapsed time. It is good to make a list of all sources of wait, as the first area you fix may not present enough savings. These records will also assist in solving future, similar performance problems. Figure 2.2 lists some common causes of poor performance.

- **Transaction volume increases or decreases**

- **Failing hardware components**

- **Application changes**

- **Operating system changes**

- **Procedural changes**

Figure 2.2 Common Cause of Poor Performance

2. Gather Data About the Problem

Performance statistics are the most important element in the data gathering process. Baseline numbers that were gathered before the problem occurred should be compared to reports generated at the time the problem occurred. As with the problem analysis step, basic questions should be asked:

- <u>What changed?</u> Recent changes in hardware, software, and communications should be investigated, along with any recent tuning efforts. The most likely cause of a sudden performance problem would be the introduction of a change in the environment.

- <u>What was happening at the time the problem occurred?</u> Recent hardware and software errors may reflect symptoms of the problem, or may be the cause. You may need to check operator procedures. The most likely cause of sporadic but chronic problems is environmental interaction.

- Has this happened before? If there are prior indicators that similar problems have occurred before, you may wish to conduct a trend analysis. Small indicators becoming larger problems over time may point to a tuning effort. The most likely cause of a steadily increasing problem is resource contention.

3. Determine a Solution

After careful analysis in problem identification and data review, you are ready to propose a solution to the problem. In this process, two heads are often better than one. You may wish to have a fellow worker check your logic. Some important questions to ask are:

- Does this problem require more than one solution? Many problems are complex, requiring more than one "fix." If this is the case, you must determine the proper sequence and scenario for effecting multiple changes.

- What are the expected results? A full understanding of the problem should yield a quantitative statement of anticipated results. Whenever possible, testing should be conducted prior to implementation of a solution. In some cases, reports may need to be created to capture pertinent data.

- What will change? If, as a result of the solution the system environment or procedures will change, some user communication may be necessary. When multiple solutions are possible, the effects of the various options should be discussed with the people involved.

4. Implement the Solution

In implementing any system change, carefully consider any potential impacts to the environment. Whenever possible, make changes one at a time. Be sure to keep detailed records of your activities in case something should go wrong. Ask yourself the following questions:

- <u>Who or what will be impacted by this change?</u> If processing schedules will change, test job streams must be run, or otherwise normal events will be impacted, it is best to communicate with others involved.

- <u>What are the priorities?</u> Understanding the priorities (processing and otherwise) in a work environment can be a difficult proposition. Never assume that your changes or time frames are most important. Impacts to on-line time and batch processing can be critical for the company. It is best to understand how your proposed implementation fits into the overall picture.

- <u>Can we recover?</u> In the unlikely event that things go wrong, it is best to have a contingency plan. Before you begin, make sure current backups are available, and plan exactly how you will recover if things go wrong. In a complicated scenario, it may be best to identify critical points in the process and plan recovery from each step.

5. Measure the Effect of the Solution

Actual results need to be compared with anticipated ones. The criteria you established in proposing your solution are key to determining the effectiveness of your results. Detailed records of the results and the analysis should be kept for future reference. Consider the following questions:

- <u>Are the results what I expected?</u> If the answer is no, reevaluate your thought process. Was your original data valid? Were tests executed properly? Perhaps you solved one problem, but another lay buried by the first. If an evaluation of your analysis does not present an explanation, you must assume your problem identification was incorrect. This means going back to step one.

- <u>Are any further changes required?</u> If the results show improvement, will further changes bring even better results?

Is there a second problem to be resolved? If you determine that there is more work to be done, continue the process at step one.

- <u>At what interval will I recheck my results?</u> If your solution appears to be a good one, you will want to recheck the results to be sure. Depending on the situation, this might involve testing from a different angle, or periodically checking results to be sure. You may wish to involve the user community or a third party to aid in observations.

6. Repeat the Whole Process if the Problem is not Solved

If the problem still exists, you must go back to step one and start over. Here are some common pitfalls to consider when trouble-shooting a difficult problem:

- *You were Treating Symptoms, not the Problem.*

  Some problems are extremely difficult to identify. Vendors can sometimes provide special expertise.

- *You Correctly Identified One Problem, but Multiple Problems Exist.*

  If your results look correct, but performance problems still exist, reinitiate the problem solving process.

- *Your Analysis was Correct, but Your Input Data was Wrong.*

  Recheck the data you used for analysis. Make sure that you are working with the correct input data and baseline figures.

- *Your Analysis was Correct, but Your Test Logic was Wrong.*

  Your problem identification is correct, but your testing or recovery scenario was incorrect. Rethink your logic and solution path.

To be effective, the Reactive problem solving process requires ongoing measurement and periodic review of performance statistics.

A baseline measurement is a necessary tool for problem identification, and current data is needed to verify that a problem has been corrected. Record keeping is key to the tuning process.

Problem solving is an excellent learning process, and documentation provides a powerful tool for future efforts. Use of a formal problem solving methodology provides for both documentation and measurement.

2.3 Proactive Performance Measurement

Another viable approach to the tuning effort is *Proactive Performance Management*. The goal of this process is to prevent problems and/or reduce problem severity. With the proactive method, tuning is a planned event with changes occurring in a controlled environment. There are many advantages to using the proactive performance management. Figure 2.3 lists a few of the resulting major benefits.

- **Problems are solved more easily. They are generally less severe, and take less time to solve.**

- **The system environment is stable, because change control is an integral part of the process.**

- **System time is more productive, because the planning process is designed to meet current and future needs.**

- **User perceptions are more favorable, because problems and interrupts are less frequent.**

Figure 2.3 Advantages to Proactive Performance Management

As with the Reactive process, there are formal methodologies to accommodate Proactive Performance Management. Let's look at the basic steps in using the Proactive method.

Where the Reactive approach deals solely with problem solving (an historical approach), the Proactive method describes current and future events. It answers the questions "Where are we now," and "Where do we want to go?" Let's examine the following five basic Proactive Tuning Steps in detail:

1. Define Performance Objective

2. Develop Measurement Procedures

3. Measure Performance at Regular Intervals

4. Forecast Resource Consumption

5. Verify Performance Quantitatively

A Word About Terminology

The terms *objective* and *standard* are often used interchangeably. There is a subtle difference between them. *Objectives* are goal oriented, and are created to improve value or productivity. They may require additional resources. *Standards*, on the other hand, are oriented toward the status quo. They draw a boundary past which trouble occurs. A standard must be able to be enforced with existing resources.

Much information is available on how to create performance objectives and standards. We will not attempt to go into these topics in depth. For our purposes here, we will use one term, *performance objectives*, to simply indicate a quantitative statement of acceptable performance levels.

1. Define Performance Objectives

The first step in creating a proactive performance methodology is establishing performance objectives. Performance objectives are critical for assessing the productivity of both machine and people resources. Success is easily achieved when the goals are clearly understood. The best resource for understanding the requirements of system performance will be the people who use it. User needs are the critical element in establishing acceptable levels of performance. System users should be included in every decision process. Many shops have formal methods for communication, such as standards committees. Whether created formally or informally, performance objectives must be understood and approved by all parties involved. The best results are seen when objectives are written, and periodically reviewed. Determining what constitutes acceptable performance can be tricky. Care should be taken to fully understand user needs. For example, users may agree that an on-line system up time of 98 percent is very acceptable. But what does that 98 percent actually mean? For the end user, a 2 percent down time may mean 13 or 14 minutes without on-lines on any given day. This kind of outage may be acceptable. However, a 96-minute outage once during a week might be devastating to business. For on-line systems scheduled up 80 hours per week, this type of outage meets the performance objective. It clearly does not meet the need.

A performance objective should be created for every component in your environment, including response time, paging rate, channel utilization, CPU usage, and storage requirements. Product recommendations and vendor requirements can be valuable assets.

Once created, performance objectives must be translated into *Threshold Values.* Threshold values are the numbers needed to monitor the performance of each system component. They tell you whether performance objectives are met. Threshold values must be able to be quantitatively measured using your available tools.

2. Develop Measurement Procedures

It is now time to develop reporting systems and performance monitors for each system component. The objective is to be alerted to any potential performance problems before they occur. For this reason, performance monitors are generally set lower than threshold values. Understanding the capabilities of your performance tools is critical. The old cliche, "using the right tool for the job" more than applies here. Figure 2.4 lists some commonly used performance monitoring aids. Note that the list includes automated tools and observational aids. Sometimes the best insights can be gained through conversations or indirect sources. You may be surprised to discover what creative reporting mechanisms exist in the form of people and events, as opposed to raw data. Your most important resources, however, will produce information that is quantitative and repeatable.

The timeliness of reporting is as important as the data itself. Your objectives should tell you how frequently to gather data. An historical base of information is essential to both Proactive performance management, and Reactive problem solving. Ongoing

- VSE/PT (only available for VSE/SP

- Explore for VSE (available from IBM for VSE/ESA)

- CICS PARS data or output of an OEM CICS monitor

- VSE Job Accounting

- IDCAMS LISTCAT

- VSE/SP or VSE/ESA Systems Activity Display

- Hardware Monitor Data

- Network Monitor Tools

- VM data from VMMAP, Explore for VM, or other VM tools

- Console Logs

- Trouble Logs/Incident Reports

- Application Change Logs/Change Control Reports

- VSAM Monitor data

- SQL Monitor data

- Maintenance Logs

- User Descriptions

- Direct Observation

Figure 2.4 Commonly Used Performance Monitoring Aids

data collection should be a high priority. A periodic review of historical data compared to the current status is also important.

3. Measure Performance at Regular Intervals

Performance measurement tools have become so versatile and easy to use that there exists a danger of producing too much data. Your measuring effort can be made easier by analyzing your reports before measuring your performance. Here are some simple questions to ask:

- <u>Is the data accessible and understandable?</u>

  Data is worthless unless it is properly understood. All persons monitoring performance and data must speak the same language. This may involve teaching end users some technical terms, or you adopting some of their terminology. Data in its raw form may be meaningful to you, or you may have to create formats that tie reports directly to the performance objectives. For data to be understood it should be concise, clear, and meaningful. Data must also be understood in its relationships to other data. Understand that techniques such as "averaging" can be helpful or harmful, depending on system performance requirements. Understanding performance against a template of business activity hours, for example, may be more helpful than 24-hour averaging.

  If you find that the data you are producing is not being utilized as planned, you may wish to consider whether it is understandable and meaningful.

- <u>Does the data relate directly to performance objectives?</u>

  An understanding of performance objectives should allow you to identify "significant indicators." Significant indicators are those measurements that allow you to determine if you are moving toward or away from a threshold value. Your data collection and reporting processes should relate directly to these measurements. If you find that data takes too long to review, or that results are not clear, you may wish to examine the relationships with performance objectives.

- Is data produced at proper intervals?

    For measurements to be effective, they must be taken at
    proper intervals. Threshold values will be either EVENT
    related or LOAD related. Capturing an event requires an
    understanding of all the precursors involved in creating that
    event. This type of reporting may be intense, but of short
    duration. Analyzing system loads may involve the routine
    capture of data at a set frequency (hourly, daily, weekly, etc.).
    Events can be lost in load reporting, and visa versa. The
    timing of data capture is critical. Without a doubt, much time
    and resource is wasted in the production and archival of
    useless data. If you are unhappy with the amount of data
    being produced, or if events still seem to slip by, you may wish
    to analyze data capture intervals.

4. Forecast Resource Consumption

Once you are capturing performance data on a regular basis, the
next logical step is to create a trend analysis. In forecasting
resource consumption you have a short-term objective, and a long-
term objective. The short-term objective is to predict potential
problem areas and prevent or reduce them via controlled change.
The long-term objective is to identify potential resource shortfalls,
and to take steps to attain those resources. The terms *short* and
long are subjective, and will mean different things in different
environments. For our purposes, *short term* means looking forward
within the constraint of current resources. *Long term* means using
the same trends to compare with a 3-5 year business plan, and
predicting resource availability.

Forecasting Short-Term Resource Consumption

Short-term resource analysis utilizes your current hardware and
software configuration. Using your measurement reporting, you
create a trend analysis, or forecast, based on current usage. These
forecasts allow you to speculate as to when resources will be tested
and when problems will occur. Your should create a forecast for
every component in your environment, and tuning activity should
occur proactively as a result. Determining where problems will
occur before they occur has many advantages. Not the least of

these are fewer and less severe problems, and more time to accomplish changes. Forecasting will not only point to system and resource requirements. It may suggest different staffing needs, or changes in procedure. It is important to remember that some needs may not require technical solutions.

As with reactive problem solving, it is important to forecast the *impact* of the changes, as well as the solutions. Understanding relationships, time frames, and user needs is critical. A change plan, including recovery methods, is recommended.

Most environments use some form of a *Change Management System*. The purpose of a *Change Control Procedure* is to prevent problems resulting from the change process. A good change control procedure will consider the following elements listed in Figure 2.5:

- **Scheduling a proper time frame for change.**

- **Approvals by those impacted by the change.**

- **Documentation of procedures altered or created by the change.**

- **Review of security procedures or accesses needed to make the change.**

- **An audit trail documenting pertinent information about the change, including the reason it was made, and the anticipated results.**

- **A presubmitted recovery plan.**

Figure 2.5 Elements of the Change Control Process

As you tune, your threshold values may change. It is important to review those values throughout each tuning effort.

Forecasting Long-Term Resource Consumption
The same usage rates that predict your tuning requirements can predict long-term resource needs. While looking long-term may not

be a task you perform frequently, it is very important. A picture of future growth and need is the best argument for obtaining new resources. For this reason, it may be best to tie long-term forecasting to your budget cycle. Matching forecasts to the long-term business plan is an excellent way to communicate resource needs.

Adding on is not always the most cost effective method for the long term. If you need more DASD, more memory, more ports, etc., you may need a new CPU! Raising these issues well in advance of the need increases the chances of obtaining them when they are needed.

Trends should always be translated into a measurable statement of need. It is costly and embarrassing to add resources and still not meet performance requirements. Therefore, much care should be taken up front to insure that forecasts represent appropriate resource measurements.

5. Verify Performance Quantitatively

Forecasting needs and making tuning changes does not end the process. Proactive resource management is a continual cycle of monitoring and evaluating. The objective of the VERIFY process is to quantitatively determine that you have achieved the expected results of changes or predicted trends. You may also find that as a result of effective system tuning, your targets have moved. Consider the following questions:

- Have my threshold values changed?

  As a result of improved performance, you may wish to lower your threshold values, thus improving performance standards. Alternately, you may discover that threshold values, for whatever reason, are not viable, and need to be moved back. In either case, changes to measurement system may need to take place.

- Can further improvements be made?

  Measurement and forecasting will continually reveal areas where resource usage can be economized. Vendor specifications and industry standards can help you determine what is possible. You may wish to create testing models that will show how your unique system usage compares to these measurements. As you identify areas for change, reuse the proactive performance management process.

3

Overview of the
Components of VSE/ESA

This chapter is an overview of the components of VSE. It is also an
overview of this book. Individual chapters will follow to provide
more detail for each component. In this chapter, our mission is to
identify each area we will cover in depth later in this book. When
this book deals with an area in an overview fashion or when a
subject is very complex, references to other books are made for the
advanced user to pursue.

3.1 VSE/ESA

This book focuses on the VSE/ESA environment, and VSE/ESA is
fully covered in each chapter. Because VSE/ESA is comparatively
new, a separate chapter is included to discuss what was added,
what was made better, and what performance issues were created
by VSE/ESA (refer to Chapter 4).

Special emphasis is placed on the tuning of newly migrated
systems. This is important because many users simply move to
VSE/ESA, without updating the key system parameters that allow
optimum benefit from VSE/ESA features and new capabilities.

3.2 SCP

The term System Control Program (SCP) refers to the VSE resident nucleus which is comprised of the supervisor plus phases loaded during IPL and tables built at IPL time or during ASI processing. The SCP performs the following functions which will be discussed in detail in the System Control Program chapter:

> Storage Management
> I/O Scheduling
> Task Initiation and Termination
> Paging
> Error Recovery
> Console Management
> File Management
> Program Loading

Each of these areas is heavily involved in affecting VSE performance and most can be tuned through simple parameters. Additional SCP functions not as intimately connected with performance management will also be briefly reviewed. Because POWER is required to create dynamic partitions, a discussion of issues related to the initialization of address spaces and the allocation of dynamic partitions is included in the SCP chapter and also in the POWER chapter.

3.3 Virtual Storage Tuning

The largest performance challenge remaining in VSE/ESA 1.2 is virtual storage availability. A separate chapter on the tuning of virtual storage is provided. Both virtual storage usage reduction, and the maximization of the size of each partition are covered in detail. Support for VTAM and POWER in the private area is discussed. Reducing the size of shared area components is explored at length. Tuning of the shared-to-private-area one-megabyte boundary is also included.

3.4 Hardware Tuning

Effective tuning of the VSE/ESA system often requires an understanding of the hardware configuration, and how the operating system exploits hardware features. A separate chapter is provided that consolidates tuning information related to the hardware configuration and operating system parameters that affect how VSE uses the hardware. Usage of new hardware options made available by VSE/ESA is emphasized.

We also look at how hardware resource bottlenecks can be managed in the VSE environment. Parameters that reduce the amount of hardware required, or that allow you to reserve hardware resources are discussed.

3.5 Lock Manager

The VSE Lock Manager is the common facility used by the VSE operating system and all of its subsystems to control access to resources. In a standalone environment, the Lock Manager performs well, however in a DASD sharing environment, it is typically the single most important performance bottleneck in VSE.

The Lock Manager is discussed in detail as part of Chapter 14 on DASD Sharing. Techniques to measure the performance and to reduce the cost of this VSE component are covered. Issues such as restricting DASD volumes defined with the SHR parameter, controlling access without the Lock Manager, tuning of the external lock file, and reducing the number of lock requests are pursued through examples. Additional discussion on the negative performance effects of DASD sharing is included where appropriate.

The DASD Sharing chapter covers tuning VTOCs, the Librarian, POWER, VSAM, and various system utilities. This chapter emphasizes managing the shared DASD environment. Alternatives to the use of DASD sharing are also discussed.

3.6 POWER

VSE/POWER is the VSE spooler. We will call it simply POWER in this book. With VSE/ESA, POWER is required for support of

Dynamic Partitions and is no longer considered an optional component.

POWER tuning is covered in detail in its own chapter. POWER startup parameters are discussed in the VSE System Specifications chapter. Certain system facilities required by POWER to manage dynamic partitions are discussed in the chapter on the SCP. Shared POWER tuning is covered in the chapter on DASD Sharing.

The chapter on POWER covers the usage and tuning of SLI libraries. The parameters used to define the POWER disk files and POWER startup commands that are related to tuning are discussed with working examples to illustrate performance problems and fixes.

3.7 Librarian

The VSE Librarian manages data used to run the operating system. It also manages user source and executable programs, Job Control Language (JCL), and even dump information. The names of the data types we will look at are, PHASE, OBJ, SOURCE, PROC, and DUMP data. We will also look at library allocation, storage requirements, and utilities in some detail. The process of selecting sublibraries to place in permanent and temporary search chains is covered in detail.

Examples of good and bad search chains will be discussed, including several problems in the default systems as shipped by IBM. We will discuss the importance of library reorganization, and review samples of JCL to accomplish this often difficult task. Library related performance issues are also discussed in a number of other areas where they are relevant.

3.8 VSAM

VSAM tuning is discussed separately in its own chapter. VSAM is the primary file-management tool provided as part of VSE and doubles as a disk space-management tool. VSAM is also a basic access method of VSE and as such is used by a number of VSE components.

Libraries may be defined in VSAM space. DL1 and SQL/DS databases are defined as VSAM space. Sequential files may be automatically allocated in VSAM controlled disk space as part of SAM managed VSAM. These subjects are discussed in the appropriate sections. This chapter covers the basics of defining VSAM files to best minimize CPU consumption or to reduce DASD space requirements.

The VSAM chapter covers VSAM file definition parameters to optimize for minimal DASD space, for minimal I/Os, and for minimal storage usage. The use of parameters like FREESPACE, BUFSPACE, IMBED, REPLICATE and other basic performance options is discussed in detail.

The advanced user is referred to J. Ranade's book *VSAM Performance, Design, and Fine Tuning* for additional information on this subject.

3.9 SQL/DS

SQL/DS is the VSE relational database. A full chapter is provided that describes the structure of SQL/DS and discusses tuning of the SQL partition and of the CICS/SQL application and ISQL interfaces.

An overview section introduces the new SQL/DS user to the terminology and parameters used to control the performance of the database. An internal tuning section covers the use of bufferspace and the NCUSERS parameter to control SQL/DS resource usage and to manage its performance. Additional information for the tuning of SQL/DS in a CICS environment is also included. The amount of DASD space required for a given DBSPACE is covered in tabular form in the hardware tuning chapter.

The more advanced user is referred to Martyn and Hartley's book *DB2/SQL: A Professional Programmer's Guide.*

3.10 CICS

CICS is the standard transaction processing environment for VSE. A proper treatment of CICS would require a book by itself. In this book we perform an overview of CICS and emphasis basic tuning issues and quick fixes for problems.

CICS is very sensitive to paging induced delays. It employs private multitasking to support a large number of transactions running for a larger number of terminals. CICS implements its own program and workspace memory management functions. It gathers limited performance statistics while it is operating.

CICS tuning is discussed in its own chapter (Chapter 11). Tuning issues related to paging, CICS DSA size, VSAM LSR usage, MRO, journaling, and other areas are covered in detail. Use of VSE and CICS facilities to monitor the performance of your CICS system and measure improvements brought about by your tuning efforts is also addressed.

A more complete treatment of CICS may be found in S. Piggot's book *CICS: A Practical Guide to System Fine Tuning*.

3.11 VTAM

VTAM is the only commonly used teleprocessing interface available in VSE. BTAM is not covered because its use is diminishing. Because it is complex and often a source of performance problems, VTAM tuning is discussed in its own chapter.

Tuning options for VTAM that apply to NCP (the software in the communications controller), the VTAM partition, and to the VTAM application are all reviewed. The critical problem of VTAM partition size is covered in detail. The usage of the limited IBM provided measurement tools is also discussed.

The tuning related operator commands, VTAM startup and configuration parameters, VTAM shutdown storage requirements, network topology induced delays, and LAN (Local Area Network) interfacing are covered in examples. VTAM buffer space management is discussed at length.

The IBM manual *VTAM Network Implementation Guide* (SC31-6404) contains a chapter titled "Tuning VTAM for Your Environment." This is a source of additional VTAM tuning information. Additional information on the design and structure of VTAM and Networks is available in Kapoor's excellent book *SNA: Architecture, Protocols, and Implementation*.

3.12 VSE/VM Environment

VM is an operating system that allows the physical hardware configuration to be partitioned via software into a set of virtual

CPUs. VSE was frequently run as a guest of VM before VSE/ESA was introduced, in order to provide enough virtual storage to hold all of a shop's applications.

This chapter covers tuning of VSE in a VM environment. Although a trend away from VM has been observed in users migrating to VSE/ESA, this environment is still considered important and is discussed in its own chapter (Chapter 16).

The VM chapter discusses the sources of VM overhead, and reviews performance parameters provided by the VM and VSE systems that can reduce this overhead. The benefits of the CMS program development environment are also discussed as an alternative to the use of the ICCF facility.

The advanced VM user is referred to J. Savit's book *VM and CMS: Performance and Fine Tuning.*

3.13   VSE System Specifications

The System Specifications and Commands chapter serves as a reference and a review of all VSE tuning related parameters. It contains information gathered from over ten different VSE manuals. Examples of ASI procedures, POWER startup commands, CICS file definitions, and network definitions are included to assist in understanding the effects of these commands.

Command syntax is reviewed, commands and control statements are used in examples, and sample output from commands is reviewed. Certain very detailed information about commands is also presented for the advanced user. The discussion in this chapter is usually more in depth than the parameter discussion in the individual tuning chapters.

4

VSE/ESA Performance Benefits

This chapter discusses the new features of VSE/ESA and emphasizes those that provide for improved performance. The term VSE is used to refer to VSE releases prior to VSE/ESA. The term VSE/ESA is used anytime a VSE/ESA feature or function is referenced. This is the same convention used throughout this book. Most of the performance techniques discussed for the older VSE releases still apply to VSE/ESA.

Each of the performance related VSE/ESA new features is briefly covered here. Where further detailed discussion is required, it is done in a separate chapter or section. Cross references to such sections are given where applicable. The IBM manual *VSE/ESA: Evolution and Support of ESA/390* (GC33-6502) is an excellent summary of the new VSE/ESA facilities. The IBM manual *VSE/ESA Performance Considerations* contains a great deal of VSE/ESA specific performance and tuning information.

4.1 Cookbook for Tuning Migrated Systems

Migration to VSE/ESA offers some immediate benefits. However, most of these benefits require that you change your environment. The following lists some changes you should consider after moving to VSE/ESA, in their rough order of importance:

- Review your current I/O configuration for low-cost changes that exploit Dynamic Path Selection and Dynamic Path

Reconnection, or which provide more than two paths to your high-use DASD strings.

- If you see any paging delays, add real memory to your VSE/ESA system. VSE/ESA supports more than 16M real. VSE/ESA also requires some more real memory to perform its function than prior systems.

- If you used CICS MRO only because of virtual storage constraints, consider eliminating MRO. It costs a minimum of 15 percent CPU, and always elongates response time.

- If you had previously detuned CICS buffers or did not fully exploit LSR because of virtual storage constraints, review your LSR specifications. With VSE/ESA, you can usually afford additional buffers and a large LSR pool. If you expect to run more transactions on your CICS system after moving to VSE/ESA, this is especially critical.

- If you encounter many CICS storage compressions or cushion releases, consider exploiting the increased DSA size that is possible under VSE/ESA.

- If you used the xMXT parameters to reduce CICS storage usage, it may be possible to increase the amount of CICS multitasking to utilize the additional virtual storage provided by VSE/ESA.

4.2 Dynamic Channel Subsystem

VSE/ESA added support for the XA mode I/O subsystem. Support for the XA mode I/O subsystem (on XA and ESA mode processors) is arguably the single largest potential benefit for users of VSE/ESA. To understand this we need to compare the 370 I/O support to XA I/O support.

VSE/SP supported only two paths to a DASD. VSE/SP attempted to select an available path by tracking where previous I/Os had been performed, but this processing and switching away from a busy path was all done in software. Also, VSE/SP would try to perform I/O on a path and only learn through an interrupt that the path was not available. Because VSE/SP used a relatively poor method to determine which path to use and because VSE/SP I/O paths were frequently busy, this resulted in delays in starting I/O requests. In addition, once an I/O was started, the requirement to complete each I/O upon the path it was started resulted in excessive RPS reconnect failures. All this meant that VSE/SP I/O performance was difficult to predict and that minor changes in the DASD I/O load could result in wide swings in system performance. VSE/ESA changed all of this as we see in Figure 4.1.

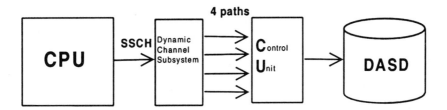

Figure 4.1 Dynamic Channel Subsystem

VSE/ESA now supports up to four paths to each DASD. The operating system does not select the path, it simply issues the Start SubCHannel instruction (SSCH). The hardware determines which path is available, and starts the I/O on an available path without any false starts. In addition, VSE/ESA does not require that an I/O complete upon the path that it was originally scheduled on. This is called *Dynamic Path Reconnect* support. It allows VSE channels to be driven much harder before serious performance problems are encountered. The old 370 DASD channels were often considered to be saturated at less than 40 percent utilization because of extra rotations caused by RPS reconnect failures. Benchmarks have shown that XA mode channels can be driven at 80 percent or greater utilization by VSE before serious DASD I/O problems are observed. Some test cases using caching control units have even shown acceptable I/O performance in the 90 percent channel utilization range! The Hardware Tuning chapter includes a benchmark showing 85 percent channel utilization on 3390 DASD with very little path contention.

The XA mode I/O facilities supported by VSE/ESA also offer a reduction in supervisor overhead to support I/O requests. This is a result of a reduction in the number of interrupts, and in a streamlined I/O scheduling path. Because less single threaded supervisor processing occurs, the fixed operating system overhead component of device service time is reduced, and the maximum channel utilization possible is also increased.

The new I/O support is often only a potential performance improvement because many VSE/ESA users do not migrate to that system with an I/O subsystem that exploits XA only capabilities. After all, if VSE users could not use a feature, they did not purchase hardware for that unusable feature. Thus, all new VSE/ESA users are advised to review their I/O subsystem for low cost changes that allow VSE/ESA to exploit the XA mode I/O support. One exception is a user who has two paths provided for VSE/SP channel switching. Such a user can take advantage of XA in two path mode and will usually see I/O service time improvements. The larger the VSE/SP channel utilization, the larger the potential savings. If your pre-XA DASD channel utilization was low, then you will receive no hardware benefit from the XA I/O subsystem, nor from the addition of I/O paths. If your pre-XA DASD channel utilization was more than 35 percent, you should add paths to these DASD to gain large improvements in device service times.

All users with multiple paths will gain some improvement, but changes may be required for maximal benefit. The first areas to be considered are adding I/O paths, switching to control units capable of extra paths, followed closely by caching DASD control units.

4.2.1 Additional Channel Support

The older VSE systems supported up to a maximum of 16 channels. VSE/ESA supports the XA I/O subsystem, and allows up to 256 channels (see Figure 4.2). Many customers have additional channel capability in place that VSE/ESA can exploit as soon as it is installed. If your processor is able to support more channels, then you will wish to consider this option. Additional channels are very desirable if you are to exploit all of the benefits of the dynamic channel subsystem. In particular, if you wish to provide additional paths to high use DASD strings, you will need to review your current processor channel configuration and possibly add additional channels. At such a time as you add 3390 DASD and 3990 control units, you will certainly need additional channels to achieve the potential performance of these devices.

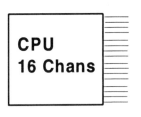

Figure 4.2 VSE/ESA Extra Channel Support

4.2.2 ESCON Support

VSE/ESA supports both ESCON conversion channels and native ESCON channels. This allows access to some of the benefits of ESCON (better reliability and increased cable length) without the need to replace all of the existing parallel devices.

VSE/ESA Version 1 added support for the 9034 ESCON converter (model 1). VSE/ESA Version 1.2 extended this to full ESCON support. It implemented conversion of serial channels to parallel I/O subsystems. The basic support was extended by VSE/ESA Version 1.2 to include the 9035 ESCON converter (model 2). This added conversion of parallel channel to serial 3990/3490 I/O subsystems. VSE/ESA Version 1.2 added support for pure serial environments. The only ESCON facility not supported by the original VSE/ESA releases was connection through a director (and this is supported from VSE/ESA when the director is owned by either MVS or VM). VSE/ESA 1.3 adds support for the ESCON director.

VSE/ESA supports DASD up to 9km from the processor using the laser serial channel. 3490 tapes units are supported up to 23km distant from the processor using the laser serial channel. Other devices can be up to 3km distant.

4.2.3 ECKD Support

VSE/ESA supports and exploits the *Extended Count Key Data (ECKD)* facility. The new ECKD commands are required for the nonsynchronous operation of ESCON channels. The supervisor

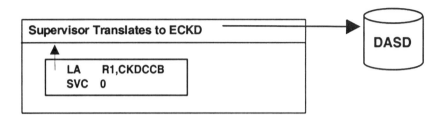

Figure 4.3 ECKD Channel Program Translation

translates CKD channel programs into ECKD channel programs whenever possible. In addition, VSE/ESA VSAM, the Librarian, virtual storage paging, and the Fast Copy utility all generate native ECKD channel programs (see Figure 4.3).

The use of ECKD channel programs results in significant performance improvements. The automatic translation of older channel programs ensures that ECKD benefits are available without changing existing software. VSE/ESA ECKD support allows the use of nonsynchronous operations with 3390 DASD. The 3390 in conjunction with nonsynchronous operation offers higher throughput at a lower level of channel utilization. In addition, the 9345 DASD and 3380 DASD are supported in ECKD mode when they are attached via a 3990 control unit.

4.3 Real Storage

VSE/ESA added support for additional real storage. Older VSE releases could only use 16 megabytes of main storage, and contained no support for extended storage. VSE/ESA still does not support extended storage, but does now support up to 384 megabytes of main storage (see Figure 4.4). This is made up of 256 megabytes of VSIZE (virtual size for partitions), plus another 128 megabytes for VIO (Virtual I/O area used by POWER).

If your VSE system is paging heavily (more than 10 pages/second is usually viewed as serious, but any paging at all for CICS impacts performance), then VSE/ESA can offer an immediate and visible improvement. If you migrate to VSE/ESA and can give additional real memory to ESA, this should be a top priority item.

The additional real memory that VSE/ESA now supports was needed to properly drive the basic twelve partitions, and is an

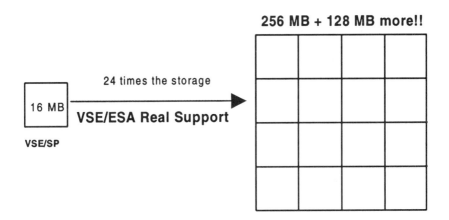

Figure 4.4 VSE/ESA Enhanced Real Support

absolute requirement for a system with any significant usage of dynamic partitions. If you migrate to VSE/ESA and intend to exploit dynamic partitions, you should first carefully review your current paging load.

Note that VSE/ESA real storage requirements are larger than for older VSE releases. If your system was paging on VSE, then additional real storage should be added before migrating to VSE/ESA. One area of increase is in the supervisor size (including copyblocks). The typical VSE/ESA 370 mode supervisor requires 512KB, and the typical ESA mode supervisor requires 576KB.

Real storage tuning is further discussed in the chapter on Paging. Additional information is included in the chapters on CICS, POWER, and VTAM.

4.4 Cache Support

VSE/ESA supports caching control units such as the 3390-3. The CACHE console command was added to control this facility, to display the status of the facility, and to allow access to some basic performance statistics maintained by the controller.

Only basic cache controller support was originally added to VSE/ESA. For example, DASD fast write was not supported, nor was any type of file-level cache enabling supported. VSE/ESA 1.3 added support DASD fast write. Only the basic read-level cache is supported at the control unit and volume level. The read cache is not controllable at a file level.

Note that cache support is a **very** important tuning option available to VSE/ESA users. Although high end DASD controllers are required to use this option, the performance benefits can often justify their purchase and usage. Cache support is discussed in some detail in the hardware tuning chapter.

4.5 Access Register Support

VSE/ESA added support for the ESA hardware Access registers. Access Register mode allows for high performance access to data across address space boundaries. Selecting a MODE=ESA supervisor enables Access Register support. Without Access Register support, a program either needs to run in the same address space as a task whose storage it needs to access, or a slow protocol involving movement of data using a common storage buffer is required. Refer to Figure 4.5 for a diagram comparing Access Register mode processing to 370 mode cross partition access. A MODE=ESA supervisor running on an ESA processor is required to support execution of POWER in a private address space. POWER requires access registers to reference data in a different address space for performance reasons.

4.6 ES/9000 Processor Support

VSE/ESA runs on all uniprocessors in native mode, including all uniprocessor ES/9000 models. However, native VSE/ESA is officially supported on only the air cooled ES/9000 processor models. VSE/ESA is fully supported in a Logical Partition (LPAR) on all multiprocessor CPUs. And, VSE/ESA is supported under VM as a guest system. VM/XA or VM/ESA are required to run VSE/ESA in ESA mode as a VM guest. Multiple Preferred Guest (MPG) mode is supported for V=R and V=F guests for VM/XA and VM/ESA. VSE/ESA can use up to 384MB of real memory but makes no use of extended storage, so you should not configure memory as extended storage.

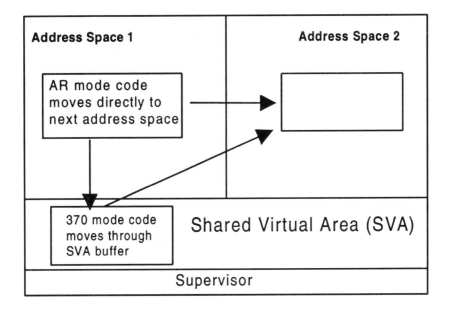

Figure 4.5 Access Register Mode vs 370 Mode

4.7 CICS/VSE V2

CICS/VSE Version 2 is supported by VSE/ESA. VSE/ESA does not support older releases of CICS. CICS V2 contains essentially all of the important MVS CICS V2 features plus certain functionality from the MVS CICS Version 3. CICS is still a major user of CPU time and source of I/O requests for VSE/ESA. The new release of VSE CICS has the following benefits:

    Improved MRO performance
    Coldstart up to 50 percent faster
    WARM shutdown up to 50 percent faster
    XRF Support improves VSE CICS availability
    COBOL II Support
    Improved transaction routing

    Please note that, although CICS MRO support has been enhanced, MRO function shipping is still not a performance option, and its use is discouraged. If your shop used MRO to bypass CICS storage constraints, you should review the need for MRO, and eliminate it if possible.

The addition of XRF to VSE CICS provides for increased availability of CICS services. XRF stands for Extended Recovery Facility. XRF allows a backup CICS system to assume the load of a failed primary CICS. To use XRF two CICS systems are required (these may be on one processor, or split across two processors). One CICS system is active, the other is an alternate. The active system processes all of your CICS work in the normal fashion. The alternate CICS is constantly monitoring the status of the active CICS. If the active CICS fails, XRF transfers all resources and activity to the alternate CICS with very little disruption of ongoing work.

COBOL II may now be used to develop CICS transactions. COBOL II added many new functions missing from the old DOS/VS COBOL. This brought COBOL up to the ANSI 1985 standard level. In addition, COBOL II applications may be easy moved between VSE and MVS. This can facilitate application development and improve programmer productivity in a multisystem environment.

The CICS V2 transaction routing support has been enhanced to support APPC paths (peer-to-peer via LU6.2). Transaction routing destinations may also be selected dynamically with the new CICS. This support is equivalent to that provided by MVS CICS V3.1.

CICS performance measurement and tuning is discussed in more detail in a separate chapter. The VTAM chapter is also useful for CICS response time tuning. A more detailed treatment of CICS tuning may be found in S. Piggot's book *CICS: A Practical Guide to System Fine Tuning*.

4.8 VTAM 3.3 Support

ACF/VTAM V3.3 brings significant new function to VSE/ESA. VTAM may now be run in a private address space, separate from the VTAM applications. Support was also added for the BSBUF and XDBUF buffer pools, autoinstall terminals, parallel transmission groups, and the X.21 SHM/MPS feature. These are minor changes listed to illustrate IBM's commitment to bring the VSE and MVS VTAMs closer together. VSE/ESA Interactive User Interface dialogues were enhanced to support the new specifications and to facilitate VTAM network definitions and management.

4.9 VSAM 2.1 Enhancements

VSE/VSAM support for VSE/ESA 1.1 and 1.2 includes the following enhancements:

- Utilize asynchronous ECKD architecture features for 3390 and 9345 DASD.

- Share options 4 support extended across VSE/ESA systems. This allows multiple OPEN OUTPUT across VSE systems (previously unsupported). Note that the use of share option 4 across VSE systems may have a severe performance impact.

- Improved performance of share options 4 for CICS. VSAM previously issued lock requests that caused the whole CICS partition to wait when share options 4 was specified. VSAM now releases control to CICS anytime a lock can not be obtained.

- Read-only catalogs are now supported. This permits a catalog to be updated by VM CMS users, while the data is read by VSE programs. Previously, VSAM attempted to update the catalog, even for dataset read requests, which required the catalog to be read-write to both the CMS and VSE guests with a risk of catalog corruption.

- Ensured read integrity for clusters opened by multiple ACBs. This is a benefit when a cluster is opened via an alternate index (AIX) and also opened through the base path. The implementation is compatible with MVS/DFP.

- The IDCAMS CANCEL STEP now results in the highest current return code being issued as the JCL completion code.

4.10 Librarian Enhancements

The following enhancements were made to the VSE Librarian for VSE/ESA:

- ECKD channel programs are used where applicable.

• Librarian Applications Programming Interface (API) is provided to permit general purpose program access to Library data. This change makes it feasible to use the VSE Librarian as a type of general system database. The DUMP library, and VSE file transfer are examples of how the Librarian is used in this fashion.

4.11 Address Space Size

VSE/SP allowed its twelve partitions to be allocated to any of nine private address spaces or the system partition. However, the maximum size of an address space was restricted to 16 megabytes minus the total size of all shared space areas. These shared space areas included the supervisor, the SVA, and any partitions specifically allocated to the shared address space. VSE/ESA supports the original nine address spaces using the same computation of private area size. VSE/ESA adds additional address spaces, one for each dynamic partition. VSE/ESA 1.3 adds additional address spaces so that each static partition can occupy a unique address space. Figure 4.6 below illustrates nine static partition address spaces plus several dynamic partition address spaces.

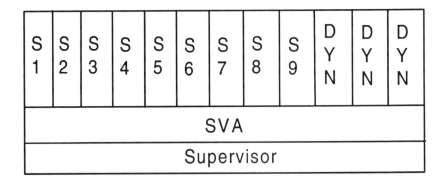

Figure 4.6 VSE/ESA Address Spaces (SHARED=HIGH)

Because POWER and VTAM were required to be in the shared address space, the maximum address space size was often only 8MB or 9MB. This was a serious growth inhibitor for many VSE users who were size constrained on their CICS partitions, and often on their database partitions as well. Many databases like virtual storage almost as much as CICS does.

VSE/ESA supports VTAM in a private area partition. If your system is run in ESA mode then POWER may also be run within the private area. This results in at least 3MB of virtual storage being returned from the shared area to increase the size of the private area.

Many VSE users had detuned their systems in order to fit critical production applications into the available virtual storage. Any such detuning should be reconsidered after moving to VSE/ESA. Such detuning applies especially to POWER, CICS, and VTAM. These are the first places you should check, because their performance can affect that of the entire system.

VSE/ESA increases the size of an address space to either 11 or 12 megabytes (11 for certain large VSE/ESA configurations, but 12 megabytes are usually available). Most VSE shops will gain from one to three megabytes in their private area. VSE/ESA increased the private area size by moving VTAM and POWER out of shared storage. The additional one to three megabytes of virtual storage can be used to tune CICS or SQL/DS partitions. This type of tuning (and retuning) is discussed in the chapters on CICS and VTAM (Chapters 11 and 13).

Customers often found it necessary to reduce their CICS DSA size in order to run CICS with VSE/SP. If the size of your CICS DSA was reduced below an optimal value and many storage compressions resulted, you should increase the size of the CICS DSA after moving to ESA. Likewise, if your CICS shutdown statistics indicate that too few LSR buffers are allocated (this is shown through LSR buffer pool waits), the number of LSR buffers of each size may now be reviewed and corrected. And, any previously resident CICS programs that were removed may now be made resident again.

4.12 Dynamic Partitions

VSE supported a maximum of twelve partitions. VSE/ESA supports these original twelve static partitions plus up to a theoretical maximum of about 200 dynamic partitions. The dynamic partitions each occupy their own address space and thus each may be the maximum size of the total available private area.

VSE users were constrained by the number of available partitions. This was a result of the large number of permanent partitions. These included POWER, VTAM, one or two CICS partitions, a database partition, and often various OEM packages each requiring its own partition. The twelve partitions of VSE were often reduced to four or less usable batch partitions. Once these batch partitions were split between application development and production, waiting for an available partition had become a dirty word in many shops.

Often VSE users were running on processors that VSE could not fully drive with only twelve partitions. Dynamic partitions permit additional work to occupy such available processor capacity. The addition of dynamic partitions can allow work to be completed in less elapsed time, offers growth in the total amount of batch work that can be run, and allows functionality to be added to VSE/ESA through additional permanent server partitions.

Each dynamic partition occupies its own address space. Thus, dynamic partition support includes support for additional address spaces and additional virtual storage size. A dynamic partition is created by POWER when a job of its class is detected. The dynamic partition is released by POWER as soon as this POWER job completes.

Dynamic partitions are organized by class, and by partition number within class. The number of different available dynamic partition classes is 23. The maximum number of classes that may be defined is 10. The maximum number of partitions available within a single class is 32.

VSE/ESA is limited to a maximum virtual storage size (VSIZE) of 256MB. A typical VSE system with twelve static partitions could easily consume over 100MB of this capacity. This leaves about 150MB for use in creating Dynamic Partitions. The minimum Dynamic partition size is 1MB so this limits the maximum number of dynamic partitions to less than 150. VSIZE is only consumed when a dynamic partition is created, so it is possible to have more space defined for dynamic partitions than exists as available VSIZE. POWER will not create a dynamic partition if enough VSIZE is not available, so no fatal problem results from excess definitions.

The dynamic partitions are wholly managed by POWER. A dynamic partition is created when a POWER job of the required class is seen, and it is freed upon completion of that POWER job. Dynamic partitions are automatically limited by VSE/ESA to the available virtual storage. Additional page data space must be allocated in order to take advantage of the dynamic partitions. For additional discussion on the management of dynamic partitions, refer to the chapters on POWER and the SCP.

4.12.1   Dynamic Partition Restrictions

The following list identifies the VSE/ESA facilities that are not supported within dynamic partitions. Essentially all normal application programs will run without alteration in a dynamic partition. Most of the features listed below are used only by IBM and other vendor's system software.

- PFIX macro is not supported. This is a feature only used by IBM and OEM system software and does not impact most applications. A program may acquire Real System storage via new options for the GETVIS macro to offer the same function.

- EXEC pgm, REAL is not supported. This affects only certain timing dependant software.

- BTAM (an old telecommunications access method). VTAM applications are fully supported.

- ISAM (Indexed Sequential Access Method) is an old predecessor to VSAM. However, the VSAM ISAM Interface Program (IIP) is fully supported in a dynamic partition.

- MICR (Magnetic Ink Character Reader) and OCR (Optical Character Reader) devices.

- SYSFIL – SYSRDR, SYSIPT, SYSPCH, and SYSLST may not be assigned to disk nor diskette. These are usually spooled by POWER and not a problem.

- Checkpoint/Restart facility (the CKPNT macro, and the // RSTRT JCL command).

- VMCF (VM Communication Facility). Some OEM products still support VMCF in a dynamic partition for their specific application.

- XECB (an old interface macro used to communicate with POWER). Use the XPCC interface to POWER instead.

- Partition label area. A single partition label area for all dynamic partitions of a given class is supported.

- XPCC/APPCVM.

4.13   VSE/ESA 1.3 Features

IBM announced VSE/ESA Version 1 Release 3 in June of 1992. This release included features that were part of the original VSE/ESA statement of direction, and also addressed a number of GUIDE requirements. In this section we will briefly look at the VSE/ESA 1.3 content. Additional information on the performance implications of this release is included throughout the book, where it is relevant, and where it was known at the time of publication. The following list summarizes the VSE/ESA 1.3 features:

- 31-bit addressing support. This increases the maximum size of an address space to 2 gigabytes.

- Additional virtual and real storage. This increases the total virtual size of the system to 90 gigabytes, and allows VSE/ESA to exploit 2 gigabytes of real memory.

- Support for data spaces is added. An MVS compatible macro interface is provided to define and manipulate data stored in a special type of address space. The MVS DSPSERVE services are implemented in VSE/ESA.

- VSE/VSAM LSR support enhanced for 16 pools of buffers. The LSR buffer pool may also be allocated above the 16M line to exploit the new 31-bit addressing support.

- CICS/VSE 2.2 implements support for 31-bit addressing and offers immediate virtual storage constraint relief to VSE/ESA users by its use of VSAM buffers in an LSR pool above the line.

- Virtual disk facility is added. This allows emulation of FBA DASD in a data space. Because virtual disk accesses can take place in memory, the performance of jobs using them can be greatly increased.

- Caching support enhancements. The 3990-3 DASD cache control unit support is improved to support DASD Fast Write and the Dual Copy feature.

- The Distributed Workstation Feature allows program development activities previously performed under ICCF or via CMS to run in a Cooperative Processing mode on an OS2 based PC. This new facility will gradually replace ICCF which will no longer be enhanced.

- VSE/ESA now supports up to 1024 real devices.

VSE System Control Program

This chapter discusses the VSE *System Control Program* (SCP). VSE is a multi-tasking system. The function of the SCP is to perform I/O and coordinate resource management for each VSE task. The term System Control Program refers to both the VSE Supervisor program and those areas built at IPL time to support the supervisor.

We will look at the various components of the SCP in some detail. In this chapter we look at the nature of VSE from the viewpoint of someone interested in tuning the operating system. To tune VSE, we must have some familiarity with how VSE is assembled and how the pieces work with each other. Additional performance information on certain SCP components will be found in later chapters of this book. The SCP components that concern us are listed in Figure 5.1

Storage Management
I/O Scheduling
Error Recovery
Paging
Task Initiation and Termination
Console Management
Program Fetch

Figure 5.1 SCP Components

The SCP comprises a number of functional areas related to system performance that will be discussed in detail in this chapter. Refer to Figure 5.1 for the list of SCP functional areas.

Each of these areas impacts VSE performance and can be tuned through simple parameters. Let's start with a discussion of what makes up a VSE task and how VSE tasks communicate with the SCP, then look at each SCP component and what each component does for user tasks. We are interested in how performance problems arise, and what we can do about these problems.

5.1 User Tasks and SCP Communication

When an application program is running within a VSE partition it is doing so as a *user task*. The JCL EXEC statement runs a program as the partition *main task*. For static partition the main task is created at the same time as partition, and exists with the partition until the partition is UNBATCHed. When you run a program in a VSE/ESA dynamic partition, the SCP creates the dynamic partition and the main task which stays in existence until the program completes. After the dynamic partition is terminated, the task can be reused in another dynamic partition. A VSE *task* is a unit of activity (a single execution thread). A program starts with a main task and can attach additional tasks called *subtasks*. Each task within VSE has a unique task ID and is managed using task specific control blocks.

Each task has a *task status*. Each task is either waiting for something or is able to run. A task status is a one byte code that indicates whether or not the task can run. A task that can be run has a "ready" status. A task that cannot run has one of many different wait status codes. Most of the tuning process involves analyzing task wait status values and taking steps to reduce the number and duration of these waits. Whenever a task enters a wait status, the VSE SCP selects a new task with ready status and dispatches that task. Once a task is dispatched by the SCP, it runs until the task communicates a request for service back to the SCP, or until the SCP takes away control. This chapter ends with additional discussion on task wait states, and tuning the various kinds of wait.

All user task communication with VSE is via *Supervisor Calls* (SVCs). Thus, any user program that needs to perform I/O, allocate storage, communicate with another task, load a program into memory, or display a message upon the console, does so by issuing an SVC. An SVC runs as an extension of the user task and cannot do I/O by itself. The VSE supervisor uses *system tasks* to perform I/O for SVC routines. A system task is a portion of the supervisor that runs as a separate task (with its own task ID and task specific control blocks). Let's look at SVCs and system tasks in more detail.

5.1.1 SVCs

An SVC is a machine instruction that causes an interrupt. The SVC interrupt is handled by the VSE Supervisor in a routine called the SVC first level interrupt handler. This routine runs as an extension of the user task. Any page faults that occur in this initial processing are handled just as though they had occurred for the application program. Up to this point, performance problems are handled through tuning of the application. The specific SVC is next dispatched to a specific SVC handler. Since 256 different SVC codes exist, up to 256 different routines can be selected, and we can have up to 256 different kinds of problems to tune. Figure 5.2 below illustrates how a program issues an SVC and enters the supervisor.

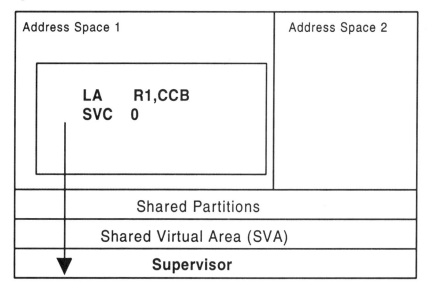

Figure 5.2 SVC Communications

Some SVC handlers are *reentrant*, but many are not. A reentrant SVC handler can service any number of user tasks simultaneously. A nonreentrant SVC handler can only service one user task. While this is happening any other user task that needs the same service waits. When a nonreentrant SVC encounters a page fault, then the SVC routine is locked out from other usage until page fault processing completes. When a commonly used SVC handler encounters many page faults, VSE performance suffers. This is one reason why even low-level paging can have a sudden and large impact on some VSE systems. We will discuss paging in depth in a separate chapter, but note that the problems mentioned here can only be effectively handled by reducing paging.

5.1.2 System Tasks and SVCs

SVC handlers run as an extension of the requesting user task. They can not perform I/O themselves. SVC 0 is not included because it simply queues the user's requested I/O, and thus does not do its own I/O. Each SVC routine that needs to perform I/O has an associated system task. A system task runs on behalf of a given user task or for the supervisor. Each system task is non-reentrant (can only run for one task at a time), and always causes a user wait until the I/O completes.

For example, SVC 4 is issued to load a program into storage. Loading a program requires that I/O be performed. In order to perform I/O the SVC 4 processing uses the DIR and SUP system tasks. Another example is the SVC 110 resource lock handler. In order to lock a resource across multiple VSE/ESA systems, I/O is required to record the request in the lock file. SVC 110 employs the LCK system task to perform this I/O.

An SVC routine that requires the services of a system task verifies that the task is available (and waits if not), then suspends the user task that issued the SVC, places the desired system task into a ready state, and exits through the dispatcher. The system task is dispatched, runs to completion, then readies the original user task, suspends itself, and exits through the dispatcher. The user task resumes execution within the SVC handler, completes its processing, and returns to the SVC issuer.

System Tasks that run directly for SVC requests include LCK, SVT, DIR, and SUP. System Tasks that run indirectly for SVC requests include SNS, DSK, ERP, and CRT. We will study these and various other system tasks in detail in later sections of this and other chapters.

5.1.3 SVC Wait Summary

We have seen several ways that SVCs are involved with performance. We will look into a number of these performance issues and the resulting problems at the end of this chapter in detail. Let us now briefly look at the kinds of wait states associated with SVC handlers.

- A nonreentrant SVC waiting for a page to be read in. Non-reentrant SVCs are always serialized, so other tasks wait for the duration of any page I/Os. This performance problem is corrected by reducing paging. The general subject of paging is discussed at length in the hardware tuning chapter.

- An SVC waiting for access to a system resource that is busy. Many SVCs require access to system resources that are serialized because they are themselves nonreentrant, or because of the need to update them. Performance problems of this type are addressed by reducing the need for the number of SVC requests or by speeding up individual requests.

- An SVC waiting for an exhausted resource. We tune these types of problems by either adding more resources or by reducing the need for existing resources.

- An SVC waiting because a system task is performing I/O or other functions on its behalf. Our primary tuning option for this type of wait is to speed up the system task. Because most waits of this type are I/O waits, this translates into tuning the individual I/O requests.

At this point, we have discussed tasks and how tasks communicate with the SCP. We have seen that tasks can be placed in a wait state as a result of this communication. Let's now look at the services performed by the SCP, and at the performance issues raised when each service is invoked. We will begin with Storage Management because many performance problems are solved by tuning this component.

5.2 Storage Management

In this section we discuss the layout of VSE storage and the parameters used to allocate this storage. We look at address spaces. We cover the shared area, and private areas. We also briefly discuss the mechanics of static and dynamic partitions. Dynamic partitions will be covered further in Chapter 7 on POWER.

5.2.1 Address Spaces

An *address space* is a view (or mapping) of virtual storage. Since current VSE releases support a virtual size of sixteen megabytes (16MB), the maximum amount of storage mapped by an address space is 16MB. VSE/ESA 1.3 supports two billion bytes (2GB or two gigabytes) of virtual storage, and the size of an address space is then be 2GB.

The sixteen megabytes mapped to an address space is comprised of the *shared area* and the *private area*. The shared area includes the supervisor, shared partitions, and SVA. Only the private area is unique to the address space. The maximum address range of the private area is the same in all address spaces. All of the private area of an address space need not be allocated to partitions.

The shared area is mapped to every address space. Please refer to Figure 5.3 for a diagram of the VSE/ESA Virtual Storage layout when SHARED=LOW is specified. SHARED=LOW places all shared area components in the low address range. This is the preferred option and is the VSE/ESA default value. Refer to Figure 5.4 for a diagram of virtual storage for a VSE/SP system or a VSE/ESA system with SHARED=HIGH specified. SHARED=HIGH defines the SVA in the high address range. Note that SHARED=HIGH results in two boundaries for the shared area. Since each shared area boundary is aligned to a megabyte boundary, we see a disadvantage for SHARED=HIGH systems. A SHARED=LOW system will allow an average of .5 megabyte additional private area size by eliminating one of these rounded boundaries.

There are two components of every address space. These are the *shared area* and the *private area*. Each VSE system has a single shared area. The *shared area* includes the storage common to all views of the VSE system (where a view is all storage addressable by a task). Shared storage reduces the size of the private area. One tuning objective is to minimize the size of the shared address space, so as to maximize the size of the private area. The sizes of the supervisor area, VIO/VPOOL storage, SPSIZE storage (shared partition storage), and SVA storage are added to determine the total amount of common mapped storage. Let's spend some time looking at, and defining, these terms.

The *VIO* (Virtual I/O) area is virtual storage not mapped into any address space, but instead mapped only to the page datasets and accessed using the VSE page manager. VIO storage is addressed by page number. The primary uses of VIO storage are:

- Holds the POWER queue file

- Stores message module for CICS/VSE

- Acts as temporary library for OPTION LINK

The *VPOOL* area is storage reserved for VIO buffer space It acts as a window into the VIO area. You define VPOOL storage via the

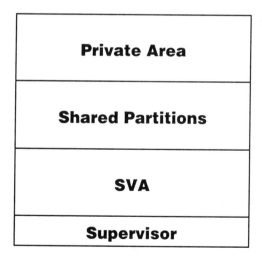

Figure 5.3 VSE/ESA SHARED=LOW Virtual Storage Layout

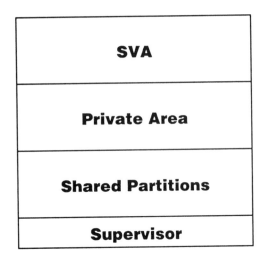

Figure 5.4 VSE/ESA SHARED=HIGH Virtual Storage Layout

VPOOL parameter of the ASI IPL control statement. Note that the VPOOL parameter is valid for all system modes, but the VIO parameter is invalid in a MODE=VM/VMESA supervisor. In a MODE=VM/VMESA supervisor, only the VPOOL parameter may be specified. This VM VPOOL area contains the entire VIO area.

Use the *SPSIZE* parameter to define the maximum size of the storage for shared partitions. The SPSIZE parameter is part of your IPL time SYS command. Later, we will look closely at SPSIZE when we are tuning the size of the private area.

The *SVA* is the Shared Virtual Area. This is common mapped storage that contains the *SDL*, the virtual library area, and the system *GETVIS* area. The *SDL* is the System Directory List, a directory containing the names and locations of all memory resident programs plus directory information for selected IJSYSRS.SYSLIB programs. Resident programs are stored in the SVA. The *SVA PSIZE* is the amount of user program memory required for the *virtual library* portion of the SVA. This is the part of the SVA used to load resident programs. The PSIZE parameter of your IPL SVA statement is used to specify the size of the virtual library. The *SVA GETVIS* is the size of the system common GETVIS area portion of the SVA. GETVIS area storage is dynamically allocated using SCP services. (Refer to Figure 5.5 for an example.)

```
┌─────────────────────────────────────┐
│                                      │
│        System GETVIS(large)          │
│        Must Never Fill Up!!          │
│                                      │
├─────────────────────────────────────┤
│                                      │
│        Virtual Library (large)       │
│       SVA and MOVE mode phases       │
│                                      │
├─────────────────────────────────────┤
│        System Directory List         │
│         72 bytes each entry          │
└─────────────────────────────────────┘
```

Figure 5.5 SVA Layout

In a MODE=VM or MODE=VMESA system, only a single 16M address space is available. Thus, in VM systems, the shared address space is the only address space supported by VSE. All partitions defined in a VM system are mapped into that one address space. (Refer to Figure 5.6 for an example.)

A *private address space* maps storage unique to one partition's view of the VSE system. VSE supports multiple private address spaces. The maximum size of each private address space is 16M minus the size of all shared address space storage.

Up to nine private address spaces may be defined to encompass the twelve static partitions. An additional private address space is automatically created by POWER using VSE/ESA system services for each active dynamic partition. POWER creates the dynamic partition when a job is started, and this address space exists for the life of the job. Thus, a system with the maximum of about 150 active dynamic partitions could have over 150 address spaces. The private address space associated with a dynamic partition is released at the end of the POWER job running in it.

Switching between address spaces was a relatively expensive CPU operation on old hardware, and it was often desirable to minimize address space switches to save CPU time. For the newer ES/9000 processors, the CPU cost of switching is very small. No significant performance benefit exists for packing several partitions

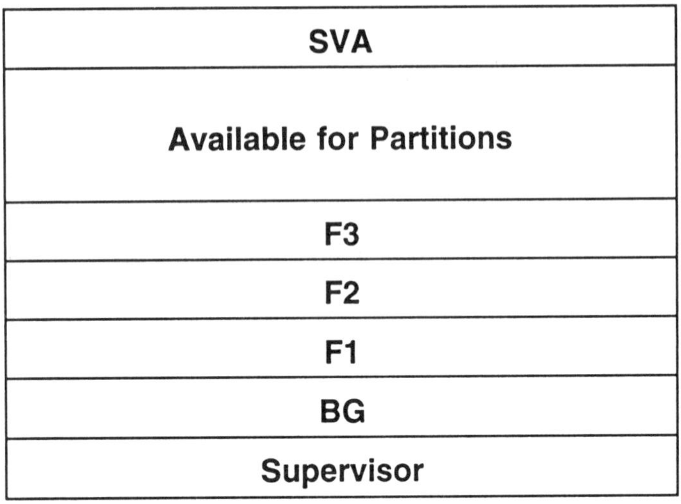

SVA
Available for Partitions
F3
F2
F1
BG
Supervisor

Figure 5.6 VM System Virtual Storage Layout

into a single address space. It is suggested that you define each partition within its own address space in a modern VSE/ESA system. This offers the maximum flexibility with no real cost.

5.2.2 Partition Storage

Each partition has a storage allocation. Partition storage is divided into two areas. These are the *program area* and the *GETVIS area.* Figure 5.7 is an example of a static partition split into these two areas. The first 128 bytes of the program area is a save area.

Note that the beginning of the partition is the program area, and the end of the partition contains the GETVIS area. Dynamic partitions have a third section called the *Dynamic Area.* (See Figure 5.8 for an example.) The dynamic area is an additional GETVIS area.

The standard GETVIS area is reset at the end of each step, and the dynamic area is preserved for the life of the Dynamic partition. The dynamic area provides private area storage that takes the place of system control blocks and OEM workspace that would otherwise need to be placed in the System GETVIS area. The

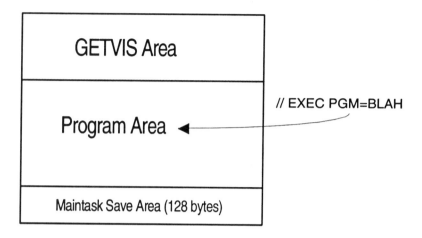

Figure 5.7 VSE Static Partition Layout

system control blocks placed within the dynamic area include the Job Control Work Area (JCWA) and workspace for label processing by $IJBSLA.

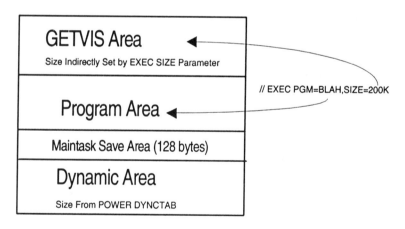

Figure 5.8 VSE/ESA Dynamic Partition Layout

The *program area* is loaded with the phase named by the JCL EXEC statement. Any portion of the program area not occupied by this phase is available for use by the phase. No operating system service is provided to allocate this storage and it must be manually accessed. If the phase named by the EXEC statement does not fit in the available program area, then the current job is canceled.

The *GETVIS* area makes up all storage not part of the program area. To obtain the size of the GETVIS area, subtract the size of the program area from the partition allocation. GETVIS storage is managed by VSE supervisor services and SCP facilities used for all allocation and/or release of this storage. The names of the macros used to allocate and free storage are *GETVIS* and *FREEVIS*. The GETVIS macro is used to allocate storage, and the FREEVIS macro is used to release storage.

The default size of the program area is determined as part of the partition definition. This size may be overridden by the SIZE= parameter of the JCL EXEC statement. The program loaded by the EXEC statement must fit within the program area.

5.3 I/O Scheduling Steps

In this section we discuss how VSE performs I/O. Resident supervisor code performs the I/O function. This code includes the I/O Scheduler, Interrupt handler, Error Recovery, and the Missing Interrupt Handler (MIH). In Chapter 17 (Hardware Tuning) we will cover I/O tuning including identification of high use datasets, file placement, VTOC placement, and similar issues.

In this section we are concerned with learning how VSE works, but will also identify many basic tuning issues. VSE performs an I/O function as shown in Figure 5.9.

1.	An application program issues SVC 0.
2.	The supervisor allocates Channel Queue entry for I/O.
3.	The virtual I/O request is translated to a real request.
4.	The supervisor communicates the I/O to the hardware.
5a.	Other ready tasks run during the I/O processing.
5b.	The I/O subsystem hardware executes the I/O.
6.	A completion interrupt is received and processed.
7.	The channel queue entry is freed.
8.	The application program is told of completion.

Figure 5.9 I/O Scheduling Steps

Let's follow an I/O through the VSE supervisor in the following subsections. We observe the above logical sequence, but instead label the various sections by the system resources needed, and by the areas we can tune.

5.3.1 SVC is Issued

One of the most common functions performed by the VSE supervisor is to schedule all I/O requests. User programs communicate I/O requests to the SCP via SVC 0. The parameter passed to the supervisor for SVC 0 is called a CCB. A *CCB* is a Channel Command Block. It identifies the logical device to be communicated with, and also is used to supply the actual I/O instructions. The SVC 0 handler is given control by the SVC interrupt. It first validates the parameter address. Next, it verifies that a channel queue entry is available.

5.3.2 Channel Queue

VSE tracks all I/O operations in an internal table called the channel queue (CHANQ). A channel queue entry is allocated at the time an SVC 0 is issued and remains queued to the device until the I/O has completed. (See Figure 5.10.)

If a channel queue entry is not available at the time an SVC 0 is issued, the task issuing the request is suspended until a CHANQ entry is freed by the completion of another I/O request.

The maximum number of channel queue entries supported by VSE/ESA 1.1 is 255 and this full number of entries should be allocated. VSE/ESA 1.2 will support up to 1024 devices and additional CHANQ entries. When you take advantage of this additional device support, you should adjust the number of channel queue entries accordingly.

5.3.3 Channel Program Translation

The SVC 0 request made by an application passes a Channel Program to the supervisor. This Channel Program is not directly usable by the hardware because it contains virtual addresses. Although the CPU supports virtual addresses the I/O channels do

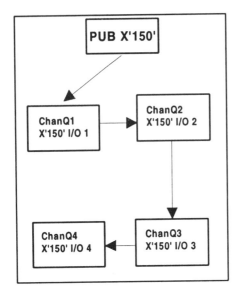

X'150' -- 4 I/Os

Four channel queue
entries linked from
PUB table entry

Figure 5.10 Channel Queue

not. I/O channels only support real addresses. The supervisor translates the user channel program and builds a new channel program containing real memory addresses. This new channel program is used to perform the requested I/O function. (See Figure 5.11.)

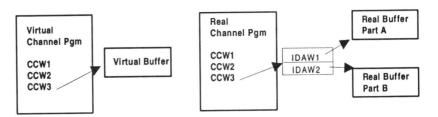

Virtual I/O to Real I/O in Copy Blocks

Figure 5.11 Channel Program Translation

The supervisor uses copy buffers to hold the translated channel program. If insufficient copy buffers are available, then the SVC 0 processing is suspended until the completion of other I/O requests releases enough copy buffer space. If your performance monitor indicates copy buffer waits, then you need to increase the number of copy buffers, or reduce the number/size of I/O requests to reduce the need for copy buffers.

You control the amount of copy buffer space via the BUFSIZE parameter on the SYS IPL control statement. If you decide that additional copy buffers are needed, you cannot just simply increase the value currently specified on the SYS statement. This is because VSE uses the value you specify as a minimum value that is rounded up by the supervisor. Thus, when you determine that you need more copy buffers, you should proceed by getting the actual current value from the 0J39I message produced by the prior IPL, and increasing that value. Note that ESA mode supervisors round in very large increments, and that if you cross a segment boundary by an increase in BUFSIZE, you could reduce the size of the private area by 1MB. Any excess storage in the shared area resulting from this rounding can be used to load CICS phases into the SVA. This has the effect of reducing the storage requirements for the CICS partitions. Because CICS is often the largest partition, moving CICS phases into the SVA can have the same effect as increasing the size of the private area.

The supervisor stores real memory addresses into the copy buffers for all data areas used in the I/O request. To provide real addresses, the supervisor temporarily fixes (TFIXes) the buffer memory in real storage for the duration of the I/O request. This decreases the amount of available real storage, and can contribute to paging problems.

One tuning objective is to minimize the average amount of real storage tied up by TFIX requests at any given moment. One easy way to effect this is to use DASD caching for files that receive many heavily chained I/O requests. (This includes VSAM and high use libraries.)

The FASTTR option is provided to improve the performance of channel program translation. This option causes the copied channel programs to be saved for possible subsequent reuse. The FASTTR option is usually only effective for certain batch jobs, and can even slow down CICS, SQL/DS, VTAM, POWER, and most VSAM. The average amount of TFIXed storage is increased by the FASTTR option. This has the effect of increasing paging. Consequently, this option is discouraged unless known to be effective in your environment. FASTTR is a supervisor generation parameter and all IBM supplied supervisors are generated with FASTTR. This parameter may be disabled via STDOPT for the entire VSE/ESA system, or it may be turned off for a single jobstream with the JCL OPTION NOFASTTR.

5.3.4 Paths to Devices

An I/O transfer occupies a path to a device. This path leads from the processor to a control unit, and from the control unit to the device. If all channels from the processor to a device are busy, then an I/O request must wait for a channel to become available. One or more channels may be used to connect a single control unit to the processor. When a control unit has only a single device attached to it, or a channel is not used by many control units, then a single path may be adequate. However, multiple devices are frequently attached to a single control unit, and multiple control units are attached to a single channel. In these cases, it is beneficial to employ multiple channels between the processor and each control unit. Figure 5.12 below illustrates the components of the path from the CPU to a DASD device.

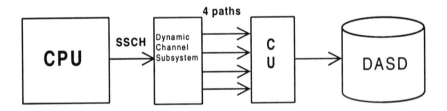

Figure 5.12 I/O Path Components

VSE in 370 mode communicates the I/O request to the hardware via a Start I/O Fast instruction (SIOF). These old VSE/SP and VSE/ESA 370 mode systems support only two channel paths to a control unit. This support is called channel switching (CHANSW). In a channel switching environment, a path is allocated to an I/O request at the time the I/O is started. The path originally allocated is the only one that may be used within this I/O request. This 370 mode I/O can result in excessive waits for I/O even when channels have a relatively low percentage utilization.

VSE/ESA supports XA mode I/O by issuing a Start Subchannel (SSCH) instruction after an I/O in queued to the channel queue. This newer ESA or XA mode support allows for up to four channel paths to new control units. The name of this hardware is the Dynamic Channel Subsystem. As the name implies, an I/O request is not limited to a single path, but instead may be started on one path, transfer data on a second path, and finally complete on yet another path. XA mode I/O allows a channel to be run at close to saturation before I/O degradation is seen.

5.3.5 I/O Interrupt Processing

When an I/O request completes, the completion status is communicated to VSE via an I/O Interrupt. When an interrupt signalling successful I/O completion is received, VSE frees the channel queue entry, and signals the completion to the application that originally issued the SVC 0 request. See Figure 5.13 below for an example of an I/O wait. Note that the application need not be waiting for I/O completion. (Multiple I/O buffers or private multitasking as done by CICS and VTAM each provide for full I/O overlap.)

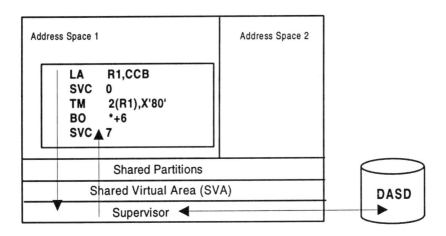

Figure 5.13 I/O SVC 0 through Completion Interrupt

An I/O that fails is handled by error recovery. Because error recovery is a complex process that introduces delays that can be difficult to spot, we will separately discuss it in the next section.

Once an I/O completes, the application that requested the I/O is resumed. This occurs only after all higher priority tasks that are ready to run have been serviced. Thus, a task is not guaranteed to be given control as soon as each I/O is completed. This factor, and differences in I/O times due to channel/device load, plus paging delays, account for much of the variation in the elapsed time duration of a job that is run many times.

5.4 Error Recovery

When an I/O request fails because of an error, the error recovery component of I/O scheduling is performed. The function of error recovery is to retry an I/O operation or to otherwise correct the value of data transferred by a failing operation. Error recovery is performed by three system tasks. These are the SNS task, the DSK task, and the ERP task. These tasks are single threaded.

The sense task (SNS) is activated when any I/O failure is encountered. The function of the SNS task is to read out the extended status provided for errors. When an I/O error occurs, the path used for the I/O is left busy until this special read (called a sense) is performed. For this reason, the sense task is the highest priority task in VSE. (It is the highest priority system task, and system tasks are higher priority than any other kind of task.) The code for the SNS system task is resident within the supervisor.

The disk recovery task (DSK) handles all DASD recovery. This code is resident within the VSE supervisor. The code is resident to prevent a deadlock in the advent of an I/O error while attempting to load a nonresident DASD error recovery routine. Disk error recovery is not usually a major performance issue.

The error recording task (ERP) performs several functions. These are recovery of non-DASD errors, the formatting and display of error recovery console messages, and the logging of device status to the recorder file. All ERP processing is performed by non-resident code. This code is contained within $$A transients that are loaded into, and execute within, the A-transient area. The A-transient area is contained within the supervisor.

Because many program fetches are required for ERP processing, ERP waits can be common, and can degrade VSE performance. This is most often seen in an environment with a lot of non-cartridge tape processing. Some OEM products permit high-usage $$A transients to be placed resident in MOVE mode. This is the only real tuning option for an environment constrained by ERP processing.

5.5 Paging

In a virtual storage environment, the storage area is broken up into *pages*. A page is a 4KB block of storage. All of the storage used by a *virtual* program does not have *real* storage associated with it. When a page of storage that does not have a matching block of real storage is referenced, then a *page fault* occurs. To handle a page fault, VSE must allocate a block of real storage (also called a page frame). If no pages of real memory are available, then VSE must "steal" another page frame of memory. The original contents will be written out to a page dataset if a valid copy is not on currently on disk. If the requested storage exists and is on disk, then VSE must perform an I/O to read this data into the page just allocated. Figure 5.14 illustrates the paging process. You will observe that pages do not occupy contiguous real memory, nor are all pages resident within real. Note that page 4 and page 6 are not actually resident in real storage in our figure, and that page 6 is being read into real memory.

The I/O done by VSE to manage virtual storage is called paging I/O. All VSE paging I/O is done by the page manager (PMR) system task. VSE only loads nonresident pages in response to page faults. This is called *demand paging*. Most VSE paging is done on a demand basis, and a task that encounters page faults will be elongated by the time to service the paging request. VSE does not do block paging at this time, but instead reads and writes only single pages. VSE tasks may request that nonresident pages be brought into memory before they are needed, and asynchronously with other task processing. The VSE PAGEIN macro implements such anticipatory paging. CICS uses the PAGEIN macro to reduce paging of transaction programs.

In a storage constrained system, paging can result in page I/O thrashing. This occurs when VSE is doing little more than paging. VSE does not perform anticipatory paging. This means that a task that is dispatched after being inactive long enough to lose much of its storage, will encounter large paging overhead when it is finally dispatched again. In turn, this can result in VSE partition balancing creating a situation where page thrashing will occur even when adequate real storage would otherwise be available. Put

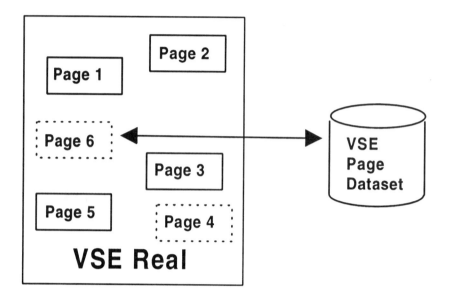

Figure 5.14 Pages and Paging

simply, VSE is NOT designed to page at high levels.

Paging cripples a transaction processing system. This is because all time spent paging is not available to service any terminal. Even ten page requests per second will often very visibly impact a CICS system. CICS is also impacted by any VTAM paging delays. Because CICS performance is a key element of most shops policy, real memory constraints are one of the most important tuning issues.

VTAM can also be seriously impacted by paging. This is a result of VTAMs large working set, and the impact of a page fault on the task VTAM is servicing plus any other tasks waiting for VTAM. Each page fault suspends the processing for a single VTAM user until it is handled. Because VTAM makes large transient demands upon virtual storage, it is often one of the first VSE components impacted by paging. Note that VTAM does employ page handling overlap and can continue processing of VTAM private tasks after a single VTAM task is suspended by a page fault.

5.5.1 Pagefaults within POWER

POWER is the VSE spooler. As such, it is a critical component, and POWER waits impact the entire system. POWER implements private multi-tasking. This allows POWER to view each service it performs for each controlled partition, as a separate POWER task. POWER also supports an SCP feature called Page Fault Overlap (PFO). This feature allows POWER to service another POWER task when a page fault is encountered by one task. The POWER task that was interrupted is suspended until the page fault can be handled. In spite of this feature, paging encountered by POWER can still be serious. Any POWER page fault elongates the interrupted task by the time to service the page fault. Any resources held by an interrupted POWER task remain held until the pagefault can be handled.

5.5.2 Pagefaults within SVCs

Many SVCs are single threaded, and page faults within such SVCs result in long periods of time where these SVCs are unavailable. This results in subsequent task wait states and task queuing. The only effective way to tune a system encountering waits for SVC routines due to page faults is to reduce paging. Refer to Chapter 17 (Hardware) for detailed information on tuning paging.

5.6 Task Initiation and Termination

The SCP is responsible for initiating and terminating tasks. These actions are performed within the resident supervisor, SVA resident phases, and by some POWER code. Two kinds of tasks are handled. These are called *main tasks* and *subtasks*. A *main task* is the first task associated with a partition. Any additional tasks created/attached by the maintask are called *subtasks*.

Task initiation is performed when a task is created. For the main task, this automatically occurs when the partition is allocated. For a subtask, this occurs when an ATTACH macro is issued. The SCP manages all tasks using task related control blocks called the *TIB* and the *TCB*. The word *TIB* is the *Task Information Block* and is used to track the task dispatching status. The *TCB* is the *Task*

Control Block and acts as workspace for supervisor processing on behalf of the task. These task related control blocks are part of the supervisor for the static partitions and the system tasks. For dynamic partitions and subtasks, the control block storage is dynamically allocated from the system GETVIS area. For dynamic partitions, additional storage is allocated by POWER from within the POWER partition to manage the dynamic partition. Once a static partition exists, the main task is automatically reset and/or recreated by termination. Task initiation is not usually a source of performance problems. Let's now look at the terminator. (See Figure 5.15.)

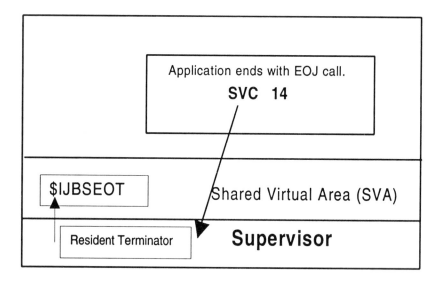

Figure 5.15 Task Termination Flow

Task termination is performed by the resident terminator. This is comprised of supervisor code plus the SVA resident phase named $IJBSEOT. $IJBSEOT is given control by the supervisor cancel exit. The termination process is complex, and contains a number of performance bottlenecks. Let us summarize the actions performed by the resident terminator, then look at these performance issues.

1. The terminator waits for all pending I/O requests to complete. This is done to ensure that critical dataset

updates are completed before resource enqueues and I/O buffers are released.

2. Any task related resources are freed. This includes task level enqueues, and various supervisor tables.

3. If a subtask is being terminated, the termination process is complete and the terminator exits. If a main task is being terminated, the terminator continues.

4. The program area storage is released and the entire partition is reset. This is done via SVC 59 to release all occupied pages back to the page manager. All partition dynamic storage (GETVIS storage) is freed by this SVC.

5. The main task is finally reset and reinitialized by $IJBSEOT. It fetches $JOBCTLA into the partition, and initializes the partition main task save area to begin execution within $JOBCTLA.

Because task termination waits for any outstanding I/Os, it can be a source of performance problems, especially when I/O errors occur or an interrupt is missed. Item one (wait for I/O completion) is a major performance issue. Because enqueues (VSE locks) are not released until after completion of outstanding I/O, long resource waits may occur. For large partitions, the process of releasing and reinitializing partition storage consumes a significant amount of CPU time. We will now discuss the task initiation and termination process and associated performance issues in more detail in the following sections.

5.6.1 Initiation – Creating Partitions

VSE creates and manages two kinds of partitions. These are the static partitions and the dynamic partitions. Static partitions are normally defined as part of the BG ASI IPL procedure. Dynamic partitions are created as needed to run jobs by POWER.

Static partitions are managed by the SCP and Job Control. The JCL ALLOC command is used to define the size of static partitions. The ALLOC command reserves the virtual storage but does not start the partition. A static partition is started by either the manual START command or automatically by POWER. POWER can automatically start partitions during initialization via the PSTART command.

Dynamic partitions are created and managed by POWER. Dynamic partitions are defined to POWER within the DTR$DYNC library member. This member is loaded by POWER when the PLOAD DYNC command is issued. POWER creates dynamic partitions as needed to run jobs of designated classes. Dynamic partitions are automatically released by POWER at the end of the POWER job for which the dynamic partition was created.

The management of dynamic partitions was added to POWER in VSE/ESA. When many dynamic partitions are started at the same time, several performance bottlenecks can be observed.

1. POWER requires additional storage for each active dynamic partition. Monitor POWER storage to ensure that adequate storage is available. The PDISPLAY STATUS command can be used to accomplish this.

2. Starting a dynamic partition consumes somewhat more CPU than starting a static partition. If many small jobs are to be run, you may wish to consider the use of static partitions rather than dynamic partitions. If your jobs run more than a few seconds elapsed time, then the performance impact of creating the dynamic partitions is negligible.

3. Starting a dynamic partition involves reading and executing the statements in an initialization procedure. If LIBDEFs or DLBLs or other time consuming statements are included in this procedure, you may see delays in the start of processing within the dynamic partition. LIBDEFs and DLBLs can also cause locks that may result in long waits during dynamic partition startup.

4. Dynamic partition management is serialized within POWER. When many small jobs are run in dynamic partitions, POWER's ability to adequately service other jobs appears to be impacted. Move small jobs to static partitions, or use a server dynamic partition rather than a job to accomplish the task.

5.6.2 Dump Waits

When a task abnormally terminates, the SVA resident phase $IJBSDMP is used to perform abnormal termination. $IJBSDMP handles abnormal termination message processing and dump processing. It is activated for all abends, even when a dump is not required. $IJBSDMP is also used to handle other kinds of dumps such as those requested by the VSE PDUMP, DUMP, and JDUMP macros (via simulated calls to $$BPDUMP, $$BDUMP, and $$BJDUMP).

$IJBSDMP is not reentrant. The phase in the SVA is serialized by SCP code. When a task needs $IJBSDMP and it is found to be busy, then the task is suspended until $IJBSDMP becomes available. This is called a *dump wait*.

Although not usually a serious problem, dump waits can seriously impact system performance under certain circumstances. For example, if a dump is being produced, and the POWER data file fills up, no other task will be able to perform $IJBSDMP until the data file full condition is corrected. This can gradually stop all VSE processing. Operators can easily miss this condition as the POWER messages can scroll off the screen. It should be suspected whenever a problem description includes the phrase "nothing is going to end of job."

5.6.3 Terminator Waits

Whenever any task terminates, $IJBSEOT will be executed. This is a nonreentrant SVA resident phase that is single threaded. $IJBSEOT is used for all normal and abnormal task terminations.

One of $IJBSEOT's main functions is to wait for I/O completion. If an I/O request cannot complete because of error recovery or because of a lost interrupt, the VSE system will gradually come to a grinding halt. The normal symptom of a terminator wait is jobs hanging rather than going to EOJ.

Terminator waits can be very serious because an incomplete job does not have any of its output available. If an IPL is performed to recover from a terminator wait, then all output from running jobs is lost, and the jobs must be rerun to reproduce this output.

Fortunately, we can usually avoid IPLs to recover from terminator waits by using standard VSE operator commands. The commands we will discuss are ONLINE, CANCEL cuu, and CANCEL FORCE. Various OEM products offer additional online and console commands to assist in cleaning up terminator hangs.

The VSE ONLINE command is often effective in recovering from missing I/O interrupts. The format of this command is **ONLINE cuu** where *cuu* is the unit address of the I/O device. This command cannot cause problems, and should be used whenever a terminator wait is suspected. Of course, the trick is to identify the device you are waiting on (the *cuu* above). The *cuu* is usually a tape device and you can safely try the tape devices known to be used by the job in question. Nothing bad will happen as a result of issuing an ONLINE command for a device that is not experiencing problems. When the ONLINE command works, the job that was hung will simply go to EOJ. If the ONLINE command is ineffective (nothing happens when it is issued), the terminator can be forcibly released via the CANCEL I/O command. The format of this command is **CANCEL cuu** where *cuu* is the unit address of the I/O device. The CANCEL command should only be used as a last resort because it cancels the job hung up in a terminator wait. If a terminator wait is due to something other than an I/O wait, another form of the CANCEL command may help. This is the **CANCEL pp,FORCE** command (where *pp* is the partition ID). Only after each of these options has been exhausted should a system IPL be considered.

5.7 Operator Console

VSE supports only a single operator console. That console is a CRT designated at IPL time. This CRT receives all console traffic. In a busy VSE system, console processing can impact the performance of VSE. Waits due to outstanding replies, console buffers, hardcopy file I/O, and the SVC 0 path for console I/O can all impact performance.

Two system tasks are used to support the console. These are the ASY and CRT system tasks. When an I/O interrupt signalling console input is seen, VSE activates the ASY task. The ASY task reads the data, moves the console input data to an internal supervisor buffer, and handles certain very basic console control commands (such as REPLID). The CRT task is activated to update the console display and the hardcopy file.

Each console input or output request is handled using a VSE console buffer. If no buffer is available when needed, the requesting task is suspended until one becomes available. Console buffer waits are normally not a serious problem.

VSE does not require a console. You can IPL a VSE system without an operator console. This major action can be used to eliminate a single point of failure, and to reduce console processing overhead. In general, either a console management product or an automated operations solution is required in order to run VSE without an operator console. A number of IBM and OEM products are available.

5.7.1 Tuning CRT Transients

The operator console CRT display and the hardcopy file are managed by the CRT system task. The code for this task is non-resident. All such code is packaged into $$BOCRTx transient routines. These are loaded into the CRT transient area where they execute. Additional processing is performed by $IJBHCF within the SVA. This is illustrated by Figure 5.16 below.

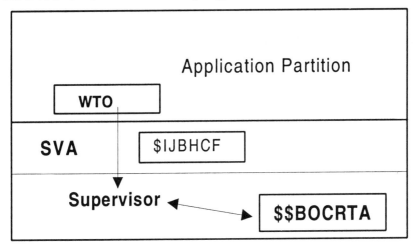

Figure 5.16 CRT Transient Execution

CRT transient area processing can seriously impact console throughput. This is a result of the five to seven CRT transients that are required to handle each write to the console. The overhead of loading transients can be eliminated by using the **MOVE** mode option of the SET SDL command. The IBM suggested list of MOVE mode transients includes a set of common $$BOCRTx transients. It is suggested that most $$BOCRTx transients be made resident to improve performance and to eliminate any confusion in tuning the console. Figure 5.17 below lists the CRT transients which must be made resident for adequate console performance. This list includes all CRT transients used in a typical environment except for $$BOCRTK which has only a small use count (you could add this one as well if you have ample SVA space).

```
$$BOCRTA,MOVE
$$BOCRTC,MOVE
$$BOCRTG,MOVE
$$BOCRTH,MOVE
$$BOCRTZ,MOVE
```

Figure 5.17 Resident CRT Transients

Console processing can amount to 5% of all CPU time spent in VSE when a lot of console traffic is produced. It is suggested that non-essential console traffic be eliminated to reduce this overhead. This can be easily accomplished with any console management product. Many POWER and VTAM messages can be removed from the display without any operator impact. An additional benefit of reduced traffic is an easier to read console, resulting in fewer operator errors, and fewer reruns.

5.7.2 DOC Mode Console Commands

VSE includes several commands to assist in managing the console CRT. The commands we will discuss include the K command, and the D command. The commands are summarized in Figure 5.18.

The K command is used to control deletion of console lines. Use K S,DEL=Y to permit automatic deletion of lines when the console is full, and it is scrolled. Messages of types A, D, and E are not automatically deleted using this option, and are manually deleted by placing the cursor under the line, and pressing enter.

Command	Function
K E	Delete lines
K S,DEL=Y	Auto-deletion
D L	Scroll back
D F	Scroll forward
D E	End scroll

Figure 5.18 DOC Mode Console Control Commands

You may choose to use K S,DEL=D to force automatic deletion of all messages when the screen becomes full. This is the default option for VSE/ESA. However, it is easy to miss a required response, stopping a partition until this is noticed and corrected, so this option is not suggested unless your operators are experienced.

The K E command may be used to forcibly delete lines from the console. Operands of this command allow you to select a range of lines to delete, and to delete all lines (the default). Selected messages may be deleted by placing the cursor on the line to be deleted, and then pressing ENTER.

The D command allows the operator to scroll the console display. The D L command initiates a scrolled console display. The D L,B command scrolls the console backwards, the D L,F command scrolls the console forwards, and the D E command resumes the current console display. When the console is scrolled back, delays may occur when critical console traffic is needed. Although VSE displays a warning message for most such cases, it is a good idea to caution operators to not leave the console scrolled back for longer than is needed.

5.7.3 Message Reply Waits

Performance monitors report on delays required to process console requests. With few exceptions, all waits are of interest to systems programmers. Some programs leave a permanent reply outstanding on the console. Such a reply can skew the average wait time reported for console requests. CICS will leave a reply outstanding on the console when configured to do so.

Any excessive console wait not attributed to a long term reply should be investigated. Our console wait checklist includes:

1. Verify that all $$BOCRTx transients are in move mode.

2. Ensure the hard copy file is not encountering long I/O waits.

3. Verify console buffer waits are not impacting performance.

4. Verify that operators are promptly replying to messages.

5. Verify that all nonessential messages are being deleted by a console management product.

5.8 Logical Transient Area

The Logical Transient Area (LTA) is a single area within the supervisor used to load $$B transients (except $$BOCRTx transients), that are executed when requested by a task. Common macros and conditions that use the LTA include OPEN, CLOSE, and end of volume. Application programs request LTA services via an SVC 2 issued from within a user partition. Figure 5.19 illustrates this process.

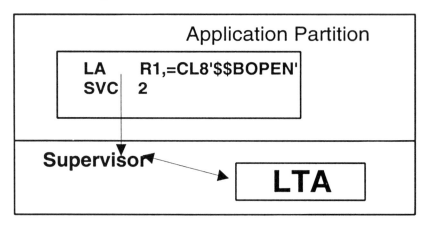

Figure 5.19 LTA Execution

The LTA is single threaded. In a VSE system running a number of partitions, even a small amount of OPEN and CLOSE processing can cause some delays. A performance monitor that reports LTA waits (code 81 waits) can be used to determine if the LTA is a problem area in your environment. The LTA is not always a serious problem. However, significant LTA waits have been observed when certain disk and tape management products are used, and when various conditions occur in normal VSE processing.

If you determine that LTA waits are a problem in your shop, the following checklist should be used:

1. Ensure high-use logical transients are in **MOVE** mode. Your performance monitor should identify transient usage. Appendix B contains a list of high use transients.

2. Verify that all tape and/or disk manager performance options have been selected. These vary by product, and you are referred to the documentation for your product.

3. Investigate the use of an OEM product to add support for multiple logical transient areas. One additional LTA can reap great benefits. In a ten-hour production period, Pete Clark observed a 34-minute LTA wait savings from one extra LTA with over transient 170,000 requests.

5.9 System Tasks

System tasks are used by the supervisor any time the supervisor needs to perform I/O. Refer to Figure 5.20 for a list of all VSE system tasks. System tasks may be run on behalf of the system or for a user. System tasks can also fail. When a failure occurs within system processing, the VSE system normally needs to be IPLed. When a failure occurs within user processing, only the affected user task is terminated.

All system task processing is single threaded. This is a result of using reserved control blocks that are part of the supervisor area. Whenever a system task is required and is already busy, then the system task requestor is suspended. A performance monitor will report system task waits, and the VSE console STATUS command can be used to display waits occurring at the time the command is issued.

System task waits that often impact VSE performance include those for the lock manager, error recovery, console management, and fetch. Tuning these areas is covered in other chapters. Fetch processing is discussed in the next section.

```
SNS 01      Sense and MIH Task
DSK 02      Disk Error Recovery
RAS 03      CPU/Channel Recovery
PMR 04      Page Manager
PGN 06      Page In Handler
SUP 07      Phase Readin Handler
DIR 08      Directory Search
CRT 09      DOC Console Manager
ASY 0A      Asynchronous Operator Communications
ERP 0B      Error recovery and logging
LCK 0C      DASD Lock File Handler for Lock Manager
LOG 0E      Security Logger Task
SVT 0F      AVR Volume Read and Library Table Update
IMR 11      Migration Aid Log Task
AR  20      Attention Routine
```

Figure 5.20 System Task Names

5.10 Fetch Routine

The supervisor handles all requests to load programs within the *Fetch Routine.* The fetch routine is comprised of several SVC routines, plus two system tasks, DIR and SUP. Fetches occur frequently, and most program fetches requires I/O. Because this process is non-reentrant, fetch is often a VSE performance bottleneck.

In the following sections, we will discuss each of the components of fetch processing. We will see where delays are introduced, and what can be done to improve performance. Additional tuning information can be found in the Librarian chapter. (See Chapter 8.)

5.10.1 SVCs Used by Fetch

Figure 5.21 illustrates the SVCs that cause programs to be loaded.

SVC 1	Load and execute a program.
SVC 2	Load and execute logical transient into LTA.
SVC 3	Load a $$A transient into PTA.
SVC 4	Load program.
SVC 48	Load a $$BOCRTx transient for CRT task.
SVC 65	Load a program into GETVIS area.

Figure 5.21 SVCs Used to Load Programs

Each of the SVCs listed can be analyzed by most performance monitors. A raw count of SVCs can be used to determine what kinds of fetches are contributing to any performance problems. All fetches are of interest because they consume significant CPU time and often require I/Os. The duration of system task waits can be used to measure whether or not fetch waits are a serious issue in your environment.

5.10.2 Fetch System Tasks

Two system tasks are used to perform a fetch. These are the DIR task and the SUP task. These tasks are the principal source of delays due to fetch processing. This is a result of all fetch related I/O being performed by the DIR and SUP system tasks.

The DIR system task is invoked to locate the directory entry information for the desired program and to save this information in an internal work area called TCB Fetch Work. The DIR task is not required when the directory entry information is provided as part of the SVC parameter list. If directory information is provided, it is moved into the fetch work area without using the DIR task at all. Like all system tasks, the DIR system task is single threaded. Because the DIR task may have to search as many as 31 directories, its processing can take a long time. Fetch waits due to the DIR task being busy are common.

The SUP system task is used to read a program into memory. It attempts to read the whole program or a large piece of the program in a single I/O operation. When a library is fragmented, this cannot be done, and the SUP task can become a bottleneck. When a fragmented program is fetched, it can only be read one block at a time. Tuning fragmented libraries is discussed in the chapter on the Librarian. (See Chapter 8.)

The SUP task may be skipped for transients by placing them in MOVE mode. The LTA tuning section above discussed this option. Normal program phases cannot normally be placed into move mode. However, some OEM products extend fetch processing to support MOVE mode non-transient phases. Programs that do not modify themselves can often be placed in the SVA. Placing a program in the SVA eliminates SUP overhead, but does increase shared area virtual storage requirements. The SVA option needs to be carefully weighed, but can be very effective.

Delays in the SUP task occur when frequently used libraries are on the same DASD volume as other high use datasets. When SUP has to wait because its I/O request is queued up after a long I/O request, then SUP delays will result. Examples of conflicting I/O requests include large VSAM I/Os, lock file I/Os, paging I/Os, and long VTOC searches. These delays are identified by observing the I/O queue depth and by comparing the average time to complete SUP task I/Os to the predicted time for the device. In general, high use libraries should be separated from the VSE Lock File, busy VSAM files, your tape and/or disk manager catalog, and other similar high use files.

We have seen that the fetch process is a complex one, that is prone to waits from many sources. A more detailed treatment of tuning fetch is done in the Librarian chapter (Chapter 8). Refer to that chapter also for fetch tuning cookbook techniques.

5.11   Diagnosing VSE Wait States

One approach to tuning a VSE system begins with an analysis of recorded wait states. This is easily accomplished using most performance monitors. A good performance monitor reports the percentage of time spent in each kind of wait. A monitor that is capable of basic statistical reporting can further simplify this task.

Common wait states should be analyzed, tuning done, and performance remeasured to verify the efficacy of the tuning operation. Changes to the system should be made one at a time to permit determination of relative benefit, and because multiple tuning changes often interact with each other.

5.11.1   Exhausted Resource Wait

One easy type of wait state to handle is the *Exhausted Resource Wait*. Whenever a resource is depleted, an Exhausted Resource Wait occurs. For example, waiting for I/O copy buffers is an Exhausted Resource Wait.

Two general procedures for tuning this type of wait are frequently used. You may add additional resources, or you may make the current usage more efficient. Thus, for our example of a copy buffer wait, you can add more copy buffers, or you can speed up the individual I/Os.

Running out of CHANQ entries, console buffers, Operator Reply Elements, or waiting for the LTA are additional examples of this type of wait. Let us finish by summarizing our tuning options for some exhausted resource cases.

- Channel queue waits can be corrected by adding more channel queue entries, or by tuning I/O requests (discussed in Chapter 18, the hardware chapter). Note that using additional buffers to eliminate I/O requests counts as tuning I/O.

- Console buffer waits can be corrected by providing more console buffers, or by speeding up console I/O (use of MOVE mode CRT transients, and suppression of messages that are not needed).

- LTA Waits can be reduced by reducing time spent in the LTA (use of MOVE mode, and LTA I/O request tuning) or by adding a multiple LTA product from an OEM vendor.

5.11.2   Routine Busy Wait

Whenever a task needs access to a routine that is already running for another user, and that routine is serialized, the requesting task is suspended until the requested routine becomes available. Most

SVC waits are examples of this type of wait. One good example is the SVC 0 CCW translation processor discussed earlier in this chapter.

The normal procedure for this type of wait is to reduce the time required by the serialized routine. We do this by tuning specific SCP (and other) components. Thus, we can attempt to improve the performance of the VSE lock manager, or tune fetch processing, or speed up the page manager. Another technique is to reduce the need for the serialized routine. In the case of the VSE lock manager, this can be accomplished by moving resources off shared DASD volumes.

Another example of a Routine Busy Wait is the Logical Transient Area (LTA). Note that an LTA wait is an example of an Exhausted Resource Wait, as well as a Routine Busy Wait. We can improve the performance of the LTA by placing critical transients into MOVE mode. We can reduce the extent of LTA waits by adding support for multiple logical transient areas, or through a change in access methods.

5.11.3   Fetch Routine Waits

Waits for the fetch routine are easily identified by wait codes involving the DIR and SUP system tasks. Any task that is waiting for DIR or SUP is waiting for fetch completion. The tuning process for fetch waits is simply to reduce the time in the two system tasks.

The DIR system task handles directory searches. We can improve this by reducing the number of I/Os or by speeding up the individual I/O requests. We reduce DIR I/O requests by making the directory search chain shorter. We speed up I/Os by reducing arm contention, employing DASD caching, or by reducing channel busy. We can also eliminate directory searches for IJSYSRS.SYSLIB phases by placing their directory entries into the SDL.

The SUP system task handles program read in. We can improve this by reducing the number of I/Os or by speeding up the individual I/O requests. We reduce SUP I/O requests by reorganizing frequently used libraries (see Chapter 8). We speed up individual I/Os by reducing arm contention, employing DASD caching, and reducing channel busy (see Chapter 17). We can also eliminate frequent program fetches by making highly used programs resident in the SVA, and by placing high-use transients into MOVE mode.

5.11.4   Wait for Paging

When a page fault is encountered, the task that attempted to access the nonresident storage is placed in a page wait, and a request to bring the page into memory is queued to the page manager. When the page is made available by a subsequent page manager I/O, the task is made ready again.

Page waits can be tuned by reducing the number of page faults, or by making page I/O run faster. We reduce page faults by adding real memory, reducing the working set of a program, or by reserving memory for applications prone to paging. We improve page I/O by reducing conflicting I/O to busy paging volumes, moving paging datasets to faster types of DASD, or by mapping page datasets to virtual storage address ranges so that parallel page requests can be processed.

Not all page faults cause paging. The first reference to a storage frame does not cause a page fault if real storage is available to be assigned to the virtual frame upon reference. Programs can be written to improve the amount of available real storage. For example, CICS uses RELPAG to free virtual pages that it no longer needs. When this storage is subsequently referenced for reuse, the page manager can often simply reassign some of the original real storage with the result that a page operation does not occur. A page fault occurs, but VSE/ESA does not have to do any paging I/O to disk. Instead it simply uses a free page frame.

When a page I/O is required, VSE normally disables the interrupted task until the page I/O completes. The VSE dispatcher gives the highest priority task that is ready to run control during this type of page wait. A task can request that it be given control by employing *Page Fault Overlap* (PFO). POWER is an example of an IBM component that uses PFO, and POWER is not as seriously impacted by paging as other products such as CICS that do not use the PFO facility.

5.11.5   Waiting for I/O

I/O waits are the most common wait state in most VSE systems. They can also be the most challenging to tune. Some of our I/O tuning options include:

- Favoring one task's I/O over other tasks. The PRTYIO command may be used to accomplish this.

- Employing buffering options to reduce I/Os. VSAM allows easy bufferspace specification within JCL.

- Speeding up individual I/Os by tuning the I/O hardware subsystem.

- Changing from slow to faster I/O devices.

I/O tuning is extensively discussed in other portions of this book. Remember that improving the I/O service of one task may impact other tasks. This is especially true when the PRTYIO facility is used. (Refer to the PRTYIO section of Chapter 18.) It is less true when a task's I/O is eliminated or improved through buffering.

5.11.6 READY Task Wait

Tasks can be ready to run, but unable to run due to unavailable CPU capacity. Ready task waits arise when the CPU is saturated. This can continue for extended periods. Refer to Chapter 17 for a detailed discussion of CPU tuning. One "quick fix" could be to use partition balancing. Partition balancing gives several partitions equal access to the CPU. Refer to the PRTY command discussion in Chapter 18 for details.

5.11.7 Task Status Codes

Figure 5.22 summarizes the common task status codes. This information is provided for advanced users, and is not required to perform the general tuning techniques covered in the rest of this book. The basic tuning process can be performed by using the cookbook section of each chapter. However, much of the advanced tuning process involves identifying those wait codes common in your environment, analyzing their causes, and taking corrective action.

In the left column, we list the hexadecimal status code value along with the IBM supervisor acronym for its meaning. The right column lists an explanation of the status code. These are the status codes listed by the IBM STATUS command. The same codes are also used by some OEM products. Most performance monitors can identify the percentage of time a task is waiting on each possible wait source.

Status Code	Reason for code (Wait Reason)
66-EOT	$IJBSEOT is busy
6F-CNS	Console buffer bound
72-DIR	Wait for DIR system task
75-BUF	Waiting for free copy block
76-ICF	Wait for ICCF
79-CHQ	Wait for free CHANQ entry
7D-AVR	Wait for volume label read/AVR
81-LTA	Logical Transient Area (LTA) is busy
82-I/O	Wait for I/O or ECB post
83-CPU	Running or waiting for CPU
84-SUP	Wait for SUP task
85-FCH	Task in DIR/SUP system task
86-PMR	Wait for page fault
89-DMP	Wait for $IJBSDMP
8E-RUR	Wait for locked resource

Figure 5.22 Task Status Codes

Chapter

6

Virtual Storage Tuning

This chapter discusses the tuning of virtual storage. This means reducing the amount of virtual storage needed, and also includes increasing the amount of available virtual storage by maximizing the size of the private area. We expand upon the basic knowledge of the VSE storage layout we acquired in the previous chapter. You should be familiar with the material in the SCP chapter (Chapter 5) before reading this one.

6.1 Cookbook for Increasing Private Area Size

Private area size is a major issue for VSE/SP users. The amount of virtual storage available for a single partition is still a key concern for most VSE/ESA users. Some proven techniques that may be used to increase the size of the private area include:

- Reduce the shared area size. ESA mode systems round the shared/private area boundary up to the next megabyte. This is a result of the one-megabyte segment size. Because of this effect, small reductions in shared area size can increase private area size by a full megabyte.

- Do not specify SHARED=HIGH in your IPL time SVA command. SHARED=LOW is the default and will save about .5 megabyte by eliminating rounding to a segment boundary. (ESA segments are one megabyte each.)

93

- Specify only the amount of SPSIZE required. The SPSIZE value directly reduces the private area size. This parameter unconditionally reserves storage, even if it will never be used by shared partitions.

- Run VTAM in private. VTAM in shared directly reduces the size of the private area. The performance cost for running VTAM in private is negligible.

- Run POWER in private on ESA mode processors. No increase in CPU time will occur, and the increase in the size of the private area will allow tuning of all of your other work.

- If you are MODE=ESA or MODE=370, you should specify VPOOL=64K. The cost of mapping a page to VPOOL is very small and larger VPOOL values appear to have no performance advantage. VPOOL directly reduces the size of the private area.

- Review VTAM buffer parameters carefully. Certain VTAM buffers always come from the shared area, and these should be reduced to the amount that is required. The default values provided with VTAM for LPBUF, SFBUF, and WPBUF may be too high for your system.

- Avoid over-allocating storage space to the System GETVIS and SVA areas. Unused space here is of no benefit, and directly reduces the size of the private area.

- Tune programs in SVA storage. Monitor usage and only keep the most used programs in the SVA.

6.2 What Determines Private Area Size?

The term *private area* refers to the window in our 16-megabyte virtual storage address space that is available for use within a private address space. The private area is all space not allocated to the shared address space, and not required as basic overhead by VSE. The address range of the private area of VSE may be mapped to any number of address spaces. Please refer to Figure 6.1 for an example of a SHARED=HIGH VSE system. The *shared area* is the supervisor, shared partitions, and SVA in the figure.

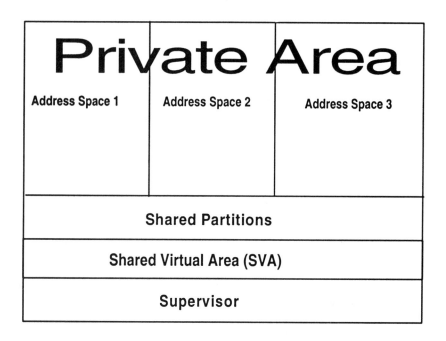

Figure 6.1 Private Area

The size of the private area for typical VSE/ESA systems will usually not be less than ten megabytes, and may even be as large as eleven megabytes. Because VSE aligns the boundary between the shared area and the private area to the next one-megabyte segment boundary, a small change in the usage of the shared area can cost or save one megabyte of private area storage.

$$PrivateArea = 16M - (SVA + SysGETVIS + SharedParts + Supvr)$$

Equation 1 Private Area Size

The private area size is decreased by adding to the shared area. For example, adding phases to the SVA can increase the size of the shared area. And, partitions defined within the shared area all reduce the available private area size.   Note that your SVA allocation and System GETVIS allocation are what impact the size of the shared area. Thus, large amounts of unused SVA or System

GETVIS space should not be allocated as this directly reduces the size of the shared area. And, extra shared partition space should never be allocated via the SPSIZE parameter unless it is required for current use.

6.3 Tuning the Shared Area

The size of the private area is increased by reducing the size of the shared area. Let us look at what comprises the shared area to understand what we can potentially reduce. The shared area contains the following:

1. Supervisor nucleus (and IPL time SCP tables)
2. Shared partitions (within SPSIZE area)
3. SVA (SDL, virtual library, and system GETVIS)

These three components each contribute to the four or five or even six megabyte shared area seen in the typical VSE/ESA system. We will look at each of these in turn, and see what can be done to reduce its size. Figure 6.2 below displays the minimum and typical values for each component of the shared area.

Component	Minimum	Typical	Large
Supervisor	500KB	540KB	768KB
SVA	1000KB	1200KB	2000KB
System GETVIS	600KB	900KB	2100KB

Figure 6.2 Shared Area Components

6.3.1 Tuning the Supervisor Area

The supervisor area includes the phase loaded at IPL plus tables allocated during IPL. The $$A$SUPx phase itself is usually a pre-assembled version supplied by IBM and little benefit exists in trying to customize a smaller version unique to your shop. A typical supervisor size for 370 mode is about 480KB. A typical ESA mode supervisor size is about 490KB. Additional storage is added to this basic requirement by various IPL time tables. The total size for a VSE/ESA supervisor is around 600KB, which is certainly significant. In this section we will concentrate on what can be accomplished using the IPL time parameters to reduce the supervisor tables.

Copy blocks (CCW translation work areas) are one of the most important items allocated at IPL time. It is critical that enough copy blocks be allocated for your configuration and I/O usage. However, extra copy blocks offer no benefit, and any unused area should be reclaimed by reducing the number of copy blocks.

6.3.2 Reducing the Shared Partition Size

The shared partitions occupy space you reserved via the SPSIZE parameter at IPL time. Reduce the SPSIZE value to reduce the size of the shared area. Note that the shared partitions must fit within the area provided. An **INVALID ALLOCATION** message will be produced if the ALLOC command fails.

Reduction of the size of the shared area is a three step process. First, reduce the size or number of shared partitions. Second, use the MAP command to observe the amount of available shared area. Third, reduce the SPSIZE value to the amount now required.

VTAM should never be included in the shared area. On an ESA capable processor, POWER may be placed in private and should not be part of the shared area. Review any partitions that you have placed in the shared area and decide if they can be run in the private area. If you must run one or more shared partitions, you should review each virtual size and reduce it if possible.

6.3.3 Tuning SVA Size

You provide parameters at IPL to reserve storage for the SVA. The SVA is comprised of the System Directory List (SDL parameter), the virtual library area (PSIZE parameter), and the system GETVIS area (GETVIS parameter). You are not defining the actual size of these components. Instead, the amount of storage that you specify is added to the storage size automatically determined to be required for the system.

The IPL time SVA command SDL, PSIZE, and GETVIS parameters determine the amount of virtual storage reserved for the SVA. You may not be using all of this storage. Any unused storage may be reclaimed. If you are loading phases into the SVA that are not required, you should remove these phases and reclaim the storage reserved for them. You reclaim unused SVA storage by reducing the appropriate IPL SVA command parameter value.

The System Directory List is usually a small area. You specify the SDL parameter of the SVA command to determine the number of user SDL entries allocated. This value is added to the number of SDL entries required by the system. The SDL storage is given by Equation 2 below. The value determined is rounded up to the next page boundary.

$$SDLSize = (SDL*72) + (SystemCount*72)$$

Equation 2 SDL Size

The virtual library area is often overallocated. You may review your current SVA status via the LIBR utility LISTD SDL command. The SVA TOTAL SPACE, USED SPACE, and FREE SPACE lines include values expressed in KB (1024-byte units) and also as a percentage. In Figure 6.3 below we see that over 60KB of SVA is currently unused and potentially could be reclaimed by reducing the SVA parameter.

```
STATUS DISPLAY           SDL AND SVA
-----------------------------------------------------------
SDL    TOTAL ENTRIES :     396    (100%)
       USED  ENTRIES :     248    ( 63%)
       FREE  ENTRIES :     148    ( 37%)

SVA    TOTAL SPACE   :    2072K   (100%)
       USED  SPACE   :    1405K   ( 68%)
        - PFIXED AREA:      93K   (  4%)   START AT: 271808
       FREE  SPACE   :     667K   ( 32%)
```

Figure 6.3 LISTD SDL Command Output

You may review your GETVIS allocation status via the GETVIS SVA command. In Figure 6.4 we see that over 700KB of GETVIS currently unused and potentially could be reclaimed by reducing the SVA GETVIS parameter.

```
GETVIS USAGE OF SVA
    AREA SIZE : 2,012 K-BYTES     HIGH WATER MARK   :  1,580 K-BYTES
    ALLOCATED : 1,122 K-BYTES     LARGEST FREE AREA :    740 K-BYTES
```

Figure 6.4 GETVIS SVA Command Output

The GETVIS SVA command displays the amount of storage allocated to the SVA, the amount used, and the amount remaining. Any unused SVA storage may be reclaimed by reducing the IPL time SVA parameter values. In the figure, we observe that we have 890KB of free System GETVIS, but that the maximum free chunk is 740KB. A maximum available chunk smaller than the free area is a result of System GETVIS area fragmentation. Fragmentation is common for any system that has been active for any amount of time.

Certain VSE features may have required that you load phases into the SVA in the past. If these features are not being used, you should remove the phases that are not currently required to be SVA resident. MRO usage is a common example of this issue. The CICS Multiple Region Option (MRO) requires that the DFHCSEOT, DFHIRP, and DFHSCTE phases each be made resident within the SVA. If you are not running MRO, then these phases should be removed from the SVA list.

Another example of this issue is specification of MOVE mode for the CRT transients. If you were running with an active VSE console in the past, you probably placed a number of the CRT transients into MOVE mode. If you have switched to running a disconnected VSE console, any transients related to processing of the DOC mode screen updates may now be removed from MOVE mode.

Care should be taken to not impact performance by removing highly used phases from the SVA. You should use a performance monitor that reports on phase usage statistics for your current SDL SVA and MOVS mode entries to determine that the phases you remove are infrequently used. And, you should verify that performance has not been impacted after phase removal has occurred.

6.4 Reducing the Size of the Largest Partition

You may need is to reduce the amount of virtual storage required by your largest private area application. This is an alternative to increasing the size of the private area. It may also be required by an increase in the size of one of the shared area components (SVA, System GETVIS, Supervisor). In this section we will discuss several common large applications, and what can be done for each. Additional information on this subject will be found in the chapters on CICS tuning, VTAM tuning, and database tuning.

6.4.1 Reducing CICS Size

CICS is often the largest application run in a partition. CICS should never be run within the shared area. CICS storage is comprised of the program area and the GETVIS area segments. Program area storage is allocated for CICS fixed needs and for DSA usage. If these areas are currently overallocated, you can reduce your CICS partition size by simply reducing the DSA size or the GETVIS area size. The DSA size is reduced by making the EXEC statement SIZE parameter smaller. The GETVIS area size is made smaller by reducing the partition allocation.

DSA requirements are normally decreased by reducing the number and size of resident programs (by updating the PPT). You can also save DSA space by reducing the number of tasks that CICS can run at once (the MXT, AMXT, CMXT parameters). Each of these options can reduce storage but also can impact the throughput of CICS.

CICS GETVIS storage is used mainly for VSAM buffer space and work space. The use of Local Shared Resources (LSR) in your CICS system is the best option available to reduce CICS GETVIS area requirements. If you are not currently using LSR, you should be. LSR is a virtual storage constraint relief tool. Its use also results in both I/O and CPU time savings. If you are already using LSR, then you should review your current LSR pool specifications. The

CICS shutdown statistics will enable you to determine if the LSR buffers are currently overallocated. A reduction in LSR space results in a reduction in CICS GETVIS usage. The LSR pool typically need not be larger than 20 percent of the VSAM buffer space allocated for the same files without LSR active.

If several CICS systems are being run then selected CICS phases may be placed within the SVA to reduce working set requirements and to save CICS partition storage. Many CICS phases are SVA eligible. A list of suggested phases to move into the SVA is found in the CICS tuning chapter.

6.4.2 Reducing VTAM Size

VTAM does not need to be run in the shared area, and should never be run there under VSE/ESA. This one change often reclaims as much as 3MB from the shared area. If you find a need for additional shared area savings, you can next look at the VTAM buffers allocated from the System GETVIS area. Refer to the chapter on VTAM Tuning for a detailed discussion of VTAM buffer types, sizes, and storage usage.

VTAM should always be started with a size parameter of ISTINCVT (the program executed to start VTAM). This ensures that all available partition storage is allocated to the GETVIS area, with nothing lost to round off of the program area during initialization. VTAM will load programs in the GETVIS area, and it will use the remaining GETVIS area for buffer space.

When VTAM was run in a private address space on VSE/SP, then all VTAM users had to be run within the same address space. The result of this was often a forced need to run MRO in order to separate the large transaction processing CICS from the terminal owning CICS. MRO used in this fashion results in a significant performance "hit." VTAM need not run in the same address space as CICS under VSE/ESA, and no similar performance penalty is incurred by running VTAM in private.

6.4.3 VSE/ESA 1.3 Considerations

VSE/ESA 1.3 implements support for 31 bit addressing, virtual DASD, dataspaces and a number of other features. This offers the following virtual storage constraint relief and performance tuning options:

- VSAM buffers and LSR pools of buffers may be allocated above the line. This is probably the most important change for new VSE/ESA 1.3 users because it offers CICS users an immediate increase in virtual storage equal to the size of their VSAM buffers. Typical users will save from one megabyte to four megabytes of storage below the line.

- The virtual library portion of the SVA may use storage above the line. This can result in an increase in the size of the private area. Only programs written to exploit 31 bit mode can be run above the line. Some IBM code and much OEM vendor code can be loaded above the line. The typical VSE/ESA 1.3 user will be able to load as much as a megabyte of SVA code above the line.

- System GETVIS may be allocated above the line. VSE/ESA operating system components and OEM software can allocate system storage without reducing the size of the private area.

- CICS/VSE 2.2 supports 31 bit addressing. This allows user transactions written in assembler to be loaded above the line. It is expected that COBOL II transactions will also be able to be run above the line. This offers future virtual storage constraint relief and room for growth, but does require that existing applications be changed to exploit VSE/ESA 1.3 capabilities.

7

POWER

This chapter discusses tuning of VSE/POWER (which we will refer to as simply POWER). POWER is an acronym for **P**riority **O**utput **W**riters, **E**xecution processors, and input **R**eaders. Originally an optional component of VSE, POWER is now required with VSE/ESA to control the dynamic partitions. The primary function of POWER is spooling. Although *spool* is now a part of the technical vocabulary, it is itself an acronym for "Simultaneous Peripheral Operations OnLine." This chapter is oriented towards POWER Version 5 with VSE/ESA. Although many of the tuning tips apply to prior releases of POWER, most of the storage estimates and the command examples are for VSE/ESA systems.

Partitions are often described as POWER controlled. This means that the partition was started by POWER, that POWER can spool its input and output, and that other services are available. A partition may also be described as "under the control of POWER." POWER manages input and output in a set of work queues that it maintains. Separate queues exist for Input (Reader), and Output (Printer, Punch, Transmit). An application programming interface is provided for POWER so that programs can create, read, and control the contents of the POWER queues.

Because POWER handles all unit record input and output for a POWER controlled partition, and because many tasks may be bidding for its services at the same time, it can introduce delays in processing. In this chapter, we are interested in how POWER works, what performance issues can arise during its processing, and what tuning options are available to correct any performance problems.

7.1 Cookbook for POWER Tuning

The primary source of information on your POWER system is the POWER status summary. The POWER PDISPLAY STATUS command produces this report. The format of the output of this command is discussed in section 7.10.1. The **D A** command is also useful to determine the current status of the various POWER tasks. The **D DYNC** command displays the status of the dynamic partitions that are under the control of POWER.

The following list includes common POWER performance problems and their fixes.

1.   Shared POWER is not a performance option. If you are not sharing POWER files, then do not enable this option. If you are currently sharing POWER files, look at alternative ways to communicate data between VSE systems such as the use of PNET. If you must share POWER files, review the timer values that control this process. See the Shared POWER section of this chapter and also refer to the Shared DASD chapter for additional information.

2.   Although the POWER QFILE is not the bottleneck it once was, it should not be placed with other high use files, nor should it ever be on the same volume as the VSE lock file.

3.   Choose the POWER Data File block size with care. A size of 4KB is suggested as a minimum starting value, with larger values often preferred.

4.   Run POWER in private on ESA mode processors. This increases the private area size with no CPU increase caused by running POWER in private.

5.   Spool using virtual 3800 POWER printers in each partition or use an OEM product to block print requests to POWER (the FAQS FPS feature does this).

7.2 POWER Startup

POWER is usually automatically started as part of the IPL process using an ASI procedure. This procedure contains POWER autostart commands which define POWER options, and bring the various static partitions under the control of POWER. Figure 7.1 below illustrates a POWER startup procedure.

```
// EXEC PGM=IPWPOWER
FORMAT=NO
PSTART BG,AOI
READER=FEC
PRINTERS=FEE
PUNCHES=FED
PSTART F2,L2
READER=FEC
PRINTERS=FEE
PUNCHES=FED
PSTART RDR,FEC,A
PSTART PUN,FED,A,,VM
PSTART LST,FEE,A,,VM
PLOAD DYNCTAB
PVARY DYNC,ENABLE,S,T,U
/*
```

Figure 7.1 Sample POWER Startup
Procedure Example

The POWER autostart parameters follow the execute of IPWPOWER (or your POWER startup phase). Additional information is provided in the Specifications Summary Chapter (Chapter 18.)

7.3 POWER DASD Files

POWER uses a number of DASD files, each of which is under your control, and each of which can impact performance. In this section, we will look at the POWER DASD files that we can tune (see Figure 7.2). The files we are going to review are:

> Queue File (QFILE)
> Data File (DFILE)
> Account File (IJAFILE)
> SLI libraries

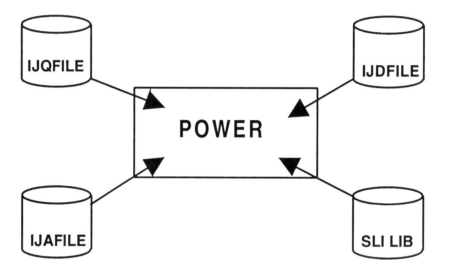

Figure 7.2 POWER DASD Files

7.3.1 QFILE

The POWER Queue File (QFILE) is used to track all files spooled by POWER. Thus, the QFILE functions as a directory, and as a series of work queues. The QFILE does not contain any actual spooled data. All actual spooled data is maintained in the data file.

The QFILE should not be over allocated. Too large a queue file results in wasted VIO space, additional POWER startup overhead, and an increase in time for I/O requests to the QFILE area. The maximum number of QFILE records used is reported as part of the POWER status summary. If many unused records are detected in your QFILE, you should reduce the size of the QFILE. Altering the size of this file requires a time-consuming coldstart of POWER.

The QFILE used to be a major singlethread point, and thus a source of serious performance issues, but all of the most critical problem areas were resolved with POWER Version 2.3. However, the QFILE can still be a source of minor performance problems in VSE/ESA. The QFILE should be placed on a DASD not used for the POWER data file. It also should not be placed on a high use DASD volume. In particular, avoid placing the POWER QFILE on the same volume as the VSE Lock File or IJSYSRS.

7.3.2 Data File

The POWER Data File (DFILE) is the file where all data (including reader, printer, punch data) is stored by POWER. The file is preformatted by POWER as a series of fixed length blocks. The blocks are organized into block groups. Individual blocks are not allocated, instead POWER allocates in units of block groups.

The DFILE may occupy multiple extents. POWER spreads its I/O activity across all DFILE extents provided, and additional extents improve the amount of POWER I/O concurrency. For the best performance, each POWER DFILE extent should be of the same size as the other extents, and each extent should be on a separate DASD device.

The DFILE block length is specified by the DBLK parameter of the POWER macro. The default block length is 2016 bytes. The DFILE blocks are organized into DBLK groups. The DBLK Group size is specified by the DBLKGP parameter of the POWER macro. The default DBLK group size is ten blocks. Both parameters are explained in detail under POWER Parameters below. Both of these parameters default values are a potential source of performance problems.

The DFILE parameters may not be altered without a coldstart of POWER. Whenever POWER is coldstarted, the DFILE is formatted, and any existing spool file information is lost. The contents of the data file may be backed up via the POWER POFFLOAD command. Periodic backups of the POWER data file are recommended.

7.3.3 Account File

The POWER Account file (IJAFILE) is used to record information about each job that POWER runs. The VSE job accounting information is typically part of the POWER Account file records. For most customers, the POWER account file is the input source for their cost accounting system. The volume of activity to this file is relatively small, and thus its placement is not critical.

When the account file fills up, all POWER processing stops until it is archived or deleted. This file should be over allocated to prevent this problem. Regularly scheduled archive runs should be employed to ensure that the POWER account file does not fill up during production processing.

The account file need not be shared even when a shared POWER system is specified. From a performance standpoint, it is a good idea to not share the account file because the separate POWER account files can be easily merged by most accounting software. If you do choose to share the POWER account file, it is even more critical than normal that you over allocate this file to prevent stopping ALL shared systems when it fills up.

7.3.4 SLI Libraries

POWER reader files may merge control cards and data cards from a VSE source statement library. This is called the POWER *Source Library Include* facility (SLI for short). The * $$ SLI statement is used to insert a source library member into a reader file. This insertion mechanism is illustrated by Figure 7.3. Note that POWER searches the LIBDEF SOURCE chain for the POWER partition, not the one for the partition where the job is running. The SLI facility may also be used to insert ICCF members into a jobstream. Note that a SLI statement is not expanded until the job containing it is run, and the SLI statement is encountered. This means that a SLI statement in a DISP=L job may have a different effect each time the job is run.

The SLI facility is powerful, but can introduce performance problems. The primary tuning option available to the user of the SLI facility is to minimize the length of the source library search chain in the POWER partition. It is best to have only a single SLI

```
* $$ JOB JNM=SLIJOB
// JOB SLIJOB
* $$ SLI INCNAME <---- // ASSGN ...
                       // EXEC PGM=blah
                       Data1
                       Data2
                       /*

/&
* $$ EOJ
```

Figure 7.3 SLI Include

library, and this as the first entry in the POWER partition's type
SOURCE search chain. If multiple SLI libraries are used, care
should be taken to have the most frequently used library first in
the chain if at all possible. Each additional SLI library adds
several I/Os to the cost of a SLI request. Since reading of a typical
SLI member usually only involves a single I/O, this is a VERY
substantial effect!

It is important to have a dedicated directory for SLI usage. This
eliminates searching through directory entries that can never be
used by POWER. If the SLI directory is on a low use DASD, the
amount of arm movement is also reduced, which improves the
speed of the search and retrieval operation.

You should also monitor fragmentation within the SLI library,
and perform periodic SLI library reorganizations if many members
do not occupy contiguous library space. Although most members fit
in a very few library blocks, fragmentation of a two block member
still makes the difference between a single member read I/O and
two I/Os (one I/O for each member block).

The SLI library is tuned in the same way as any other VSE
library. If the SLI facility is heavily used, it is particularly
important that this library be carefully tuned, as delays in POWER
can impact the whole VSE system. Please refer to Chapter 8
(Librarian) for further information on tuning VSE libraries.

The SLI facility allows ICCF members to be inserted into a
jobstream, in addition to the source library include facility we have
already discussed. If you employ ICCF, you should consider this

method of getting ICCF data into VSE batch jobs. This is done via the following POWER SLI statement special format:

```
* $$ SLI ICCF=(memname),LIB=(libnum)
```

In this example, "libnum" is the ICCF library number and "memname" is the ICCF member name. The ICCF SLI statement is relatively efficient, and is an excellent method to merge ICCF data into VSE jobstreams. It is extensively used by IBM supplied configuration dialogues to supply ICCF information that is catalogued into various VSE startup and control procedures. If the ICCF library file (DTSFILE) is very busy or on an active DASD volume, then the performance of ICCF member SLI requests will suffer. If poor ICCF SLI performance is observed, then the DTSFILE should be moved to a lower use volume, or spread across several low-use volumes.

7.4 POWER Parameters

In this section we review the POWER parameters that are related to tuning. These parameters are also reviewed in the chapter on VSE commands. For a complete discussion of all POWER parameters you are referred to the IBM manual *SC33-6571 IBM VSE/POWER Administration and Operation*. The POWER parameters we will look at here are listed in Figure 7.4.

```
DBLK=
DBLKGP=
DASDSHR Option
```

Figure 7.4 POWER Performance Parameters

7.4.1 DBLK Buffer Size

The data file block size is specified via the **DBLK=** parameter of
the POWER macro. Too large a value causes both REAL and
VIRTUAL storage problems. Too small a value increases the I/O
done by POWER. Sadly, the default value (typically 2016 bytes) is
not large enough and most VSE users do a great deal of
unnecessary POWER I/O.

The minimum value for the DBLK parameter is 1000 bytes. The
maximum value is 12288 bytes. If you omit this parameter, or
specify a value of zero, then the default value is used. The DBLK
parameter value may only be changed with a POWER coldstart.
Whenever you warmstart POWER, the current DBLK value defined
within the queue file is the value that is used.

A suggested starting value for the DBLK parameter is 4KB. This
is the preferred value for all except the most storage constrained
environments. If your environment includes many large spool files,
you may wish to consider increasing the DBLK value further.
Values as high as 12KB have been found to be very effective in
some environments.

Too large of a DBLK size causes problems by using too much
storage for your environment. Real storage and partition GETVIS
storage is required for DBLK buffers. If you are unable to provide
the amount of real storage needed by POWER for your DBLK
buffer specification, you should reduce the buffer size to one that
fits in your available real storage. You should only reduce the
DBLK specification below 4KB if there is no other way to reduce
the real storage constraint, and then only when POWER spooling
is not heavily used. Refer to the discussion on POWER storage
usage in section 7.6 below.

7.4.2 DBLK Group Size

The data file block group size is specified by the **DBLKGP=**
parameter of the POWER macro. Too large a value causes
fragmentation of DASD space. Too small a value causes overhead
in the operator commands used for repositioning printouts. The
default value is ten blocks to the block group.

If you process large printouts frequently, then you should
consider increasing the DBLKGP value. However, because the

DBLKGP is the unit of allocation for the data file, too large a value results in wasted space for each small report or small input card file processed by POWER. Also, because the DBLK group size is associated with the DBLK block size, it is important to decrease the DBLKGP value when the DBLK block size is increased. It is also important to increase the DBLKGP value when the DBLK block size is decreased.

Although a large DBLKGP parameter permits faster access of the group containing a desired page number, it can also increase the total number of I/Os required to locate the page. Once the group has been found, half of the blocks within the group will have to be read on the average to find the required block. Thus, a very large DBLKGP value is almost always something to be avoided.

No correct value exists for the DBLKGP parameter for all VSE shops. The default of ten blocks is a very good starting point. If you greatly increase the DBLK block size, you should consider reducing the DBLKGP value. Most environments do not need to increase the DBLKGP value. However, good results have been seen with values as large as 50 in environments that process very large spool files.

7.5 POWER Spooling

POWER receives each individual print or punch request issued by a controlled partition. A significant amount of fixed overhead occurs for each request given to POWER. This fixed overhead is often more than half of the CPU time used to print lines to POWER. When multiple print requests are chained together and passed to POWER as a single request, much of the fixed spooling overhead can be eliminated. It is not easy to change a program to write a whole page with a single request.

However, POWER offers a simple way to achieve the same effect. Whenever a program prints to a 3800 printer, the 3800 logic module blocks many single lines into a chain that is passed to POWER as a single request. You can enable this processing by simply defining virtual 3800 printers as your spooled print devices. This can be done even when you have no real 3800 print devices.

The Goal Systems FAQS product contains a Fast Printer Support (FPS) option that automatically blocks together print lines into a single large request for POWER to process. Both the POWER virtual 3800 option and the FPS option save up to 50 percent (more for VSE/ESA 1.3) of the CPU time of a print bound application.

7.6 POWER Storage Requirements

POWER requires both real and virtual storage. Real storage is reserved for POWER via the ALLOCR statement for the POWER partition. POWER partition virtual storage is reserved via the ALLOC statement. POWER requires virtual storage in the program area, GETVIS area, VIO space, and System GETVIS area.

In this section we will look at each of the types of storage needed by POWER. We will review why POWER uses storage, how you allocate storage to POWER, how much storage is needed, and how to measure storage availability in your system. POWER uses storage from three areas in its partition:

- The Fixable Area (the ALLOCR size up to 512KB is mapped to the start of the POWER partition).

- The Pageable Area (follows the Fixable Area at the start of the POWER partition and continues up to the SIZE= value).

- The partition GETVIS area (the POWER partition ALLOC value minus the SIZE value).

Estimates are provided below for POWER storage requirements. We also look at how to determine how much storage is being currently used in a system. If you wish to compute the exact amount of storage required for your environment, refer to the IBM manual *SC33-6571 IBM VSE/POWER Administration and Operation*.

7.6.1 Real Storage

POWER requires real storage. A suggested minimum ALLOCR value is 128KB. Note that extra real storage allocated to POWER does not cost anything. This is because unused real storage from an ALLOCR specification is still available for paging purposes. POWER requires some real storage just to initialize, plus additional real storage during execution for each task. The real storage required during POWER execution is called *fixable* storage. The actual amount of fixable storage used by POWER is displayed as part of the status summary. This report is produced automatically at POWER shutdown time, and may also be requested during POWER operation via the PDISPLAY STATUS command. You should review the output of this command to tune POWER real storage. Fixable storage is reported in the FIXABLE STORAGE USED BY VSE/POWER line. Note that this value does not include all real storage required by POWER. Additional storage is used at initialization time. You should refer to the NUMBER OF TIMES TASKS WERE WAITING FOR PFIXED STORAGE line to judge whether or not more real storage is needed. If this line is not zero, then additional real storage should be allocated to POWER. If this line is zero, then adequate real storage is currently allocated to POWER. You may leave this storage allocated or remove it by adjusting the POWER partition ALLOCR value downward.

Each change to the POWER ALLOCR value should be done at the same time as a corresponding change to the POWER SIZE= value. If you simply increase the ALLOCR value, you will automatically decrease the size of the POWER Pageable Area. This is a result of the Pageable Area being determined by the SIZE= value minus the ALLOCR value. You **never** want to receive messages that POWER is waiting on fixable storage or on pageable storage, because of processing delays and because the system could even become deadlocked.

7.6.2 System GETVIS Storage

POWER typically requires 20KB in the System GETVIS area. This amount of storage is not a problem, and is not readily controlled by the user. This storage is used to load the nucleus code, and control blocks for the static plus dynamic partitions. It is allocated at POWER startup, and released when POWER terminates. The amount of System GETVIS storage used by POWER is displayed as part of the status summary in the **SYSTEM GETVIS STORAGE USED BY POWER** line.

7.6.3 Virtual Storage

POWER requires virtual storage in both the program area and the GETVIS area. You reserve the total POWER virtual storage via the ALLOC statement when the POWER partition is defined. You reserve the program area storage and determine the size of the GETVIS area via the SIZE parameter of the EXEC statement when you start POWER. Program area usage is essentially static. Essentially all POWER dynamic storage is acquired from the fixable area and the GETVIS area.

POWER uses program area virtual storage to contain the POWER phases, user exit phases, plus certain control blocks and tables. In general, the program area storage size is static once POWER has been initialized. A good estimate of the size of the POWER program area is 512KB. You specify the size of the POWER program area via the SIZE parameter of the EXEC statement. Additional program area storage serves no useful purpose, and any large extra amount should be moved to the GETVIS area. An example of an EXEC statement to start POWER follows:

```
// EXEC IPWPOWER,SIZE=512K
```

POWER makes extensive use of partition GETVIS space for control blocks and for DBLK buffers. When inadequate GETVIS space is available, POWER waits. Most of POWER's usage of GETVIS is dynamic. Therefore, you determine whether you have enough GETVIS space allocated by looking at a POWER system after it has been running long enough to have encountered a representative load. The GETVIS used by a newly started POWER system will always be somewhat less than the total amount required during execution.

The GETVIS console command can be used to view the status of the GETVIS area in your POWER partition. This command will display the high-water mark for the GETVIS area. The high water mark value can be used to easily determine whether additional GETVIS space is required. The status summary output contains detailed statistics on POWER partition GETVIS usage and needs. Refer to the NUMBER OF TIMES TASKS WERE WAITING FOR VIRTUAL STORAGE line. If this line's value is zero, then no GETVIS shortage exists. If this line's value is not zero, then additional GETVIS storage is needed by POWER. The DYNAMIC

PARTITION SCHEDULING STATISTICS section contains a count of the number of times a dynamic partition could not be started due to a shortage of GETVIS storage.

7.6.4 POWER in Private

POWER often runs in a shared address space. Before VSE/ESA this was the only way that POWER could be run. With VSE/ESA POWER can run in either the shared area, or in a static partition defined within the private area of one of the nine address spaces. POWER can not run in a dynamic partition. (This would be hard to do since POWER manages all of the dynamic partitions.)

VSE/ESA users should always run POWER in private as illustrated in Figure 7.5. The CPU cost is zero, and the benefit is an increase in the maximum private area equal to the size of the POWER partition. This means that the typical user can increase the size of their private area by one megabyte (or more!) by simply

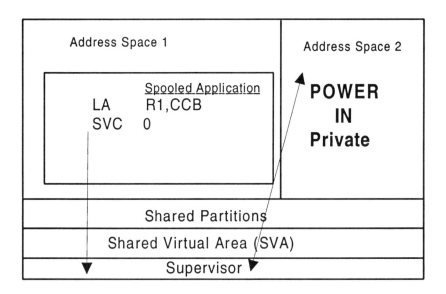

Figure 7.5 POWER Running in Private Area

moving POWER to private. Remember to reduce the SPSIZE parameter of the IPL SYS command by the size of the POWER partition.

Running POWER in private also enables the user to over allocate the POWER partition GETVIS area. In general, the GETVIS area for POWER should never be allowed to become full. The elimination of concerns about the size of the POWER partition allows this area to be properly allocated.

7.7 Dynamic Partitions

One of the most important functions of VSE/POWER is management of dynamic partitions. A *dynamic partition* is a partition automatically created and freed by POWER. Each dynamic partition occupies its own unique address space. Like other POWER controlled partitions, each dynamic partition is a member of a reader class. Because dynamic partitions are totally managed by POWER, writer only partitions are not supported. Thus, each dynamic partition requires virtual reader, printer, and punch devices for POWER to control.

Normally, POWER favors dynamic partitions over static partitions of the same class. If you would rather use the static partitions first, specify SET DYNAL=LOW in your POWER startup. When DYNAL=LOW is in effect then POWER creates a dynamic partition when the following are all true:

- A dispatchable job is encountered.

- No static partition of the required class is available.

- At least one free dynamic partition of the required class is currently available to be started.

A dynamic partition only exists for the lifetime of a single POWER job. The dynamic partition is created, the POWER job is run to completion, and the dynamic partition is then released. Sufficient virtual storage must be available for a dynamic partition to be created. The page dataset area for the virtual storage occupied by a dynamic partition is allocated when the partition is created, and freed when the dynamic partition is released.

The DTR$DYNC member is used to define and control the class, number, size, and other characteristics of the dynamic partitions. A sample DTR$DYNC member follows. Each dynamic partition can have its own ASI startup procedure. This procedure is used to

initialize the environment for the dynamic partition. For example,
the startup procedure may be used to define standard LIBDEFs or
create standard assignments for a dynamic partition.   In our
example, the startup member is DYNSTART.

```
       p1      p2    p3     p4   p5  p6        p7    p8
CLASS=  Y      10    1024   64   50  DYNSTART  01    Y
READER=   FEC
PRINTERS= FEE
PUNCHES=  FED
CLASS=  Z      1     256    64   50  DYNSTART  30    Y
READER=   FEC
PRINTERS= FEE
PUNCHES=  FED
```

Figure 7.6 DTR$DYNC Member Example

1.   The first parameter specifies the dynamic partition class via
     CLASS=Y.

2.   The second parameter (p2) is the size of the dynamic
     partition in megabytes. A dynamic partition is a minimum
     of one megabyte and is defined in increments of one
     megabyte. The theoretical maximum size is 15M (prior to
     VSE/ESA 1.3), but in practice the maximum size is usually
     10M (the size of the private area).

3.   The third parameter (p3) specifies the size of the program
     area portion of the dynamic partition. This is the maximum
     program size that may be executed within this dynamic
     partition.

4.   p4 is the size of the dynamic space GETVIS area. (Note
     that this is separate from the dynamic partition GETVIS
     area.) The Dynamic space GETVIS area is used for the Job
     Control Work Area and for label processing workspace and
     also is used by various OEM packages.

5.   The fifth parameter (p5) defines the number of logical units
     (LUBs).

6. p6 lists the name of the dynamic partition startup procedure. This procedure will be executed by POWER when the dynamic partition is created, before the POWER job is processed.

7. p7 defines the maximum number of dynamic partitions of this class that may be defined at one time.

8. p8 specifies whether or not the POWER PLOAD DYNC command can be used to activate a dynamic partition.

The PVARY command is used to control the dynamic partition configuration. Use PVARY DYNC, DISAB to disable one or all dynamic partition classes. Use PVARY DYNC, ENAB to enable one or all dynamic partition classes. If a dynamic partition startup fails, then that class is disabled until explicitly re-enabled via the PVARY command.

POWER also provides a command to display the status of the dynamic partitions. The PDISPLAY DYNC, ENAB command displays the status of only the enabled dynamic partitions. The PDISPLAY DYNC command displays the status of all dynamic partitions. See Figure 7.7 below for an example of the output of this command.

```
D DYNC
1C39I COMMAND PASSED TO VSE/POWER
1Q6AI *** DISPLAY OF ACTIVE DYNAMIC CLASS TABLE ***
1Q6AI CLS STATE    ACT/MAX ALLOC   SIZE   SP-GETV    PROFILE  LUBS
1Q6AI  Y   ENAB     2  2    10M    1024K    64K      DYNSTART  50
1Q6AI  Z   ENAB     0 30     1M     256K    64K      DYNSTART  50
1Q6AI  E   ENAB     1  9     1M     500K   124K      DYNSTART  50
1Q6AI  T   ENAB     4  8     2M    1024K   124K      DYNSTART 200
1Q6AI  U   ENAB     0  9     1M     500K   124K      DYNSTART 200
1Q6AI  V   ENAB     0  9     2M     500K   512K      DYNSTART 200
1Q6AI  W   ENAB     0  9     1M     500K   124K      DYNSTART  50
1Q6AI  X   ENAB     0  9     1M     500K   124K      DYNSTART  50
```

Figure 7.7 D DYNC Command Output

7.8 Shared POWER

POWER permits the spool files to be shared. Shared POWER means that the QFILE and DFILE are shared by two or more VSE/ESA systems. These systems see the same POWER queues (RDR, LST, PUN, XMT), and share the same DASD for all files spooled by POWER. In a shared POWER environment, one system can create a job, a second system can run the job, and yet a third system can process the output of the job. Figure 7.8 shows how several VSE systems can share POWER DASD files.

Shared POWER is not a performance option. Bluntly put, shared POWER files perform poorly. Although POWER version 4 and 5 have improved performance over earlier versions of POWER in a shared DASD environment, this is still a very important tuning consideration. Shared POWER impacts performance, and should be avoided if possible. You identify that you are not sharing any POWER files by specifying **SHARED=NO** in you POWER macro.

Two sharing options exist. These are shared queue file and shared queue file plus account file. If you are sharing only the POWER queue file, you should specify **SHARED=(Q)**. If you are sharing both the queue file and the account file, then you must specify the option **SHARED=(Q,A)**. Note that shared queue file means shared data file – the data file is shared anytime that the POWER queue file is shared.

A shared POWER account file should be avoided if possible. Although the account file I/O cost is relatively small, it is greatly impacted in a shared account file environment. When the POWER account file is not shared, a separate account file must be defined for each system. Most accounting packages allow such account files to be merged, and thus no real functional impact occurs by not sharing the account file. Also, running separate account files minimizes the impact of the account file becoming full. When a single shared account file is used, all shared systems will wait when this one file is full.

7.8.1 Tuning Shared POWER Files

If your system is running shared POWER then your major tuning option is the **TIME=** parameter of the POWER macro. This parameter is used to control the amount of time one system can

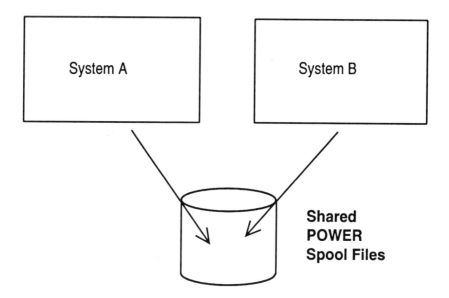

Figure 7.8 Shared POWER

monopolize the queue file, and the delay in detecting jobs created by another system. The format of the TIME parameter is:

TIME=(t1,t2,t3)

The three parameters each represent a time in seconds. The values specified do not have to be the same for all POWER systems. In fact, you are encouraged to specify different values for different POWER systems to improve the performance of key systems.

t1   The *active* time in seconds. This is the elapsed time during which the POWER on one system is allowed to give the queue file to one of its tasks. The value must be between 1 and 99 seconds. The default value is 5 seconds. Too small of a value can cause excessive overhead for long operations. Too large of a value causes other systems to wait. (On average, a system will wait for half of the t1 value of the system owning the queue file.) Once a task has the queue file, it can hold it for longer than the t1 value. For this reason, POWER automatically releases the queue file between the output of each class of a display command. Note that a small t1 value will do nothing to prevent performance problems caused by frequent operator usage of the PDISPLAY command.

t2   The *idle* time in number of seconds. This is the amount of time POWER must wait after giving up control of the queue file before attempting to regain control of it. This value may be specified from 0-to-9 seconds. The default is 0 seconds. The strongly suggested value is also 0 seconds. Specify a non-zero value to impose a penalty on a low priority VSE system, to ensure that the high-priority systems have queue file access.

t3   The *polling time* as a number of seconds. This is the amount of time an inactive POWER waits before reading the shared queue file to see if another system has queued work to it. Specify a value from 1-to-999 seconds. The default value is 60 seconds. On average, a system will wait for half of the t3 time before detecting a job. Note that this value only has an effect when the new job is added by another POWER, and the system that receives that job is inactive. Your POWER will immediately detect work placed in the queue by itself. POWER only waits for work queued by other systems, and only when it is itself inactive. Update the t3 value if the operator complains that jobs delay startup when they are submitted from another shared spool system. Changing the t3 value has no effect when POWER RJE (PNET) is used to move jobs between POWER systems.

7.9 Spooling to Tape

Thus far, our discussion of POWER has centered on spooling to DASD. POWER also supports spooling directly to tape as illustrated in Figure 7.9. This option can greatly reduce DASD I/O and POWER disk file contention. If you produce a number of large reports, the use of tape spooling can also greatly reduce the DASD requirements for the POWER data file.

Tape spooling is enabled in POWER via the **DISP=T** parameter of the * $$ LST statement. You may optionally provide the TADDR= parameter to specify the tape address to be used. If the TADDR operand is omitted, then POWER will prompt the operator to supply a tape address via a 1Q55D message.

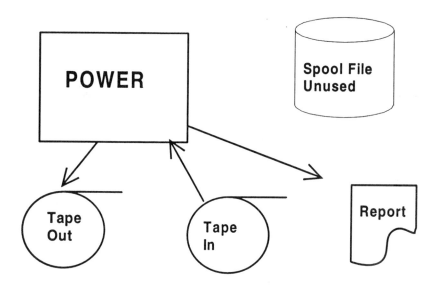

Figure 7.9 Tape Spooling

After a report has been spooled to tape, you can print it directly from tape by starting a POWER printer from a tape device. This is done via the PSTART LST,cuu,X'tape' form of the start command. Spooling to tape, and printing from tape are attractive for a number of reasons:

1. Less POWER spool DASD space is required

2. DASD I/Os are reduced

3. The tape provides built in backup of the report

7.10 Operator Commands

POWER provides a complete set of operator commands. These commands include several that are important to the tuning process. This section reviews only the POWER tuning related commands.

7.10.1   PDISPLAY STATUS Command

The **PDISPLAY STATUS** command is used to display the current POWER status summary upon the console. The information displayed is the same as POWER provides at shutdown time upon the printer. The format is slightly different to accommodate output upon the system console. Figure 7.10 contains sample output from this command.

```
1R46I      VSE/POWER 4.1.1 STATUS REPORT FOR IPWPOWER
1R46I   QUEUE FILE      IJQFILE
        TOTAL NUMBER OF TRACKS                            12 TRACKS
        TOTAL NUMBER OF QUEUE RECORDS                    750 RECORDS
        NUMBER OF FREE QUEUE RECORDS                     628 RECORDS
        MAX. NO. Q-REC'S USED IN PRESENT SESSION         130 RECORDS
        MAX. NO. Q-REC'S USED SINCE LAST COLDSTART       302 RECORDS
        NUMBER OF QUEUE RECORDS LOST DUE TO I/O ERROR      0 RECORDS
        QUEUE FILE STORAGE COPY VIO SPACE                192 K-BYTES
1R46I   DATA FILE       IJDFILE
        TOTAL NUMBER OF TRACKS                           2850 TRACKS
        TOTAL NUMBER OF DBLK-GROUPS                      2565 GROUPS
        NUMBER OF FREE DBLK-GROUPS                       2333 GROUPS
        MAX NO. DBLK-GPS USED SINCE LAST COLDSTART       2565 GROUPS
        NUMBER OF DBLK-GROUPS LOST DUE TO I/O ERROR         4 GROUPS
        DATA BLOCK GROUP SIZE                             10 BLOCKS
        DATA BLOCK SIZE                                 1952 BYTES
        SPOOL LIMIT PERCENTAGE                            90 %
1R46I   ACCOUNT FILE      IJAFILE
        TOTAL NUMBER OF TRACKS                            90 TRACKS
        PERCENTAGE OF FILE THAT IS FILLED                73 %
1R46I   GENERAL STORAGE/TASK STATISTICS
        FIXABLE STORAGE USED BY VSE/POWER                128 K-BYTES
        VIRTUAL STORAGE OCCUPIED BY VSE/POWER PHASES     419 K-BYTES
        SYSTEM GETVIS STORAGE USED BY VSE POWER           24 K-BYTES
        NO. OF TIMES TASKS WAITING FOR PFIXED STORAGE      0 TIMES
        MAX. NO. OF K-BYTES FIXED IN PRESENT SESSION      84 K-BYTES
        MAX. NO. OF TASKS ACTIVE AT ONE POINT IN TIME     42 TASKS
        NO. OF TIMES TASKS WAITING FOR VIRTUAL STORAGE     2 TIMES
        MAX. GETVIS STOR. REQUESTED IN PRESENT SESSION    72 K-BYTES
1R46I   DYNAMIC PARTITION SCHEDULING STATISTICS
        SUCCESSFUL DYNAMIC PARTITION ALLOCATION          842 TIMES
        UNSUCCESSFUL DYNAMIC PARTITION ALLOCATION          4 TIMES
1R46I   NUMBER OF NOTIFY MESSAGES LOST:                    0 MSG(S)
```

Figure 7.10 POWER PDISPLAY STATUS Command Output

The status command output contains a number of interesting pieces of information. Let us look at each of these.

The **MAX. NO. Q-REC'S USED SINCE LAST COLDSTART** item is used to determine the correct size of your POWER queue file. This file should not be vastly over allocated. If you find that your queue file is too large, it should be reduced to the high-water mark plus 10 percent.

The **NO. OF TIMES TASKS WAITING FOR PFIXED STORAGE** line shows if POWER ever exhausted its real allocation. Each time this occurs, POWER suspends an internal task until another POWER task releases the storage it owns. Console messages are produced by POWER and can be used to judge the amount of time lost due to real storage waits. If this number is not zero, then you should increase the POWER partition real allocation. You may have to increase the SIZE= value at the same time because allocating more real storage reduces the size of the POWER Pageable Area.

The **MAX. NO. K-BYTES FIXED IN PRESENT SESSION** item is indicates the maximum amount of real storage consumed by POWER. Use this to determine if you have greatly over allocated storage for POWER, or are close to exhausting your real allocation.

The **NO. OF TIMES TASKS WAITING FOR VIRTUAL STORAGE** line indicates if POWER ever exhausted its virtual storage allocation. Each time this occurs, POWER suspends an internal task until another POWER task completes and releases the storage it owns. Console messages are produced by POWER and can be used to judge the amount of time lost due to virtual storage waits. If this number is not zero, then you should increase the POWER partition virtual allocation.

The **MAX GETVIS STOR. REQUESTED IN PRESENT SESSION** line displays the high water mark for partition GETVIS usage by POWER. This value may be used to determine if the POWER partition GETVIS allocation is too large. This is only important if POWER is not run in a private address space. If you run POWER in private, you are encouraged to over allocate the partition GETVIS area to provide for growth. You can increase the size of the GETVIS area by lowering the ALLOCR and SIZE= values by the same amount if too much ALLOCR was provided. If you run POWER in the shared area you will wish to run POWER with the smallest possible partition GETVIS area to maximize the available private area.

An **UNSUCCESSFUL DYNAMIC PARTITION ALLOCATION** line displays the number of times that a dynamic partition allocation failed. The next line lists the number of these failures that were due to insufficient allocation space. This indicates the number of times a dynamic partition allocation was delayed due to a lack of virtual storage. Define additional page dataset space to correct this situation.

7.10.2   D DYNC Command

The status of the dynamic partition classes may be displayed via the POWER D DYNC operator command.   Enter **D DYNC** to display the status of all classes.   Enter **D DYNC,DISAB** to display the status of any disabled classes.   Enter **D DYNC,ENAB** to display the status of only those dynamic partition classes that are currently enabled.   See Figure 7.7 for an example of the output of this command.

7.10.3   D A Command

The D A command displays the status of all POWER tasks.   A separate task exists for each active POWER controlled partition in the system.   In addition, the status of all POWER controlled devices is displayed.   The current relative output position is included in the command output.   The current "running" job name is also part of the display.   Figure 7.11 below is an example of the output of a **D A** command.

```
D A
1C39I COMMAND PASSED TO VSE/POWER
1R48I    BG,FEC,A0I,        INACTIVE
1R48I    F2,FEC,L2,    FAQSVM5 ,56286,2
1R48I    F3,FEC,K3,         INACTIVE
1R48I    F4,FEC,J4,         INACTIVE
1R48I    F1,FEC,H1,         INACTIVE
1R48I    F2,FEE,,      FAQSVM5 ,56287,A      30816 LINES SPOOLED
1R48I    T1,FEC,T,     JCLSCHED,56326,T
1R48I    T1,FEE,,      JCLSCHED,56326,A          0 LINES SPOOLED
1R48I    RDR,FEC,A          INACTIVE
1R48I    PUN,FED,A,VM            INACTIVE
1R48I    LST,FEE,A,1,VM          INACTIVE
```

Figure 7.11 D A Command Output

7.11   POWER Networking – PNET

POWER supports networking of systems via its PNET feature.   The POWER networking feature is controlled via the PNET= operand

of the POWER macro. PNET via SNA is controlled via the SNA=
operand of the POWER macro. PNET is often used to connect
multiple CPUs at different locations. It is also an alternative to
shared POWER spool.

Figure 7.12 illustrates three nodes connected via PNET. Systems
A and B are directly connected, as are systems B and C. Systems
A and C are indirectly connected through system B. Systems C and
D are running with shared POWER. Systems A and B can both
ship jobs to System D via the System C connection.

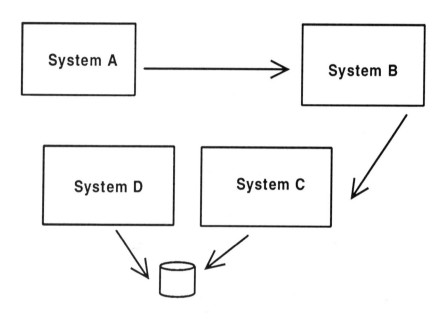

Figure 7.12 POWER PNET Systems

PNET connects nodes within a network. PNET supports the
transmission of jobstreams, output, commands, and messages
between nodes. The nodes may be connected via BSC, CTCAs, and
SNA lines. A node may be a single VSE system or up to nine
different VSE systems each connected to the others via shared
POWER. When SNA lines are used, then any two nodes may
communicate data without the use of intermediate POWER
systems, even when the nodes are not directly connected within the
network. Such indirect nodes are supported for CTCA and BSC
transmission, but the information is spooled on each intermediate
system before being passed to the next system.

7.11.1 PNET Tuning

Optimizing the performance of PNET consists of tuning several separate components of POWER and of VTAM. These are:

- VTAM pacing

- Number of VTAM buffers

- Number and size of PNET buffers

- Amount of concurrent PNET activity

Before running out and assigning all available resources to PNET, remember that the performance of transmission between POWER systems should be secondary to online system performance. Specifically, note that optimizing PNET can result in CICS degradation. CICS users perceive delays by waiting for their terminals to respond. The real dollar cost of a delay in transmitting a job or its output between VSE systems is often much lower. The default values provided by IBM take this into account, and often deliberately detune PNET transmissions.

VTAM pacing parameters affect PNETs ability to utilize a transmission channel to capacity. A low value of about three is suggested to keep POWER's real storage requirements low. Increasing this value may be done if:

1. The transmission line has capacity

2. Both POWER systems can afford the additional storage

The pacing value must be altered in two places. These are in VTAM's APPL statement that defines the PNET, and also in the MODEENT macro for the BIND parameters. If the pacing value is increased then additional LFBUF and VPBUF buffers may be required within the VTAM partition. Note that the pacing value and the number of PNET buffers should match because POWER introduces a ten second delay anytime it finds VTAM unable to accept its data.

You specify the number of buffers provided by PNET for each node via the MAXBUF parameter of the PNODE macro. You also specify a buffer size for PNET buffers. The minimum buffer size is

300 bytes. The maximum buffer size is 32000 bytes for SNA, and 1800 bytes for BSC and CTCA communications. The larger the buffer size, the smaller the number of I/Os required to transmit a given file, and the faster the file transmission takes place. Of course, large buffers also require additional real storage within the POWER partitions. Large buffers also monopolize the communication channel for longer periods than small buffers do. BSC and CTCA buffers are allocated from PFIXED storage. SNA buffers are allocated from the POWER partition GETVIS area. If storage is not a problem, then larger buffers are often one of the best ways to improve PNET performance.

PNET can use multiple transmitters and receivers for communications between two nodes. These are all multiplexed on the same transmission channel, so additional performance does not result. You may wish to define additional transmitters and receivers over a critical path so that a single large job does not stop the transmission of smaller jobs or small commands until the large job completes.

Chapter

8

Librarian Tuning

This chapter discusses the VSE *librarian*. The Librarian offers services to the operating system and to general system users. The VSE librarian manages the various types of data involved in running a VSE operating system. This data includes source programs, job control, compiler output, and executable programs. The librarian includes code that is part of the supervisor, SVA resident modules, and phases that execute within batch partitions.

We look at the librarian with several objectives in mind. The structure and performance characteristics of VSE libraries are reviewed. Common problems are discussed, commands and parameters reviewed, and suggestions are made for tuning libraries. Examples of common simple jobstreams are included.

The librarian is used by essentially all components of VSE. Some of these components are briefly covered in this chapter. Additional library related discussions beyond the level in this chapter are included in other areas of this book where warranted. For example, additional CICS, POWER, and VTAM information is provided in the chapter for each component.

VSE has its own special terminology for the different types of data managed by the librarian. VSE refers to source programs as type *SOURCE*. It refers to job control as type *PROC*. Compiler output is type *OBJ*. Executable programs are type *PHASE*. Storage displays are of type *DUMP*. Figure 8.1 depicts the different librarian data types. Additional user data types are supported beyond the IBM standard types. The LIBR utility allows you to catalog card image data into any user named type desired. The

VSE Librarian also supports a standard API that permits application programs to create and manage library members containing variable length data. The new IBM PWS support and the file transfer facility both use the Librarian as a database manager. Several OEM products also use the Librarian as a pseudo database.

VSE Type of Data	Librarian Data Type
Program Source	SOURCE
Compiler Output	OBJ
Programs	PHASE
Job Control (JCL)	PROC
Dump Output	DUMP

Figure 8.1 Librarian Data Types

8.1 Cookbook for Librarian Tuning

Many quick fixes exist for Librarian-related performance problems. Some common problems and their fixes include:

- Slow fetch due to long directory searches. Review your permanent LIBDEF chains and remove unneeded sublibraries. You may also gain an improvement by combining sublibraries. If all else fails, you can isolate the problem by moving the sublibrary from a permanent SEARCH chain to a temporary SEARCH chain.

- Slow fetch due to long program read-in. Review frequently used sublibraries and reorganize those that are fragmented.

- Slow search and fetch. Move high-use libraries to low use DASD. Consider using a caching controller for these volumes.

• Slow batch utility. LIBR utility performance can be improved when more buffer space is provided. Check the amount of available GETVIS in the LIBR batch partitions.

8.2 Library Structure

VSE libraries are a VSAM like (but non-VSAM) file structure. Users define libraries and sublibraries, and catalog members into sublibraries. The librarian performs its own disk space management from a single pool of space for both directories and members. All directories share the same pool of space within a library.

A library represents one or more units of DASD allocation. This space may be allocated using VSAM (a VSAM library) or it may be allocated manually via DLBL and EXTENT statements (called a BAM library). A library may contain one or more extents spread across one or more DASD volumes. Space owned by a library is formatted to fixed length blocks when it is allocated. Currently, the only blocksize supported by the librarian is 1024 bytes (1KB). This small blocksize results in wasted space for program storage on other than FBA DASD due to a relatively large gap (compared to the data size). Note that this 1KB size is a compromise value to optimize storage usage for small members (such as procedure and transients) and for large members (like source programs and phases for many application systems). The library architecture supports other better blocksizes, but these are not implemented in VSE at this time. When VSE implements a choice in blocksize, selecting a blocksize will become an important tuning parameter.

A sublibrary represents a directory. Each sublibrary has no space allocated to it, but instead shares the space owned by the library. Thus, any one sublibrary can occupy all space allocated to a library. Also, since space is allocated at the library level, the whole library is locked during the allocation/deallocation processing for any sublibrary. This results in potentially long lock waits during library maintenance.

A single directory can contain the source for a program, the compiled object output for this program, the phase produced when the program is link-edited, and even the JCL to execute the program. Thus, VSE libraries are not restricted to a single type or format of data. This was an important change introduced in VSE/SP 2.1 in 1984. Prior to that time, DOS used a separate library for each type of data, and each library type had its own unique format, management utilities, and performance management characteristics.

8.2.1 IJSYSRS Library

The library named IJSYSRS is the system residence library (also called SYSRES). It is automatically defined to the system at IPL time. You IPL your VSE system from IJSYSRS. IJSYSRS is never defined within VSAM space, and may occupy only a single extent. The sublibrary SYSLIB is built into the IJSYSRS library. This is the sublibrary from which the supervisor is fetched, where the ASI procedures are located, and is a default part of ALL search chains.

The default IJSYSRS library is on the DOSRES volume of a standard VSE/ESA system. A backup IJSYSRS library is provided on the SYSWK1 volume. Either of these IJSYSRS libraries may be IPLed and becomes the current system residence library for the duration of the IPL.

The backup IJSYSRS library is used to build a new system residence file as part of a fast service upgrade. It can also be automatically selected by VSE/ESA for a restart as part of the unattended node support.

8.2.2 Private Libraries

Libraries defined in addition to the IJSYSRS library are called *private libraries*. The physical layout of the IJSYSRS library and of private libraries is the same. Private libraries may occupy multiple extents, and also may be defined within VSAM space. Private libraries within VSAM space may be automatically extended in size when they fill up. This is accomplished by performing dynamic secondary allocation using normal VSAM space management facilities.

User programs should be catalogued into private libraries rather than the IJSYSRS library. These private libraries should be defined on a disk volume separate from the DOSRES volume to reduce arm contention. Private libraries must be defined to the system via a LIBDEF statement before they will be searched for programs.

8.2.3 Librarian I/O

The Librarian is implemented within an SVA phase called $IJBLBR and also within the supervisor fetch routine. All librarian I/O utilizes ECKD channel programs where applicable for improved performance. All librarian I/O is chained together to reduce the number of SVC's and improve performance, when sufficient bufferspace is available. The LIBR program buffers come from partition GETVIS, while the fetch routine uses the target area for a program load as its bufferspace. The fetch routine uses head queue I/O which is system priority I/O scheduled before any other pending requests for a device.

8.3 Search Chains

Multiple sublibraries may be chained together to define a search chain used to locate a specific member. VSE allows each basic type of data to have its own library search sequence. Thus, a search chain is provided for the *PHASE, OBJ, PROC,* and *SOURCE* types of data. The LIBLIST command may be used to display a search chain. (See Figure 8.2 below.)

```
LIBLIST PHASE
F6-TEMP ** NO LIBRARY INFORMATION AVAILABLE**
F6-PERM LIBNAME SUBLIB     STATUS  ---PARTITIONS----
SEARCH  EXPLORE EVSEPROD      SHR 0    456789AB DYNP
        PRD1    BASE          SHR 0 23456789AB DYNP
        PRD1    SORT          SHR 0 23456789AB DYNP
```

Figure 8.2 LIBLIST Command Output

VSE supports a permanent search chain and a temporary search chain for each type of data. The temporary search chain is reset to empty at the end of each job. The permanent search chain remains set within each partition, until it is explicitly reset via a LIBDROP or altered via another LIBDEF. Because it takes time to search each sublibrary in a chain, it is a good idea to reduce the number of sublibraries in a search chain. Sufficient time is saved by reducing the length of a search chain, to make it desirable to combine sublibraries where no strong reason exists to keep them separate. For example, if software for a general ledger system and an accounts payable system are kept in different sublibraries that are always LIBDEFed, you will wish to review combining these into a single accounting sublibrary. No benefit exists for using separate sublibraries for phases. In fact, 1000 phases in a single LIBDEFed sublibrary require less storage in system GETVIS than two sublibraries with 500 phases. The single sublibrary search takes no longer than either of the smaller sublibraries does. Both of these results stem from VSE maintaining an index in storage that identifies the exact directory block a specific member resides in.

Because VSE supports both permanent and temporary search chains, you may also benefit from reducing the number of libraries in the permanent chain, and defining rarely used libraries only as needed in the temporary chain. VSE builds information in the system GETVIS area for each sublibrary, the first time that sublibrary is LIBDEFed, in any chain, in any partition.

This system GETVIS information is reused each time that same sublibrary is LIBDEFed anywhere, and the library/sublibrary open is bypassed. Thus, the very first LIBDEF to a library and sublibrary is relatively expensive. This must be considered when eliminating permanent LIBDEF chain entries. If a sublibrary would need to be frequently LIBDEFed into a temporary chain, then it should be made part of a permanent chain, or LIBDEFED in some other partition. For example, a performance improvement can be noted for frequently LIBDEFed temporary chain libraries if they are LIBDEFed under POWER, even though the POWER partition itself never references them. POWER does not reference the type OBJ search chain, so additional libraries may be *preopened* by referencing them in this chain. The POWER PROC chain may be similarly employed. POWER does use the type SOURCE chain during execution for resolving SLI includes, so care should be employed in using this chain to preopen libraries.

8.4 Managing Library Updates

In this section we will discuss what is required to manage a library that has a relatively high frequency of updates. We are concerned about lock requests, fragmentation, and library reorganizations.

All library updates require one of more *lock requests* to ensure library integrity during the update. Each time space is allocated within a VSE library, a lock is required. Each time a directory is updated, a lock is required. And, all sublibrary management requests involve their own locks.

When VSE libraries are updated over a period of time, *fragmentation* results. A library member is fragmented when it does not occupy contiguous library blocks. Fragmentation causes slower library accesses, gets worse the longer the library is reused, and can be very difficult to measure.

The performance fix for a fragmented library is a library *reorganization*. A library is reorganized by recreating it. We will look at using the LIBR utility to backup, delete, and redefine a library to accomplish this task.

8.4.1 Librarian Locks

The VSE librarian makes numerous requests of VSE lock management to ensure library integrity. In a nonshared DASD environment (DASDSHR=NO), these locks are local to the VSE system, and only involve updates to memory resident tables. In a shared DASD environment (DASDSHR=YES), librarian locks for shared DASD are made to the resident tables plus reflected in the external lock file.

Library locks can be a serious performance issue, especially in a shared DASD environment. Each time that space must be allocated, the librarian must lock the library space map for exclusive use. This results in serialization of all librarian updates for the library. Serialization occurs even when different sublibraries within one library are being updated. This is a result of the space map being managed at the library level, not at the sublibrary level. Sublibraries do not own space, libraries own space. In a DASDSHR=YES environment, these locks require disk I/Os. In fact, these disk I/Os usually take more time than the actual library updates which are being locked!

One of the best tools to reduce problems due to library locks is to ensure libraries are not used in a shared environment, and not placed on shared DASD. Large improvements in throughput result from not running multiple updates for the same library, at the same time. In fact, benchmark runs have shown that two updates for the same library can take five-to-ten times longer when run at the same time than if they are run separately.

8.4.2 Fragmentation

Fragmentation is a major cause of performance problems with VSE libraries. Library fragmentation occurs when many of the most frequent used members of a library do not occupy contiguous disk space. Fragmentation is bad because disk blocks that are not contiguous must be read with individual I/O requests.

The VSE Librarian reuses deleted member space, after all library space has been used once. Free library blocks are reused from the low end of the library allocation through the end. The Librarian does not require that a member occupy contiguous library blocks, and thus a member created in reused area will often occupy several noncontiguous segments of library blocks.

These two design characteristics result in fragmentation of library space. Library space is fragmented whenever a significant percentage of the most frequently accessed members of a library occupy non-contiguous blocks. Fragmentation severely impacts member read and update performance.

Fragmentation does not occur until after the free area of a library has been consumed by member catalogs. The librarian allocates member blocks starting at the begin of the free area, and extending through the whole free area. Thus, each library block will be allocated once before space reuse begins. However, once space reuse begins, member fragmentation typically begins to occur.

Fragmented members are read much slower than contiguous members because the librarian is able to read multiple contiguous blocks in a single I/O, but only able to read a single block that is not contiguous. For example, the librarian can read a 50-block member in a single I/O when sufficient buffer space is available, but requires 50 separate reads when every block of this member is fragmented. This can translate into a 50-to-1 performance cost. A library reorg will totally correct this problem.

Sadly, VSE libraries tend to become more and more fragmented over time. The average contiguous free space element size tends towards the 1-to-2 block range. This is because the average deleted element size is smaller than the modal member size. (The modal member size is the most frequently occurring size.) Actually, the average deleted element size begins as the modal member size, then gradually is reduced in size over time. This results from allocation of free space elements using the whole element or splitting an existing element.

Since splitting of elements always increases the degree of fragmentation, and since a fairly large number of one or two block members exist in any sublibrary, library maintenance of small members drives the size of available free elements towards the smallest size encountered.

8.4.3 Reorganizing Libraries

We have seen that fragmented libraries perform very poorly, and that all libraries upon which maintenance is performed become fragmented in proportion to the amount of maintenance. Fortunately, it is relatively easy to correct a fragmented library. All that is required is to backup the library, delete it, redefine the library, and restore the library. Note that defragmentation must be done at the library level.

Performing these operations at the sublibrary level will only further fragment a library. This is a result of space being allocated and/or managed at the library level, instead of at the sublibrary level. Fragmentation occurs even if each of the sublibraries making up a library is individually restored.

Deleting, redefining, and restoring a library can be difficult. VSE will not allow you to delete a library while any of its sublibraries are still LIBDEFed. This makes it very difficult to defragment libraries that are defined in long running partitions, especially libraries defined to POWER or VTAM! In general, these libraries can only be defragmented in a standalone mode. The GSLIBR utility offered by Goal Systems may be used to avoid the VSE restrictions for LIBDEFed libraries.

Refer to Figure 8.3 for an example of a jobstream that can be used to reorganize the library named **MYLIB**. Note that we employ separate backup and restore procedures.

8.5 Library Placement

Libraries need to be managed like any other dataset. High-use libraries should not be placed on the same volume as other high-use datasets. This is particularly true of libraries containing type

```
// JOB REORG
/* Backup all SubLibs in the MYLIB library
// TLBL TAPE,'LIB REORG'
// EXEC LIBR,SIZE=200K
BACKUP LIB=MYLIB,TAPE=181,TAPELABEL=TAPE
/*
// EXEC LIBR,SIZE=200K
DELETE LIB=MYLIB
DEFINE LIB=MYLIB
RESTORE LIB=MYLIB,TAPE=181,TAPELABEL=TAPE
/*
/&
```

Figure 8.3 LIBR REORG Example

PHASE members. The VSE fetch routine is single threaded within two system tasks, and only one fetch can be in progress at a time.

Because fetch waits are common in an active VSE system, it is desirable to ensure that high-use libraries are not blocked by other I/Os to the same volume. This is another reason why defragmenting high-use libraries is especially important when any number of high use phases are involved. It is critical that libraries not occupy the same volume as the VSE lock file, the POWER QFILE/DFILE, nor paging datasets in a high-paging environment.

DASD caching control units can be very useful for high-use VSE libraries. OEM products that permit placing frequently fetched phases in memory are also an excellent tuning option. Resident directory entries are a low cost option that can save as much as half of the fetch I/Os.

A performance monitor that reports on I/Os by dataset should be used to detect conflicts between high-use datasets, and conflicts resulting from a temporal association of I/Os that lead to excessively long seeks. Library I/O must be supported by your performance monitor. Both directory search, and member read-in I/Os should be tracked and reported on. Note that directory searches must be factored into library placement calculations. In fact, these I/Os may be more important than member read I/O requests. It is often true that more search I/Os are needed to locate a member, than read I/Os to actually process the member.

8.6 SDLEs for CICS

An application that performs a large number of fetches can improve performance by building and using local directory entries for phases. CICS does this the first time each PPT entry is used. When these local directory entries are available, all directory search overhead is eliminated, and the only cost of a fetch of a CICS program (or map) is the I/O to read the phase. CICS builds local directory entries for all maps and programs.

It is a little known fact that the directory entries built by a static partition CICS are worthless unless sufficient system GETVIS is available during CICS execution. The CICS directory entries built within the PPT are not large enough to contain a "real" VSE directory entry. For this reason, the fetch routine builds a dummy directory entry in the area provided by CICS, and allocates a "real" VSE directory entry in the system GETVIS area (called an SDLE). However, this is only done when more than the smaller of 48KB or 20 percent free system GETVIS is provided at the time that CICS builds the PPT entry. Thus, when system GETVIS is tight, CICS runs without the benefit of "real" directory entries, and must perform slow directory searches for all members fetched by CICS. This is especially bad for CICS MAP phases, which must be fetched each time they are referenced.

If you are unable to increase your system GETVIS allocation to ensure that 20 percent free space is available, you should consider declaring your MAPs as programs. This "lie" will cause CICS to manage maps in available DSA space on a LRU basis just as it manages all other programs.

When CICS is run in a dynamic partition, then the extended directory entries are placed in the dynamic space GETVIS area, and not in the system GETVIS area. For this reason, you should run CICS in a dynamic partition whenever possible.

8.7 POWER SLI Library Includes

POWER can read JCL and data from a library member. This is controlled via the * $$ SLI statement. POWER searches the normal LIBDEF SEARCH,SOURCE chain for SLI members. If you can reduce this chain to a single sublibrary, POWER performance will be improved.

POWER SLI includes often perform better than VSE procedures accessed via EXEC PROC=name. This is particularly true when the search chain employed by POWER is properly tuned. POWER SLI also supports retrieval of ICCF library members. This is not supported for EXEC PROC=name retrieval. If you must make a choice between VSE procedures and POWER includes, POWER includes are preferred on the basis of functionality plus performance.

Many shops use both VSE procedures and POWER SLI includes. Often the VSE procedures contain commonly used segments of JCL for a single utility or a frequently required jobstep. The POWER SLI members are typically used to define a complete POWER job, and often contain references to VSE procedures.

8.8 Procedure Libraries

VSE allows job control, and data, to be catalogued into procedure libraries. Procedures can be called out as needed within JCL via the // EXEC PROC=name command. VSE procedures are easily misused from a performance standpoint. This typically occurs when a user has defined a long permanent search chain for type PROC, or when many procedures are used where each inserts only a few statements. In addition, job control support for procedure libraries is not as fast as the POWER support for SLI libraries. POWER SLI also allows direct retrieval of ICCF library members into a VSE jobstream. However, POWER SLI members are not as robust as procedures in terms of parameter passing and substitution or for the nesting of procedure calls.

Job Control accesses procedures and specifies parameters via an extension of the execute command. You may code // EXEC PROC=pname, TODAY=SUNDAY to execute a procedure and set the variable named *TODAY* to the value *SUNDAY*. Variable parameters are passed to the procedure, and may be substituted into JCL statements within the procedure. Parameter substitution into data cards is not supported by VSE.

SYSIPT data is card data that is read by a user program, rather than by Job Control. Procedures may contain SYSIPT data. This is indicated by specifying DATA=YES on the CATALOG statement used to create the procedure. The DATA=YES parameter is required when data following an EXEC card is to be read by a program. Nested procedure must be all of the same type. A procedure coded with DATA=YES may invoke only those other procedures that also were catalogued with the DATA=YES parameter. The procedure override facility can not be used to replace or alter SYSIPT data.

Procedures may also have partition dependent names. For static partitions this is accomplished by specifying a $ as the first character and the partition indicator as the second character of the member name. The partition indicator is 0 for BG, else it is the second character of the partition ID. A dynamic partition dependent name is built by specifying the class of the dynamic partition as the first character of the member name followed by the $ character. The partition dependent procedure is then invoked by coding an EXEC statement with $$ as the first two positions of the member name. VSE/ESA will replace the applicable $ with the partition qualification character.

9

VSAM Tuning

In this chapter we will look at the *Virtual Storage Access Method* (VSAM). VSAM is used by VSE to manage DASD space, to define files within that space, and to access and update the data within VSAM files. We will look at the components of VSAM files, the parameters used to define these files, their performance characteristics, measurement methods, and basic VSAM tuning.

The various types of VSAM files are each covered. We emphasize tuning of KSDS's since most VSAM performance issues are related to this type of file. LSR is briefly covered here, and also in the chapter on CICS.

VSAM is a complex subject. By necessity, our study of it will be somewhat superficial. Readers interested in a more in depth treatment of this subject are referred to J. Renade's book *VSAM: Performance, Design, and Fine Tuning*. The IBM manual *VSAM:Programmer's Reference* (SC33-6535) is a fine reference for the IBM utilities discussed in this chapter.

9.1 Cookbook for VSAM Tuning

Most common VSAM performance problems involve the separate areas of record access and update. Let us look at common performance fixes.

- Use Local Shared Resources (LSR). This is the major CICS tuning option for VSAM.

- Specify VSAM bufferspace. It is the major batch tuning item for record retrieval. A good starting value has been found to be 64KB.

- Emphasize index bufferspace for random retrieval, data bufferspace for sequential retrieval. Note that you may override the bufferspace at runtime via the BUFNI= and BUFND= parameters of the DLBL statement.

- Avoid excess CI freespace. CI level freespace is wasted unless a file receives a fairly random distribution of updates.

- Avoid excess CA freespace. CA level freespace is wasted unless a file receives enough updates to justify the extra index entries and additional starting allocation required for this freespace.

- Do not reorganize VSAM files too often. Once the initial CA splits have occurred for a file, subsequent updates make use of freespace created by the initial splits. A reorganization at this point will only force these CA splits to occur again.

- Reorganize VSAM files only to recover unusable (and therefore wasted) freespace, or to reduce the number of index levels.

9.2 Overview of VSAM File Components

VSAM manages areas on DASD called VSAM SPACEs. VSAM also manages files. Files are suballocated within VSAM SPACEs. Information on VSAM files is maintained within VSAM catalogs instead of in a Volume Table Of Contents (VTOC). A VSAM catalog is a special kind of VSAM file, and the only kind that is usually addressed via the VTOC. The VTOC contains entries only for VSAM spaces and VSAM catalogs. Figure 9.1 illustrates how the catalog is addressed by the VTOC, and how the VSAM catalog in turn addresses the remaining VSAM objects.

VSAM also supports a *UNIQUE* allocation. This is a type of allocation for a specific file that is also entered in the VTOC. A VSAM file may be defined to occupy either a UNIQUE allocation or space *suballocated* from that owned by a VSAM catalog.

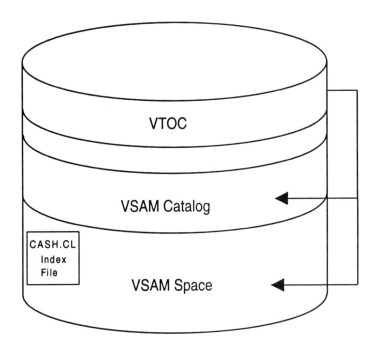

Figure 9.1 VSAM Catalog and VSAM Space

IDCAMS is a batch utility that is used to define, delete, and alter VSAM catalogs, spaces, and files. It may also be used to display information about the status of a VSAM file that is useful for tuning. The information printed by IDCAMS can be difficult to understand and interpret. A number of OEM tools exist that will display VSAM status information online and in easier to interpret formats than those used by IDCAMS.

CICS is a major user of VSAM in the VSE environment. CICS also contains a number of VSAM specific tuning parameters, and produces statistics of great use in tuning VSAM for CICS. CICS supports the important VSAM LSR feature.

In this section we will look at catalogs, spaces, and files in more detail. We are interested in how to define each of these VSAM elements. We are also interested in what general tuning actions can be taken at the time of definition, and what performance information is maintained by VSAM for our use.

9.2.1 Catalogs

A VSAM catalog contains information on VSAM spaces and files. We will refer to these items as VSAM objects. Information on non-VSAM objects may also be held within a catalog. A non-VSAM object is a file that VSAM does not manage, but for which VSAM holds descriptive information.

A VSAM catalog is itself a VSAM object. A catalog is defined to VSAM along with the unit of disk space that catalog will occupy. A single VSAM catalog may be defined upon each DASD volume. It is also a special type of VSAM file. The VSAM catalog is the only VSAM file with its own special VTOC entry (although each VSAM space is also defined within the catalog).

The catalog contains a record of all space controlled by VSAM for use by file definitions. Space to be controlled by a catalog may be added to a catalog at any time. A VSAM catalog can manage space on any number of volumes. A single DASD volume may be divided among several VSAM catalogs, with each catalog managing a separate space on that volume.

Once a catalog has been defined, VSAM files may be defined within space controlled by that catalog, or defined within their own unique space. Several types of VSAM files exist. The types of VSAM files include *Relative Record DataSets* (RRDS), *Entry Sequenced Datasets*, and *Key Sequenced DataSets*. Most performance issues involve KSDS's, so we will concentrate on this type of file.

9.2.2 KSDS

A KSDS is just what its name implies, a file that is accessed using a key rather than a byte displacement or a record number. A VSAM *key* is a portion of a record used to identify that record. It must occupy a fixed position within each record.

Each KSDS is actually two files, an index file and a data file. The VSAM catalog contains an entry for the KSDS that names each of these two files. Thus for a KSDS, the catalog contains three entries. The first entry tells us that we are dealing with a KSDS, the second entry describes the index, and the third entry describes the data. The index and data files each have their own allocation of DASD space. Figure 9.2 illustrates the separate index and data components of the **CASH.CL** VSAM KSDS.

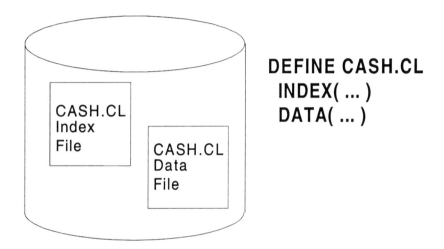

DEFINE CASH.CL
INDEX(...)
DATA(...)

Figure 9.2 VSAM KSDS Components

A KSDS also requires two types of buffers for all processing. Both index and data buffers (perhaps of different sizes) must be allocated for each KSDS. Choosing the correct bufferspace values for KSDS's is one of the most important VSAM tuning options.

9.2.3 CIs/CAs

VSAM packs records into a *Control Interval* (called a CI). A CI is the smallest unit of data transfer for VSAM. A CI is a single VSAM buffer. It is the unit of bufferspace. A CI may occupy one or more physical record on disk. A VSAM CI may be empty (and therefore free) or it may be allocated. Each allocated CI contains one or more records. The CISIZE parameter is used to specify the size of a CI to VSAM when a file is defined via IDCAMS.

A VSAM *Control Area* (called a CA) is the unit of allocation of disk space. Each file may have its own CA size. A CA is the smallest amount of disk space that may be allocated when additional space is required for a file. A CA contains an integral number of CIs. You determine the CA size when you define a VSAM file. The CA size is the smaller of a cylinder, the primary allocation, and the secondary allocation. VSAM automatically determines the CA size based upon your primary and secondary allocation specifications. If you define the primary and secondary allocations as cylinders, then the CA size is always a cylinder.

VSAM index and data files are each made up of an integral number of CIs, organized into CAs. The CI size can be different for the index and data components of a KSDS. You explicitly specify the CISIZE value in the VSAM DEFINE CLUSTER parameter. VSAM can override an illogical CISIZE specification. You should ensure that your buffer space value is consistent with your CISIZE value to prevent VSAM from overriding the CISIZE. The CA size can also be different for the index and data components of a KSDS. You separately define and tune the index and data components of a file.

Figure 9.3 below illustrates the relationship of CIs and CAs to a VSAM file component. Notice that the VSAM component is made up of one or more equal size CAs, each of which is made up of a fixed number of CIs.

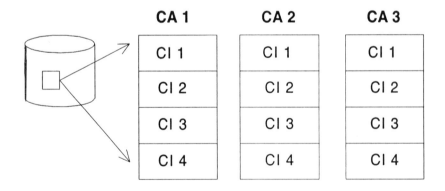

Figure 9.3 VSAM CI's and CA's

9.2.4 Index File

A VSAM index file is used to locate data records given the key of the record. The VSAM index contains the highest key for each CI within the data file plus the relative byte address of the CI containing the key. A VSAM index is comprised of a number of index CIs.

Each CA of a Data file has a single index CI associated with it. The index CI contains a single entry for each data CI within the data CA. Each of these entries contains the key of the last record within the data CI along with the RBA (Relative Byte Address) of that CI. Because keys can be large, VSAM does not store the entire key. Instead, VSAM compresses keys to eliminate repetitive information from consecutive keys. Large keys are typically compressed to less than 25 percent of their original size. Small keys are typically compressed very little. You define the index CI size used by VSAM. Additional space in the index CI is wasted and should be avoided.

A VSAM index is a tree structure and is organized into levels. Index levels are best understood by discussion. Each index CI at the bottom level of the index contains the key and RBA of every data CI in a single data CA. Index CIs in the bottom level of the index are called *sequence set CIs*. Figure 9.4 is an example of a sequence set CI. In this example, our data CA contains 4 data CIs. Observe that a separate pointer exists within the index CI for each data CI within the data CA. Each index CI must be large enough to contain the high key and the address of each data CI in a single data CA.

When more than one data CA exists, then a second level of the index is built. This new level contains additional index CIs, where each record contains the high key and RBA of an index CI in the bottom level. Thus, one record exists in the second level of a VSAM index for each data CA. These records may occupy one or more index CIs. If multiple CIs are required in the second level of a VSAM index, then a third index level is required. The number of levels in a VSAM index can grow as a result of update activity on a file. This occurs when updates alter the length of records.

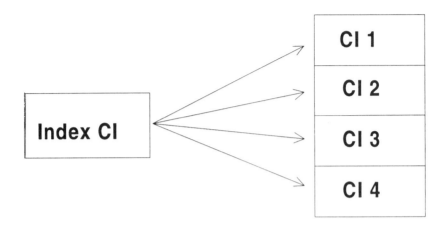

Figure 9.4 Sequence Set Index CI and its Data CA

9.2.5 Data File

The data file component of a KSDS contains the data records in logical key sequence. A single data CI may contain one or more records plus free space. Figure 9.5 illustrates a data CI.

Each record must be wholly contained within a data CI for normal VSAM files. If a record will not fit within the available space in a CI, then a new CI must be allocated in order for the record to be inserted. A special file attribute of *spanned* is provided to support records so large that they will not fit within a data CI, but this file type is infrequently used, and is not considered in our performance discussion.

Data CIs are grouped together into data CAs. The maximum size of a data CA is a cylinder. Each data CA has a single index sequence set CI associated with it. This sequence set CI must contain the high key and RBA of every occupied data CI in the data CA. If the sequence set CI becomes full, then any remaining space in the data CA is unusable. Thus, it is important to ensure that the sequence set CI size is adequate to contain a key and RBA for every data CI allocated within a data CA. If this is not done, VSAM will simply ignore and not use the excess space in each data CA, and will give no indication of the problem except that your file will require additional space over the computed minimum allocation and the file load may fail.

Data Control Interval

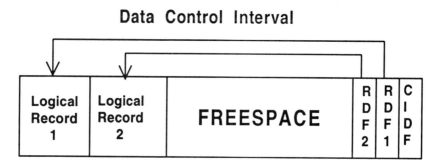

Figure 9.5 Data CI Example

9.3 Tuning Parameters

In this section we will look at the various VSAM file definition parameters that affect file access performance. These parameters are used to tune files for reduced DASD space, reduced virtual storage usage, or reduced number of I/O requests. VSAM tuning usually involves these conflicting objectives. We will look at freespace, bufferspace, imbed, and replicate here. The important LSR option is discussed in a separate section.

The remaining tuning sections of this chapter will look at tuning VSAM datasets based upon how they are used. We will separately discuss minimizing access time, then look at tuning for sequential access, random access, and for update activity.

9.3.1 Freespace

VSAM *CI freespace* refers to the unused space within a CI. CI freespace may be available within both data and index CIs. *CA freespace* refers to the unused CIs within a CA. CA freespace may exist within both data and index CAs. Freespace is of value when it is used to hold an updated or inserted record. Freespace that is never used simply makes the file larger than it need be, contributes to performance problems, and is of no real value.

Freespace may be explicitly allocated via the FSPC parameter. Freespace is also created when records are deleted or when a CI or CA *split* occurs. VSAM inserts records into existing freespace. If sufficient freespace does not exist when a record is inserted, VSAM first creates freespace by allocating a new data CI and splitting the records between the original and new CIs. VSAM only uses freespace within the target CI for a record. CI freespace in the preceding or following CIs is not available for use. It is possible to have many CIs that are half-full and split a full CI in the same area. Such half full CIs will stay as they are until they are themselves updated, or until their file is reorganized.

Freespace can be unusable or usable. Unusable freespace is any freespace that will not hold a whole record or that will never be used because a record will not be inserted into the freespace. Caution should be employed when coding the FSPC parameter. This parameter is specified as two numbers. The first number is a percentage of each CI reserved for updates when the CI is allocated. The second number is a percentage of each CA to be reserved for updates. Freespace is allocated when a file is loaded and used when it is updated.

CI freespace is a number of free bytes. VSAM does not guarantee that the number of bytes reserved for freespace is enough to hold a record, but it does reserve this number of bytes in each CI when records are initially loaded into a CI after the CI is allocated. CI freespace has the effect of reducing the number of usable bytes in a CI during the load of that CI.

Freespace is not free! The amount of space required to hold a given file is increased by the amount of freespace reserved within that file. Thus a file loaded with 50 percent freespace will require twice the space it otherwise would need. It may also take twice as long to load and to back up, than a file with no freespace. Freespace is of benefit only when these performance costs are outweighed by faster updates.

Freespace may have no effect at all. For an example let us look at a case of a CISIZE of 4096 bytes with a record size of 2000 bytes and a CI freespace of 1 percent. Obviously 1 percent of 4096 bytes is not enough to hold a single record, and our freespace specification is ineffective. Figure 9.6 shows that our 4KB CI has 86 bytes of freespace remaining after two 2000 byte records are loaded. When we specify 1 percent freespace, nothing is reserved. One percent of 4096 is less than the 86 bytes left without a freespace specification. Anytime we specify a percent of freespace less than the number of bytes left due to record fitting, VSAM reserves no additional bytes of freespace. We can see that a freespace specification of 2 percent will also reserve no additional bytes of freespace. (.02 * 4096 is 81 bytes and less than the 86 bytes of freespace left by VSAM.)

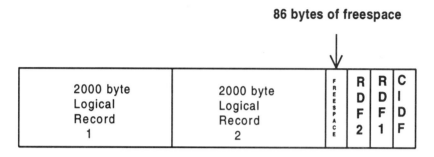

Figure 9.6 2000 Byte Records Data CI

A small CI freespace may also have a very large undesired effect. Let us look at a case of a CISIZE of 4096 bytes with a record size of 2000 bytes and a CI freespace of 3 percent. Obviously 3 percent is not enough to hold a single record, but this time we reserve half of each CI for freespace. How does this occur? The CI freespace percentage is used to compute a number of bytes. VSAM reduces the available space in each CI by this number of bytes BEFORE attempting to fit any records into the CI during initial load. Thus, our 3 percent reduces the amount of available space in each CI to less than 4000 bytes, and we only can fit a single record in each CI. In this case 3 percent is actually the same as 50 percent freespace.

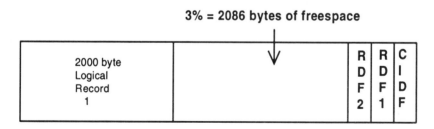

Figure 9.7 3 percent CI Freespace is 2086 bytes!!

CA freespace is a number of free CIs. If a non-zero CA freespace percentage is seen, then a minimum of one CI is always reserved for freespace. CA freespace is safer to reserve than CI freespace because it can be used if any CI within that CA is full and a split is required. Figure 9.8 below illustrates four CAs each with the

single free CI that 25 percent CA freespace would cause to be
reserved. Note that a 1 percent CA freespace specification would
have the same result. If you only require one free CI for each data
CA, then **FSPC(0 1)** is all that you need specify.

CA 1	CA 2	CA 3	CA 4
CI 1	CI 1	CI 1	CI 1
CI 2	CI 2	CI 2	CI 2
CI 3	CI 3	CI 3	CI 3
Free CI	Free CI	Free CI	Free CI

Figure 9.8 VSAM CA Freespace — Free CI's

9.3.2 Bufferspace

Bufferspace is the storage used by VSAM for CI I/O. You control
the amount of bufferspace VSAM can use. Bufferspace is arguably
the single most important VSAM tuning parameter. It is also one
of the easiest parameters to use in VSE. You may specify VSAM
bufferspace when a file is defined, and you may override this
specification at runtime via JCL parameters. Furthermore, a
number of OEM products are available to dynamically compute and
specify optimum bufferspace values.

Bufferspace may be specified at the file level, the index level, or
the data level. Index bufferspace is important for random retrieval
requests. Data bufferspace is important for sequential retrieval
requests. You can specify bufferspace explicitly at the index and
data levels via the DLBL BUFNI= and BUFND= parameters. If
you specify bufferspace at the file level, VSAM will determine which
to emphasize based upon how the file is opened and accessed. Let
us look at the characteristics of sequential access followed by
random access.

For sequential access, data buffers are the most important type
of buffer. VSAM reserves a single index buffer for use in handling

the assembler POINT or the COBOL START requests. One data buffer is reserved to handle splits, and is not otherwise used. All remaining bufferspace is used to hold data CIs. VSAM divides the available data bufferspace in half. This is done to accomplish double buffering when more than one buffer is provided. Unfortunately, the VSAM default is the worst possible. By default, VSAM reserves a single index buffer and two data buffers. Since one of the data buffers is reserved to handle splits, only a single buffer can be used, and no I/O overlap is possible.

The suggested minimum amount of space for sequential access is five data buffers plus one index buffer. This allows for double buffering, with the result of I/O overlap. It also cuts in half the number of I/Os required to read a VSAM file. In general, this will reduce the elapsed time for a job that reads the VSAM file to less than half of its original value.

Let use look at an example. Given a KSDS with a 1KB index CI size and a 4KB data CI size, VSAM will reserve 9KB of bufferspace by default. This 9KB holds 1 index buffer and two data buffers. If one reserves only 21KB of bufferspace, VSAM will have five data buffers plus the usual single index buffer. The five data buffers will reduce the number of I/Os in half for sequential retrieval operations.

For random access, index buffers are the most important type of buffer. Index buffers are used by VSAM to hold index CIs from the top levels of the index on a least recently used basis. By default, VSAM reserves only a single index buffer plus two data buffers. One of these data buffers is reserved for handling CI splits, the other is used to hold the data CI needed for a request. Because VSAM must perform one read for each level in the VSAM index, each random retrieval for the default case will usually involve L+1 I/Os (where L is the number of levels in the VSAM index).

The suggested minimum amount of bufferspace for random access is enough to hold all of the top two levels of the index, plus one extra buffer. Having two index buffers always saves one I/O for each random retrieval in comparison to the default bufferspace. This is because the top level of a VSAM index always has only a single index CI, and VSAM will maintain this CI in memory whenever possible.

Let use look at an example. Given a KSDS with a 1KB index CI size and a 4KB data CI size, VSAM will reserve 9KB of bufferspace by default. This 9KB holds 1 index buffer and two data buffers. If one reserves only 21KB of bufferspace, VSAM will have thirteen index buffers plus the usual two data buffers. The thirteen index buffers will often eliminate index I/Os for the top two levels of an index. For a typical VSAM file with a three-level index, this will result in reducing in half the number of I/Os for random retrievals.

9.3.3   IMBED

The *IMBED* index option causes one track to be reserved within each data CA for the index. The index CI describing the data CIs within this CA is written on this track as many times as it will fit. The use of this option reduces the time needed to retrieve the sequence set index CI. Since the sequence set CI is replicated around the track, the latency of the read request for this CI is reduced to a fraction of the normal latency. Also, since the sequence set CI is located in the same cylinder as its associated data CA, no additional seek is required to position to the data. However, because IMBED uses one track per data CA, its use should be carefully weighed in terms of its cost in comparison to that of other tuning options.

Imbed also has a truly terrible worst case. If a data CA is a single DASD track, then imbed doubles the size of the area required for data. Each data track is accompanied by its own index track! Figure 9.9 is an example of the IMBED worst case.

In general, IMBED should not be used until after index bufferspace options have been explored, and acceptable performance has still not been attained. If caching DASD controllers are employed, then IMBED should never be specified. IMBED causes inefficient usage of cache storage to occur.

9.3.4   REPLICATE

The *REPLICATE* index option causes all nonimbedded index CIs to be replicated as many times as they will fit on a track. Each nonsequence set index CI takes one track. The REPLICATE option reduces the disk read latency for the nonsequence set CIs to the same fraction as IMBED does for the sequence set CIs. The REPLICATE option was designed early in VSAM's history when DASD devices were much slower than they are today. This option is relatively expensive and normally should not be used.

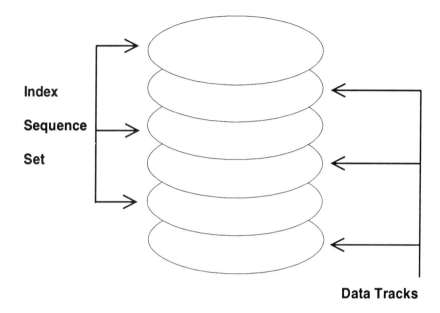

Figure 9.9 Imbed Worst Case Example

Specification of additional index bufferspace is normally much better than this option.

REPLICATE should never be used for cached DASD, as it greatly impacts the efficiency of the cache. Because cache control units are usually managed in units of tracks, all cache benefits are disabled for VSAM indices employing the REPLICATE option.

9.4 Tuning to Minimize Access Time

VSAM files may be tuned to minimize access time, or to minimize update time, or to minimize DASD requirements. These are separate and often conflicting objectives. Thus, adding freespace to minimize time for updates negatively impacts both the access time and the DASD space requirements for a dataset. Both the IMBED and REPLICATE options that improve access time result in additional DASD space being required.

In this section we concentrate on tuning to minimize access time. We look at spreading file components across several DASD volumes, using DASD cache control units, and employing LSR. The following sections treat this issue in more detail for *Sequential* and *Random* types of access.

9.4.1 Separate Index and Data

When IMBED is not specified, the index and data components of a KSDS should be defined on separate DASD volumes when feasible. This is accomplished by coding the VOL parameter for both the DATA and INDEX components of a cluster. The sequence set CI is typically read from disk. If the index is defined on the same DASD as the data, a seek will always be required to position to the data. When the index is defined on a separate DASD, a seek is not always required, and is usually shorter even when one is required. Figure 9.10 illustrates this point.

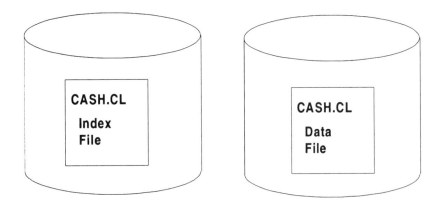

Figure 9.10 Separate VSAM Index and Data

Separating the index and data components allows the I/O load for a VSAM file to be spread across several volumes, perhaps across several paths and control units. This can be of particular importance when a file is accessed under CICS where several simultaneous I/Os may occur. It has the added benefit of spreading the I/O load so that a single volume is not as easily made into a major bottleneck by a poorly designed CICS transaction. In addition, placing several VSAM index components upon a volume permits volume level performance to be boosted by employing caching. Let us now look at VSAM tuning and DASD caching control units.

9.4.2 Cache

Modern DASD cache control units provide an important tuning tool for VSAM. Although the specification of large bufferspace values can be more effective than cache, virtual storage constraints often make large bufferspaces infeasible. Caching should be enabled for VSAM files requiring large numbers of I/O requests, but only after buffering has been reviewed. Additional VSAM buffers offer a greater performance boost than cache control units can offer. The EXCP count value displayed by IDCAMS is an indication of the number of I/Os. The OEM product Explore for VSE also contains extensive tools to identify VSAM files experiencing large amounts of I/O. Additional discussion on the use of cache support is provided in Chapter 17 on Hardware Tuning.

9.4.3 LSR

LSR (*Local Shared Resources*) is a VSAM tuning option that allows VSAM to manage a pool of buffers for multiple VSAM files. LSR requires programming in Assembler language. LSR is a major tuning option wherever a number of VSAM files are used in a single partition. Fortunately, CICS supports this option. LSR was originally implemented for relief of virtual storage constraints. It is one of the most important CICS tuning options. Refer to the chapter on CICS for further discussion of the LSR option. Some OEM VSAM dynamic buffering products enable the use of LSR for batch programs. This can be a useful option, especially for certain large accounting packages.

LSR has a negative effect on CA splits. A CA split involves formatting a new CA, and copying half of the data CIs to the new CA. Without LSR, the whole CA can be formatted with a single I/O request. The data CIs can also be read then copied with single requests. With LSR, both the format and copy operations are performed one CI at a time. This results in very long CA splits (over 5 seconds and 250 I/Os for 4KB CIs on 3380 DASD).

Elimination or reduction in the number of CA splits is a priority for files managed by LSR. LSR is very effective if most of the accesses are reads, or when most update requests replace records without altering their length. If many CA splits are expected, you should consider not using LSR. If you still wish to use LSR, you should either reduce the size of the CA or increase the size of the data CI so that CA splits take less time. The CA size is reduced by specifying either a small primary or secondary allocation. (The CA size is the smaller of a cylinder, the primary allocation, or the secondary allocation.)

Sequential browse requests can also adversely impact LSR performance. Browse does not perform read ahead I/Os when LSR is used. This results in addition I/Os for long browses. The buffers used for a browse are held in use within LSR until the end of the browse request.   This can result in a single browse request monopolizing all LSR bufferspace of a given size. Long browse requests should be avoided for files within an LSR pool. If you have an application that makes use of long browses, it may be necessary to exclude the browsed file from the LSR pool. Note that several OEM accounting applications make heavy use of long browses. You should not assume that you purchased applications are well tuned. (The exact opposite is often true.)

9.5 Tuning Sequential Access

VSAM files may be tuned to optimize sequential or random retrieval performance. Different bufferspace values, index and data CI sizes, and application designs are used for these two types of access. Tuning techniques are often in conflict for the different types of access.   We will discuss bufferspace and CI size for sequential access here, followed by random access in a subsequent section. When a file is used for both sequential and random access, tuning for efficient random access is often the best choice. LSR is also effective for files where the type of access is altered several times for a single application.

9.5.1 Data Bufferspace

For sequential processing, the amount of data bufferspace is the most important tuning parameter. Full track buffering is optimal. Because VSAM uses one-half of the data buffers at a time, two full-track buffers must be provided. The default provided by VSAM allows single buffering of one data CI, and should always be overridden for performance reasons.   If you are constrained by available virtual storage, bufferspace should be allocated based on which VSAM files normally require the most data file I/Os.

A good minimal cost bufferspace value is five data buffers. This usually results in more than twice the throughput of the default VSAM bufferspace, with only a small increase in total application storage. Figure 9.11 illustrates the suggested data bufferspace.

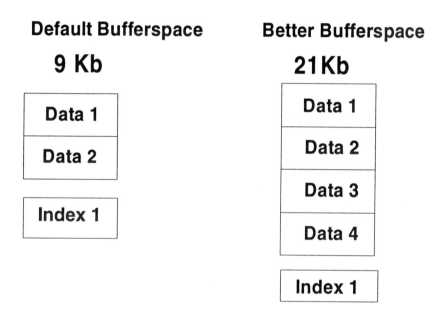

Default Bufferspace

9 Kb

Data 1
Data 2

Index 1

Better Bufferspace

21Kb

Data 1
Data 2
Data 3
Data 4

Index 1

Figure 9.11 Data Bufferspace Tuning

9.5.2 CI Size

For sequential access, the larger the data CI size, the more records are read per input operation, and fewer total I/Os are required to read a dataset. Although bufferspace can be used to cause multiple CIs to be brought into memory for a single I/O request, a large CI size is the preferred specification for a sequentially accessed dataset. A single CI read has a much shorter path length within VSAM than the chained read of several data CIs. A large CI size means that fewer index entries are required for each index CI. This results in smaller index CIs, and less total index entries, which means improved start browse performance.

A large CI size also affects the performance of update requests. On one hand, a large CI offers the most effective use of freespace. On the other hand, a large CI size results in slightly slower CI splits. The CI size should be chosen based upon the record size to reduce unusable space.

A large CI size is usually a liability for random performance. When a file is accessed sequentially and randomly, a very large CI size should be avoided. A large bufferspace for sequential access compensates for a small CI size. A large buffer size is a good compromise when a file is processed both randomly and sequentially.

9.6 Tuning Random Access

In this section we will discuss tuning of VSAM datasets that are accessed in a random fashion. Sequential file tuning was discussed previously. Note that the tuning methods are in conflict between sequential and random tuning. If a dataset is accessed both sequentially and randomly, particular care should be taken in specifying the bufferspace, freespace, and the CI size.

9.6.1 Index Bufferspace

For random processing, the amount of index bufferspace is the most important tuning parameter for record access. The optimum amount of bufferspace would be enough to hold the entire index in memory. Because this is usually not feasible, enough index buffers to hold the top two levels of the index is our second choice. The default bufferspace provided by VSAM allows for only one index buffer, and should always be overridden if possible. Figure 9.12 illustrates the default and suggested values. If you are constrained by available virtual storage, then bufferspace should be allocated based upon which VSAM files normally require the most index I/Os.

Note that the bufferspace for a base cluster opened via a path comes only from the catalog specification. The bufferspace specified in the ACB applies to the AIX only, and not to the base cluster. If this defaults (as it often does), the performance of AIX I/O will suffer. The recommended BUFSP specification for your DEFINE CLUSTER is 64K.

Default Bufferspace

9 Kb

Data 1
Data 2

Index 1

Better Bufferspace

21Kb

Data 1		
Data 2	Index 9	
Index 1	Index 5	Index 10
Index 2	Index 6	Index 11
Index 3	Index 7	Index 12
Index 4	Index 8	Index 13

Figure 9.12 Index Bufferspace Tuning

9.6.2 CISIZE

For efficient random retrieval, the data CISIZE should be large enough for efficient storage of records, but no larger. A very large data CISIZE results in a longer access time, and unneeded additional virtual storage. Reading in data that will not be needed is pointless. Because records can not span CI boundaries, a small CISIZE will waste DASD capacity on each track, and waste space within each CI.

If a dataset is used for both random and sequential retrieval, you should choose a data CISIZE that balances the different performance objectives. A small CISIZE can be compensated for in sequential retrieval by specifying additional data buffers. For sequential access, VSAM will read multiple data CIs when sufficient bufferspace is available.

If the primary access mode for a dataset is sequential, you should specify the largest CISIZE that you can afford. VSAM will always choose an efficient physical block size, and the CISIZE does not usually impact track utilization.

9.7 Tuning to Minimize DASD Space

In this section we review VSAM tuning options that are intended to minimize the total amount of DASD space required for a file. This objective is often in conflict with the objective of reducing the time for updates, and to a lessor extent is in conflict with certain options that improve access time for VSAM files. If DASD space tuning is the first objective, the performance of updates will usually have to suffer.

9.7.1 Blocksize/Track Utilization

VSAM can not choose a physical blocksize that is larger than the CI size specified for a file. Small CI sizes result in smaller physical block sizes and more wasted disk space per allocated track. Although small index CI sizes are common, the index is normally not large enough to be of concern. However, large data files are common, and the data CI size could be chosen carefully with track utilization in mind. In general, 4KB is a good minimum value for a data CISIZE, as a CI size of 4KB or more wastes only a small percentage of each disk track. For datasets that are processed randomly, larger sizes should be avoided as they increase average access time with little benefit. For datasets that are processed sequentially, a larger CI size value should be choosen to further reduce wasted space.

9.7.2 Effects of Imbed/Replicate

IMBED and REPLICATE are old options that should be carefully evaluated before being used for modern VSAM files. IMBED and REPLICATE both cost large amounts of disk space for current DASD. The effect is so large for REPLICATE that this option should not normally be used. IMBED can still be effective for some files, but bufferspace and caching DASD controllers are better tuning options. IMBED can defeat the benefits of DASD cache control units. In other words, use IMBED only if performance issues still exist after tuning bufferspace, and if cache control units are not available.

9.7.3 Freespace

Freespace can be a valuable tuning option. CI freespace should be carefully weighed before use. If a file is heavily updated throughout, then CI freespace may be the best choice. However, CI freespace can easily result in wasted space within a file, increased I/Os for both load and backup, and save relatively little time to boot. CA freespace is less risky to use, and is often as effective as CI freespace in terms of total I/O savings.

9.8 Tuning Update Performance

Record adds and updates that alter record lengths incur the highest cost of any VSAM file activity. CI/CA splits are usually the largest factor in the cost of updates. Thus, tuning a VSAM file for update performance means tuning for reduced CI/CA splits first, and faster CI/CA splits second.

Freespace is the best tool to reduce the number of CI/CA splits for small to moderate update levels. However, when freespace is overallocated, all sequential file processing is impacted. Your freespace value should be chosen based upon the measured level of update activity. You should also periodically verify that your current freespace value is still the correct value.

If updates occur at a high frequency, freespace may be ineffective. In this case, you are interested in improving the performance of the CI/CA splits you will encounter. CA splits always perform poorly when the file is within an LSR pool, so LSR should not be used for files with large numbers of CA splits unless the overall performance is known to be better with LSR than without LSR.

9.9 VSAM Tuning Statistics

Performance statistics are a requirement for tuning VSAM files. For your transaction processing system, the CICS shutdown statistics are a valuable source of information, particularly for tracking LSR performance. CICS will also produce file statistics on demand via the CSTT transaction.

The IDCAMS LISTCAT command is a native VSAM source of file level statistics. LISTCAT output includes the number of records inserted, deleted, and read, plus I/O counts for the index and data components of the file. A comparison of I/O counts to read requests is a good indication of the efficiency of your VSAM buffers.

A number of VSAM dynamic buffering products exist that will produce fairly detailed VSAM statistics. In addition to these specialized products, most VSE performance monitors include detailed VSAM statistics. An application program can also use VSAM services to access VSAM performance counters internally.

10

SQL/DS Tuning

SQL/DS is the VSE relational database provided by IBM. The advent of VSE/ESA with its increase in both real and virtual storage capacity has made large SQL/DS applications feasible. Tuning of the SQL/DS database has become a key factor in total system performance, and in the response time of many online systems.

This chapter contains an overview of SQL/DS, a discussion of SQL startup parameters, and separate tuning sections for various features. The overview section defines a number of SQL specific terms, and identifies areas of concerns with respect to performance. The Startup Parameters section covers all general tuning parameters. An internal tuning section covers SQL/DS tuning issues, and a separate external tuning section briefly discusses application and CICS related tuning issues.

This chapter only touches the surface of SQL/DS tuning. For additional information on the structure and use of the SQL language, you are referred to the book *DB2/SQL A Professional Programmers Guide* by Tim Martyn and Tim Hartley. The IBM manual *SQL/DS Performance Analysis and Tuning Cookbook* (GG24-3429) is a good source of tuning information. The book *SQL/DS Performance, Techniques for Improvement* by Dov Gilor is an excellent source for advanced tuning information.

10.1   Cookbook for SQL Tuning

• Use PRTYIO to favor the scheduling of SQL/DS I/O.

• Set PRTY to run SQL/DS at a high priority. It should run at or just below CICS and VTAM, and above all batch partitions.

• Bufferspace is critical to SQL/DS performance. Carefully review your startup options. Explicitly specify both NDIRBUF and NPAGBUF.

• If storage constrained, remember that one page buffer equals eight directory buffers. Reduce paging by reducing page buffers, and slightly increasing directory buffers.

10.2   Overview of SQL/DS

The term *SQL* is often used to refer to both the SQL/DS database and the SQL language. We will use the term SQL/DS when we refer to the database. The SQL/DS database is accessed via a single VSE partition executing the ARISQLDS program. ARISQLDS is the main SQL/DS program.

Whenever the term SQL is used, we are referring to the *Structured Query Language*. The SQL language is used to generate views of the contents of the database, retrieve records, and perform updates. SQL statements may be preprocessed and later executed by an application program or they may be dynamically generated at runtime.

A program that accesses data managed by SQL/DS is an application. The term *Logical Unit of Work* (LUW) is important to tuning these applications and is roughly equivalent to a transaction. An LUW is started when the first SQL command is issued and ends explicitly when either a COMMIT WORK or a ROLLBACK WORK command is issued, or implicitly, when a program terminates.

An SQL/DS database is called a *table* and is comprised of *rows* and *columns*. A *table* is analogous to a file, a *row* to a record, and a *column* to a field within a record. An application deals with a portion of a table called a *view*. The SQL **CREATE VIEW** statement is used to define a view pseudo record and its field names. A view contains a subset of the table and may omit part or all of the various table rows and columns. Columns are omitted from a view to enhance security, to improve data integrity, and to improve performance. Rows are omitted from a view to simplify the design of an application. The SQL statement **SELECT** is used to determine which rows and columns are used.

Overall SQL/DS capacity and performance is affected by which resources, and how many resources, are provided to ARISQLDS. The design of the SQL/DS tables determines the types of accesses that can be performed efficiently. The format of your SELECT statements determines the relative efficiency of the applications using them. SQL/DS databases often require massive amounts of I/O. SQL/DS tuning involves resource allocation, application design, and I/O subsystem tuning.

10.3 Virtual Storage Requirements

SQL/DS is a large system. The suggested minimum partition size is 4.2MB plus 204KB times your NCUSERS specification. SQL/DS is best run in the private area. Attempting to run SQL/DS in the shared area will usually reduce the available private area size to the point where a medium size CICS will no longer fit. This is easily seen when we consider than a SQL/DS partition will require from four to six megabytes and that CICS plus the SQL/DS batch utilities an additional six to ten megabytes of memory.

SQL/DS supports an interactive SQL function under CICS called ISQL. ISQL requires CICS DSA storage. Although the actual storage requirements depend upon the type of function performed, a reasonable estimate is 330KB of CICS DSA plus about 45KB per user.

The IBM manual *SQL/Data System: System Administration for VSE* (order number GH09-8096) contains detailed formulas for calculating storage requirements for various SQL/DS configurations.

10.4 DASD Requirements

SQL/DS uses two kinds of DASD. These are DBEXTENT DASD and directory DASD. The DBEXTENT and log DASD uses 4KB blocks and is the larger allocation. The hardware chapter contains a table that indicates the amount of data in 4KB blocks that can be stored on the various DASD supported by VSE. Directory space uses 512 blocks. Directory space DASD is of interest to use because of its poor utilization of DASD. Where we can fit 3784 megabytes of 4KB DBEXTENT blocks on a 3390B, we can only fit 872.8 megabytes of directory blocks on the same drive.

The DBSPACE named SYS0001 is used for the SQL/DS catalog. The maximum size of this area is defined when the database is generated. SYS0001 must be defined large enough for the maximum size of the catalog. If the SYS0001 DBSPACE fills up, you must completely regenerate your database in order to add space to it — this can take a long, long, long time. Because space defined for the SYS0001 area is not required until it is used, you should always overallocate this area.

10.5   Startup Parameters and Tuning Options

The SQL/DS startup options fall into several groups. These are:

- Options related to the number of users

- Buffering options

- Other options

We will look at each of these areas in turn. You should tune your system using all three groups of options, in the order shown. Only change one startup parameter at a time, unless otherwise directed.

10.5.1   Tuning the Number of Users

The number of simultaneous requests that SQL/DS can service is determined by the number of *agents* provided. Each LUW requires an agent. The **NCUSERS** startup parameter specifies the number of agents. If insufficient agents are provided, then requests will be queued and erratic/slow response times will be observed. However, the number of agents is limited by the amount of storage available and by the capacity of the I/O subsystem. Each agent requires about 270KB of SQL/DS storage! In addition, each agent that is added generally requires additional directory and page buffers to maintain the same level of performance, and each agent requires its own lock requests. This can also result in more erratic and slower response times.

If the **SHOW ACTIVE** command indicates that all of your agents are consistently allocated, then you should consider increasing the number of agents by increasing the NCUSERS value. When resources are available, increasing the number of agents will improve SQL/DS performance. Each time NCUSERS is increased, you must also review and perhaps increase the NPAGBUF and NDIRBUF values. After increasing NCUSERS, you should carefully monitor the paging rate, SQL/DS I/O rate, lock waits, and CPU usage. Your VSE performance monitor is a good source for CPU usage and page-rate values. The SQL **SHOW LOCK** command may be used to display lock statistics. The SQL/DS counters can be checked to see if DASDIO activity is excessive.

CICS users can access a SQL/DS database. In order to do this, a link is established from the CICS partition to the SQL/DS partition. This is accomplished by the CIRB transaction. The CIRB transaction specifies a password and the maximum number of links. The number of links equals the number of agents that must be available within SQL/DS for CIRB to execute. CICS permanently acquires agents. Thus, CICS transactions do not wait within the SQL/DS partition for an agent to become available. However, CICS transactions can be queued within CICS waiting for a link to become free. If too many links are requested with the CIRB transaction, excessive virtual storage will be wasted within the SQL/DS partition, and batch SQL performance may suffer as batch users queue up waiting for the remaining agents. If too few links are requested, CICS performance will be impacted. Any SQL users needing a link are placed into a CICS wait, and response time suffers. Because of the design of CICS, when multiple users are waiting for links, CICS CPU usage will also be increased.

Good CICS performance requires that adequate links be reserved to service all transactions that require them. If enough agents can not be allocated within SQL/DS, then the CICS CMXT value should be used to restrict the number of concurrent transactions requiring SQL services. The CICSPARS report shows how many waits for links (if any) are occurring within CICS. If significant CICS internals waits are observed, then a tuning action to increase the number of links, or to better manage them, is required.

10.5.2 Buffering Options

SQL/DS uses three different types of files. Each file occupies its own extent and has its own type of buffer. These are:

- Directory — A single extent formatted as 512 byte blocks

- LOG(s) — One or two extents formatted as 4KB pages

- DBEXTENTs — Several extents formatted as 4KB pages

Buffers are provided to hold Directory, LOG, and DBEXTENT data. Two buffer pools are used. The directory buffer pool consists of 512-byte buffers and is determined by the **NDIRBUF** startup parameter. The page buffer pool consists of 4KB (4096 byte) buffers and is determined via the **NPAGBUF** startup parameter. The page buffer pool is used for both LOG and DBEXTENT I/Os. If the above parameters are not specified, a default is chosen using the **NCUSERS** startup parameter value according to the following formula:

$$NPAGEBUF = NDIRBUF = (4*NCUSERS) + 10$$

Equation 3 SQL/DS Buffer Default Calculation

The rules for buffer specification are simple. The more buffers allocated, the less I/O required, and the less CPU used for each request. More buffers result in faster response times for each user, and faster LUWs with shorter locks. This means that more total users can be supported. If things were this simple, we could stop right here. Unfortunately, a number of additional factors are involved.

Buffer space is restricted by two major issues: real storage and virtual storage. If enough real storage is not available to support the additional virtual buffers, overall performance will suffer as paging increases. Virtual storage is a major limiting factor for SQL/DS performance simply because there is not enough of it. The 16MB addressing limit of VSE/ESA 1.2 sets a limit on the size of the SQL/DS partition, and upon the number of buffers it is possible to allocate. VSE/ESA 1.3 partially alleviates the virtual storage constraint, and it is expected that subsequent SQL/DS releases will exploit additional VSE/ESA 1.3 capabilities such as data spaces which will simplify or eliminate the buffer space management task.

The design of your data and tables also influences the benefits additional buffer space can provide. If a table has long rows, few rows will fit within a single DBSPACE page, and the ratio of requests to I/Os will be small. The number of agents performing requests for the same row, or rows in the same area also affects the efficiency of buffer use. Thus, large tables with random access see little benefit from large amounts of buffer space.

The NDIRBUF and NPAGBUF parameters are related, and usually both should be altered at the same time. Changing the number of directory buffers does not affect the number of page I/Os required to handle a given request. An increase in page buffers is required to reduce the number of page I/O requests. Increasing the number of available page buffers usually decreases the number of directory I/Os required. On the other hand, when virtual storage is limited, you can get more immediate results with directory buffers because one 4KB page buffer occupies the space needed for eight directory buffers.

10.5.3   Other Options

Several additional startup options effect SQL/DS request performance. In this section we will discuss the CHKINTVL, NLRBU/NLRBS, and startup mode options.

The **CHKINTVL** parameter determines the checkpoint interval. SQL/DS checkpoints are required for the warmstart recovery mechanism. Each checkpoint writes all modified directory and page buffers back to disk, releases all shadow pages (working copies of database pages), and flushes the current log buffer. This creates a spike of I/O activity, and delays processing of all agents until the checkpoint is completed. If checkpoints occur often, then performance suffers. If checkpoints are taken infrequently, then the time to restart SQL/DS can become very large. The CHKINTVL parameter specifies the number of log pages that must be filled between checkpoints. The default value for CHKINTVL is 10. In general, checkpoints should not be taken more often than every 15 minutes, unless your system has very high activity and a high failure rate. You must determine the correct CHKINTVL value in your environment. The COUNTER command can be used to determine the number of checkpoints that have been taken, and you can translate this into checkpoint frequency. If you encounter very few failures of SQL/DS then you may wish to increase the CHKINTVL value. If most of your system activity is inquiry, then long intervals between checkpoints are usually acceptable.

The **NLBRU** and **NLRBS** parameters determine the number and usage of lock request blocks. SQL/DS uses *Lock Request Blocks* (LRBs) to serialize access to DBSPACEs, tables, rows, indices, and other objects. NLRBS specifies the total number of LRBs. NLRBU specifies the maximum number of LRBs that an individual user can own. Each lock requires two LRBs, and each LRB occupies 24 bytes of storage. Although many LRBs are required by the SQL/DS system, the total virtual storage required for them is usually small. The default for NLRBS is calculated as follows:

$$\text{NLRBS} = \text{NCUSERS} * 2 + \frac{\text{NCUSERS} * \text{NLRBU}}{2} + 10$$

Equation 4 NLRBS Default Calculation

The basic tuning strategy for LRBs is to prevent a shortage. If too few LRBs are provided then fewer concurrent accesses can be supported, and deadlocks may result. When LRBs are exhausted, the requesting agent must wait for a free LRB, and currently held locks can create deadlocks. Deadlocks can result in agent cancellation. Using the default ensures that the number of LRBs is automatically updated when NCUSERS is altered. If lock problems are seen, then it will be necessary to manually control the number of LRBs. NLRBS and NLRBU should be both specified at SQL/DS startup if either is to be specified.

When lock problems are seen, you should also investigate your applications. More frequent COMMIT WORK requests reduce the number and duration of outstanding locks. Repeatable Read (RR) applications require more locks than those using a Cursor Stability (CS) isolation level. If an application can lock at a high level (such as LOCK TABLE or LOCK DBSPACE) then much expensive lock activity can be eliminated. This option can cause other applications to wait, but will usually greatly improve the efficiency of the application that uses it. Each application should use the most selective predicates possible and allow SQL/DS to use a single index if possible.

The **SYSMODE** or Startup Mode parameter is the last SQL/DS startup option we will look at. You specify either SYSMODE=M for multiple-user mode or SYSMODE=S for single-user mode. The usual mode is multiple-user which allows sharing of the database between online and batch users. Single-user mode is employed for batch execution only and causes the user program to be loaded into the same partition as SQL/DS. Large batch maintenance jobs are candidates for single-user mode. In single-user mode, the CPU overhead of cross partition communication is eliminated, and resource contention is eliminated. It is also possible to specify LOGMODE=N in single-user mode to eliminate logging. This can greatly reduce the I/O load for large updates, but requires that a database archive be performed before switching back to multiple-user mode.

10.6   SQL/DS Performance Bottlenecks

In this section we will look at the general causes of SQL performance problems. These items are categorized as either *internal* to SQL or *external* to SQL. We use the term *internal* to reference the SQL/DS partition and its configuration. The term *external* is used in connection to applications and CICS transactions that employ SQL services. We will look at tuning the external items first, followed by the internal items.

10.6.1   External Sources

SQL processing can be delayed by other work being performed by the operating system, or by work being done by system components that SQL is dependent upon. Thus, if a higher priority task has the CPU, then SQL will wait for CPU availability. Or, if SQL I/O requests are queued up behind other active requests, SQL can experience unusual elongation in its average time to complete an I/O. Such dispatching and queuing delays are easily identified by a batch performance monitor.

SQL CPU priority is a key factor for your production system. Many large SQL systems are CPU limited, and SQL waiting for the CPU translates directly into response time delays. Your batch performance monitor should report this as *waiting for CPU*, or as a *ready wait*. If more than 5 percent of your SQL waits are waiting for CPU, you should increase the priority of the SQL partition. If this is observed when CICS has a higher priority than SQL, you may wish to consider exchanging the priorities or even balancing the SQL/DS and CICS partition priorities.

Paging can cripple SQL processing because SQL is single threaded. When a page request is being serviced for SQL, then it is doing nothing else. If you observe more than one or two page requests per second for the SQL/DS partition, you should address paging before other issues. Your batch performance monitor will report paging by partition. If it is necessary to reduce paging by changes to the SQL/DS partition, you should reduce the number of agents before reducing the amount of buffer space (unless you know that buffer space is overallocated).

The key factor in tuning CICS SQL/DS usage is providing the right number of links between CICS and the SQL/DS partition. The CIRB transaction defines the number of XPCC links, and reserves the number of agents for the life of these links (which is usually the life of the CICS partition). The CMXT value can be used to ensure that a single CICS transaction does not monopolize all available SQL/DS services. If adequate resources are not available within SQL/DS to support the agents reserved for CICS, then the CIRB value should be reduced for better service. If CICS never uses all of the agents reserved for its use, then the CIRB value should be reduced to return the 270KB per agent of virtual storage for other uses (such as additional buffer space). If batch work is run while CICS is up, NCUSERS should reflect the total agents required for batch plus the CIRB value.

10.6.2   Internal Delay Sources

SQL performance is often impacted by the configuration of the SQL partition. SQL is run in a single VSE/ESA partition by executing the program ARISQLDS. You should carefully choose your startup options as previously described. You should monitor SQL/DS performance using the COUNTERS command, and your SQL/DS performance monitor. The buffer specifications are critical to reducing the number of I/Os performed by SQL processing. If inadequate buffers can be provided due to storage constraints, you should review a reduction in the number of agents, and the number of links from CICS may need to be reduced.

Application design is a key factor in SQL/DS performance. The power of the SQL language permits speedy development of some really poorly performing applications. The ease of update to SQL allows fast response to application design induced problems. Measuring application performance, and correcting design issues, is a part of the application development process that is required to ensure adequate SQL performance.

10.7   Gathering SQL/DS Statistics

In this section we will look at the various types of SQL/DS statistics which are used for tuning, how they are gathered, and how they are used. We will look at the COUNTER command, and several forms of the SHOW command. These commands may be entered upon the VSE console or via the EXPLORE for SQL product. The EXPLORE for SQL performance monitor contains online displays with the output of these commands.

10.7.1   COUNTER Command

The COUNTERS command may be used to query the SQL/DS internal statistics. We will look at sample output from the COUNTER command in Figure 10.1 and examine each of the values displayed. Commands are entered into SQL/DS through the console or through a CICS transaction. To enter a command to partition FB, first enter MSG FB on the console, then reply COUNTER * to the prompt. Figure 10.1 below contains a console log with sample output for a COUNTER * command issued to a copy of SQL/DS running in partition "FB." Let us list each of the values displayed, along with its explanation.

- RDSCALL is the total calls to the Relational Data System. This is the total number of requests from SQL/DS users.

- DBSSCALL is the calls to the Data Base Storage System. RDS makes calls to DBSS for buffers and data.

- BEGINLUW is the number of LUWs created in this interval.

- CHKPOINT is the number of checkpoints taken in the interval.

```
FB 011 Calls to RDS               RDSCALL :  4761
FB 011 Calls to DBSS              DBSSCALL:  53971
FB 011 LUWs Started               BEGINLUW:  4792
FB 011 LUWs rolled back           ROLLBACK:  103
FB 011 System checkpoints taken   CHKPOINT:  94
FB 011 Maximum Locks exceeded     LOCKLMT :  0
FB 011 Lock escalations           ESCALATE:  8
FB 011 Waits for lock             WAITLOCK:  0
FB 011 Deadlocks detected         DEADLCK :  0
FB 011 Looks in page buffer       LPAGBUFF:  98264
FB 011 DBSPACE page reads         PAGEREAD:  3397
FB 011 DBSPACE page writes        PAGWRITE:  603
FB 011 Looks in directory buffer  LDIRBUFF:  48729
FB 011 Directory block reads      DIRREAD :  4271
FB 011 Directory block writes     DIRWRITE:  935
FB 011 Log page reads             LOGREAD :  14
FB 011 Log page writes            LOGWRITE:  287
FB 011 Total DASD reads           DASDREAD:  22941
FB 011 Total DASD writes          DASDWRIT:  9257
FB 011 Total DASD I/O             DASDIO  :  32198
FB 011 ARI00651 SQL/DS operator command ...
```

Figure 10.1 COUNTER Command Example Output

- LOCKLMT is the number of times the NLRBU limit was reached. This counter should be zero. If you ever see it as other than zero, you must increase NLRBS/NLRBU.

- ESCALATE is the number of successful lock escalations. High values indicate that NLRBS/NLRBU may need adjusted. Your application design may also be flawed.

- DEADLCK is the number of deadlocks that occurred. This value should be small. If more than a few percent of BEGINLUW requests result in deadlocks, then serious performance degradation is occurring. Increase the number of LRBs to avoid deadlocks. You may also need to review application design.

- LPAGBUFF / PAGEREAD / PAGWRITE reflect page buffer usage. LPAGBUFF is the number of looks with the page buffer and should be far larger than PAGEREAD. The hit-ratio of your SQL/DS system is given as follows:

$$HitRatio = \frac{PAGEREAD}{LPAGBUFF}$$

Equation 5 Hit Ratio Calculation

The closer the hit-ratio is to one, the more effective your buffer space is being utilized. It is often convenient to think of the hit-ratio as a percentage. Thus, a value of .73 is 73 percent. A hit-ratio of less then 60 percent indicates that you should review and probably increase your buffer space. The only time that low hit-ratios cannot be increased is when most I/O is truly random. This occurs infrequently in most multiuser real world environments.

- LDIRBUFF / DIRREAD / DIRWRITE reflect directory buffer usage. Evaluate their importance and tune using them as described above. Because eight directory buffers fit in the space of one-page buffer, the storage constrained user should stress tuning directory buffers.

- LOGREAD / LOGWRITE counters indicate the number of LOG read and write requests to one log extent. Any I/O to the second log extent is not reported. Because log activity is a consequence of logical activity against the SQL/DS database, only applications changes can reduce these counts.

- DASDREAD / DASDWRIT / DASDIO reflect the totals of the previous counters as follows.

```
DASDREAD = PAGEREAD + DIRREAD + LOGREAD
DASDWRIT = PAGWRITE + DIRWRITE + LOGWRITE
DASDIO   = DASDREAD + DASDWRIT
```

Equation 6 SQL/DS I/O Totals

These totals are less important for tuning than the individual values. They can be used for a quick determination of relative system efficiency. In general, large DASD I/O values are always worth a tuning effort. The first step in any tuning effort is to review the available buffer space. DASD cache control units have been very effective as a "quick and dirty" tuning tool for SQL/DS databases.

10.7.2   SHOW Command

The SHOW command is used to display the status of the SQL/DS partition resources. In this section we will look at the following forms of the command:

- SHOW DBEXTENT for short on storage conditions

- SHOW ACTIVE for a summary of the agents

- SHOW LOCK ACTIVE to identify agents in lock wait

- SHOW SYSTEM for a quick overview of the system status

The SHOW DBEXTENT command displays the usage of each of the storage pools. The *SHORT ON STORAGE* item is the one of interest to us from a tuning standpoint. If an asterisk is present in this column, then the corresponding pool has less than the SOSLEVEL percent free pages (SOSLEVEL is a SQL/DS startup option). Each time that this occurs, the SQL/DS system schedules a checkpoint. A checkpoint flushes all pages to disk, and frees all shadow pages. This is an expensive process. You need to either allocate additional space to the pool, or delete unused DBSPACEs and tables. (See Figure 10.2.)

POOL NO.	TOTAL PAGES	NO. OF INUSE PAGES	NO. OF FREE PAGES	% USED	NO. OF EXTENTS	SHORT ON STORAGE
1	27189	3967	23222	12	1	
2	17298	9478	7820	58	1	
3	17298	16107	1191	94	1	*

Figure 10.2 SHOW DBEXTENT Sample Output

The SHOW ACTIVE command is used to display the status of the SQL/DS agents. The output is a snapshot of the current agent status. If a hung agent is expected, then several SHOW ACTIVE commands are usually entered in sequence. If the status of the suspect agent remains unchanged, then it is probably in a long term wait. A user status of NIW indicates that the corresponding agent has no work. The user status field is also used to determine whether or not CICS links are in use.

The SHOW LOCK ACTIVE command displays the status of all agents currently in a wait state. A status of LOCK indicates that this agent is waiting for a lock held by another agent. The WANTLOCK TYPE column shows the type of lock requested. If an agent stays in the same lock state for an extended period, you should suspect that another agent is holding the lock for longer than may be desired. In Figure 10.3 below the checkpoint agent (CHECKPT) is waiting for work (it is inactive). User GLOCK is waiting on a page lock.

AGENT	USER	WAIT STATE	TOTAL LOCKS	LONG LOCKS	WANTLOCK TYPE	WANTLOCK DBSPACE
C	CHECKPT	NIW	0	0		
1	GTEST	LOCK	17	17	IPAG	12
2	GCOMM	COMM	19	19		

Figure 10.3 SHOW LOCK ACTIVE Example

11

CICS

The VSE transaction processing system is named the *Customer Information Control System* (CICS). This chapter presents an overview of CICS tuning. For an advanced treatment of this subject, you are referred to S. Piggott's book *CICS: A Practical Guide to System Fine Tuning*. The IBM manual *CICS/VSE Performance Guide* (SC33-0703) is also a good source of additional information. Let us start by briefly looking at some common CICS performance problem fixes. We will then discuss CICS measurement, and performance problems and fixes in more detail.

11.1 Cookbook for CICS Tuning

- Use PRTYIO to favor scheduling CICS I/O.

- Set PRTY to run CICS at a high priority. It should run at or right below VTAM, and above all batch partitions.

- Reduce CICS paging via TPBAL, reducing a large DSA size, and moving heavy batch work to periods when CICS is down or less active.

- Increase the DSA size to reduce program fetch overhead and to save CPU time through reduced storage compressions.

- Redefine Maps as Programs to reduce Map fetch overhead.

- Use CMXT to reduce the number of high-impact transactions that can execute at the same time.

- Use LSR to reduce CICS GETVIS requirements, permit an increase in DSA size, reduce total VSAM I/Os, thus improving your VSAM performance.

11.2 CICS Performance Bottlenecks

In this section we will briefly look at the general causes of CICS performance problems. These items are either *internal* to CICS or *external* to CICS. The term *external item* refers to something outside of the CICS partition, or a program not controlled by CICS. The term *internal item* refers to something that is under the control of CICS (such as a transaction or internal task). Figure 11.1 below illustrates common wait sources both internal and external to CICS. We will look at the items external to CICS first, followed by the internal items.

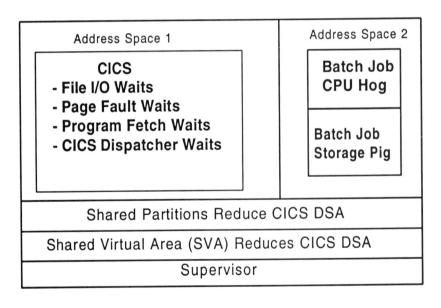

Figure 11.1 CICS Wait Sources

11.2.1 External Sources

CICS processing can be delayed by other work being performed by the operating system, or by work done for CICS by other operating system components. If a higher priority task has the CPU, then CICS will wait for CPU availability. Or, if CICS I/O requests are queued up behind other active requests, CICS can experience unusual elongation in its average time to complete an I/O. Such dispatching and queuing delays are easily identified by a batch performance monitor.

CICS CPU priority is a key factor for your production system. Many large CICS systems are CPU limited. CICS waiting for the CPU translates directly into response time delays. Your batch performance monitor should report this as *waiting for CPU*, or as a *ready wait*. Of course, CICS itself is often capable of fully utilizing your CPU, and you must account for the reduction in batch thruput that occurs when CICS is given priority.

I/O contention can also directly impact CICS response time. Just as you set a high CPU priority for CICS, you should also give CICS a high I/O priority. You should avoid allocating CICS datasets on the same DASD volumes that are used for batch files, and you should alter your buffer allocations to reduce the amount of batch and CICS I/O.

Paging can cripple CICS processing. This is a result of the single threading of the CICS system. While a CICS page request is being serviced, CICS does nothing else. If you observe more than one or two page requests per second for CICS, you should address paging before other issues. Your batch performance monitor will report paging by partition.

VTAM network delays are another cause of CICS response time issues. Your CICS performance monitor will usually report the amount of time spent in the terminal control program, and VTAM is the largest single factor in this total. Your VTAM performance monitor will report total time spent in VTAM. This is an easy way to decide how much of your problem is due to VTAM.

11.2.2 Internal Delay Sources

CICS processing and design often impact CICS performance. CPU delays occur within CICS when a transaction is ready to run, but another transaction owns the CPU. Because CICS uses a non-preemptive dispatcher, a low priority transaction can impact other transactions. A large burst of CPU activity by any transaction can block other transactions for the duration. Your CICS performance monitor will report on CPU queuing delays within CICS itself.

CICS storage management results in additional internal delays. Each storage compression results in visible delays at the time of the compress. Additional program load caused delays occur long after the completion of the storage compress. CICS shutdown statistics report on the number of storage compressions. Your CICS performance monitor will usually indicate the frequency, and causes of storage compresses.

Customers use the MXT, AMXT, and CMXT values to tune their CICS systems. These parameters introduce artificial bottlenecks into the CICS dispatcher. When improperly used they can seriously impact CICS. If you are using these values, you should periodically verify that they are doing what they are supposed to, rather than simply introducing a performance ceiling. Your CICS performance monitor will identify how often the dispatcher is constrained by these values.

11.3   Gathering CICS Statistics

In general, user perception determines whether your CICS system has "good" or "bad" response time. Unfortunately, the users who tell you that response time "stinks," do not tell you what the source of the problem might be. To perform CICS tuning, you must gather statistics. And, you must gather these statistics on an ongoing basis. Many excellent OEM CICS performance monitors exist. In this chapter we will be using only the native IBM tools.

CICS offers a number of sources of performance information. Statistics are produced by CICS at shutdown, on demand via the CSTT transaction, and can be produced automatically at user designated intervals by running the CSTT transaction during the day. You can save statistics in sequential files on disk for later processing, print them when they are produced, or have them output to the console for current reference.

Shutdown statistics are automatically produced at every normal shutdown of CICS. They report on all CICS system activity from the preceding initialization to its completion. They are used for spotting trouble spots, and to gather data for trend analysis. This report is printed as part of every normal CICS termination, and should be reviewed regularly.

You may also request that statistics be produced at any time that CICS is up via the CSTT transaction. The form CSTT AOR displays all statistics, while the CSTT SOR form of the command displays selected statistics. One or more of the types of statistics listed in Figure 11.2 may be selected for inclusion in the SOR output.

```
DUMP Dump Statistics.
DYTB Dynamic transaction backout.
FILE File statistics.
IRCM Inter-region control.
JOUR Journal control.
LINK Inter-system and multi-region links.
PROG Transaction and program.
STOR Storage statistics.
TASK Task statistics.
TEMP Temporary storage.
TERM Terminal statistics.
TRAN Transient data.
```

Figure 11.2 CSTT Statistics Selection

The command CSTT SOR CSSL TERM, DONE displays only terminal statistics. Statistics produced while CICS is operational may be found to be incomplete or inconsistent, due to activity that was "in flight" when the CSTT request was processed. The AOC and SOC forms display all or selected statistics and reset the counters. This form of the command should normally be avoided.

The CSTT transaction can also be used to produce statistics automatically, at user defined intervals, via the CSTT AUT form of the command. This allows you to analyze several snapshots of the load on CICS during peak periods, or when problems are known to be occurring.

When the CSTT transaction is used to produce statistics, the output is directed to the CSSL destination by default. The CICS supplied program DFHSTUP may be used to analyze output to this destination. DFHSTUP will produce either a summary report or interval plus summary reports. The CSTT transaction is fully described in the IBM manual *CICS/VSE   CICS-Supplied Transactions*. The manual *CICS/VSE System Definition and Operations Guide* contains detailed information on running the DFHSTUP program.

You may request that the output of CSTT be directed to the console by specifying a destination of CNSL. The default IBM systems define destination IEP1 to be the system console. If you do not have CNSL defined on your system, you should try IEP1. The command CSTT SOR CNSL STOR, DONE will send storage usage statistics to the console, assuming that you have defined a destination of "CNSL" for the system console. Note that console output should be avoided except when needed. The large volume of statistics output can overload the VSE console, and make it difficult to spot messages from other partitions.

11.3.1   CSTT Statistics Types

In this section we will look at some of the types of statistics produced by CICS in more detail. The most important displays are probably those for FILE, PROG, and TEMP. You should try these on your system to become accustomed to the format of the output. You may request all three of these types of data via the CSTT SOR IEP1 FILE, PROG, TEMP command.

FILE displays file usage statistics. The amount of output can be large because detailed information on every file defined to CICS is displayed. Detail for the number of Get, GetForUpdate, Browse, Add, and Update requests is given. LSR buffer pool statistics are also included. This is a very useful display. Issue the CSTT SOR IEP1 FILE, DONE command for an example similar to that in Figure 11.3.

PROG displays detailed program statistics. Use the CSTT SOR IEP1 PROG, DONE command for an example. A large amount of detail is produced, because every program and transaction defined to CICS is reported on. Each transaction is listed along with the program, and the number of times the transaction was entered. The number of references to every program is reported upon, as is

```
CICS ELAPSED TIME IS  0000 HOURS 50 MIN 39 SEC.  RELATIVE DAY IS   0

    REQUESTED STATISTICS  03/14/92

********************************************* FILE STATISTICS ***************
FILE    GET     GET UPD  BROWSE  ADD    UPDATE  DELETE   VSAM EXCP REQUESTS
NAME    REQSTS  REQSTS   REQSTS REQSTS  REQSTS  REQSTS     DATA     INDEX  TOTAL

DFHCSD  45      0        865     0       0       0        105        46     0

MC0001  0       0        0       0       0       0        0          0      0


*TOTALS* 45     0        865     0       0       0        105        46     0
```

Figure 11.3 CSTT FILE Output Example

the total number of fetches by program. This information describes the amount of program fetch wait you are experiencing in CICS.

STOR information is storage usage statistics. CICS reports the total number of allocation requests, release requests, and storage violations. This is only indicative of the level of internal CICS overhead for storage management, and of program problems. Use the CSTT SOR IEP1 STOR, DONE command for an example. Most CICS performance monitors measure detailed storage usage by transaction.

TASK includes summary statistics on the number of tasks executed, the number of times CICS was at the maximum number of tasks, and the peak number of tasks being serviced at the same time by CICS. Use the CSTT SOR IEP1 TASK, DONE command to display this data.

TERM outputs terminal statistics. This includes detailed statistics by terminal plus VTAM summary information. The maximum number of VTAM RPLs posted, the number of times this maximum was encountered, and the count of VTAM short on storage conditions are displayed. A separate summary of counts for auto-installed terminals is also produced.

TEMP reports on temporary storage usage. A large amount of useful information is reported including the number of PUT/PUTQ/GET/GETQ requests, and detailed temporary storage file level statistics. Use the CSTT SOR IEP1 TEMP,DONE command to see an example of this output.

TRAN produces transient data statistics. You should use the CSTT SOR IEP1 TRAN,DONE command for example output. Detailed statistics by transaction and by intrapartition dataset are output.

11.3.2 CICS Monitoring

CICS includes an extensive monitoring facility. This is a general statistics gathering facility that supports a variety of performance related information. You control what kind of information is to be gathered, the monitoring classes, and the output datasets via the Monitoring Control Table (MCT). Monitoring gathers information that is written to an external dataset. It is not necessary to wait for CICS to shutdown to retrieve monitor data. The CSTT transaction will stop the monitor and close the dataset. Another alternative is to use the CEMT SET JOURNAL SWITCH command to switch journal datasets.

The monitor journal dataset is processed using a batch program. The IBM CICSPARS/VSE product is an example of a program that can be used to display monitor data. IBM also supplies a sample program called DFH$MOLS that will format and print monitor output. Various OEM performance products also gather CICS monitor performance data and allow online and batch review of this information.

CICS performance monitor data includes global and transaction level information. Global information is snapshot data about the performance of CICS as a whole that is written periodically based upon a time value defined within the MCT. Transaction level information relates to events occurring within each transaction and is written when each transaction completes.

The CICS exception monitor data is also important for performance measurement. A number of "resource exhausted" conditions are included as exceptions. Information is logged for temporary storage full, dynamic storage full, and VSAM file strings exhausted conditions. The VSAM wait is especially interesting. It occurs when a task is waiting on a string at the dataset level or the LSR pool level, or when a task is waiting on an LSR pool buffer to become free. If any VSAM exceptions are seen in your system, this is a sign of performance problems that should be addressed.

11.4   Priority and Dispatching

CICS performance is impacted by priority values and by dispatching. Priorities are usually manifested in external waits. CICS dispatching affects internal waits. External waits reflect resource contention between the CICS partition and other partitions. Internal waits are caused by CICS processing. We will look at VSE priority values first, followed by CICS dispatching.

11.4.1   Delays Due to Priority

The priority of the CICS partition is important because all delays that affect CICS are seen by each terminal. CICS should generally have a lower priority than VTAM, but should be run at a higher priority than all normal batch partitions. CICS is a private multitasking system. This means that CICS controls and dispatches its own tasks, and that any delay external to CICS, will impact all CICS tasks. Examples of such synchronous delays are waits for CPU, paging, VTAM, VSAM, and many databases. It is important that you give CICS priority access to resources, whenever possible.

Even when CICS is run as a POWER controlled partition, it can be run at a priority higher than POWER. This is accomplished by specifying NPC (No Priority Checking) on the PSTART autostart command for the CICS partition. Note that running CICS above POWER may impact POWER processing if CICS consumes large amounts of CPU.

Use the PRTY command to establish the relative dispatching priority of the CICS partition. This reduces waits for the CPU. The PRTYIO specification can be used to favor CICS I/O requests. This parameter is best coded within the BG ASI procedure. PRTYIO reduces waits for devices. The TPBAL command can be used to improve the treatment of the CICS partition from a paging standpoint. This reduces waits for paging.

Your VSE batch performance monitor will identify the percent of time that CICS is ready to run but not dispatched because the CPU is in use by another task. Any CICS wait for CPU translates directly into increased response time. If more than a few percent of your total CICS wait is caused by CPU waits, you should increase the priority of your CICS system.

You also determine the relative priority of transactions within your CICS system. CICS transaction priority can be used to ensure that any low resource using transactions are allowed to complete before starting a transaction known to monopolize CICS resources or the CPU. You should not use transaction priorities until you are satisfied with your CICS dispatching controls, as priorities can mask dispatching problems.

11.4.2 Delays Due to Dispatching

CICS implements private multitasking. All transaction processing is done by a single VSE task, and this task is shared among the transactions by the CICS dispatcher. Because CICS performance can experience wide swings in response time with small changes in the number of tasks, the CICS dispatcher is able to be artificially constrained in several ways. The MXT, AMXT, and CMXT values are specified in the SIT to control the dispatcher. These values may also be altered while CICS is running. The effects of all three values are reported in CICS shutdown statistics, and are also provided on a realtime basis by most CICS performance monitors. Figure 11.4 below summarizes the effects of these three parameters.

Parameter	Function/Effects	Where Set
MXT	all tasks	SIT, runtime
AMXT	active tasks	SIT, runtime
CMXT	each class has its own parameter	SIT, runtime

Figure 11.4 MXT, AMXT, CMXT Parameters

The MXT value limits the total number of concurrent tasks within the CICS system. Waits caused by the MXT value are reported at CICS shutdown, and can also be displayed during CICS operation. This value is most effective when CICS tasks are *pseudo-conversational*. A pseudo-conversation transaction is one that ends during each terminal I/O. The MXT value is used to restrict the amount of virtual and real storage required by CICS. It should be specified just below the point where paging starts to become appreciable. Sadly, this value is usually best determined by trial and error. When the MXT value is reached, CICS stops processing input messages. For VTAM, such messages are allowed to accumulate in access method buffers. Thus, MXT can impact the number of buffers required.

When MXT is set too large, then CICS stress conditions result. You should consider reducing your MXT value when you have storage compression, paging, or buffer shortage delays you cannot otherwise tune. Use MXT to stop system thrashing, not to conceal problems you can tune in other ways.

When MXT is set too small, then CICS will be delayed without consuming available resources. If you encounter significant CICS dispatching delays, but your overall system has available capacity, you should raise the MXT value to utilize this capacity. MXT can be used to reserve excess CPU capacity for future needs. Note that the use of MXT can cause wider swings in response time than would otherwise be seen. This occurs when large numbers of tasks are pending, and create a backlog of work that CICS must work off.

The AMXT value limits the number of tasks serviced by the CICS dispatcher. It affects the count of tasks that CICS considers to be eligible for dispatching at one time. The default for AMXT is the MXT value. It has no effect when not specified. Set AMXT smaller than MXT to use it to limit storage requirements. AMXT is useful when a number of long running transactions are present and MXT alone does not restrict CICS in the way desired. AMXT is useful in a *conversational* CICS environment. A conversational transaction is one that continues to exist through its terminal I/Os. The AMXT value controls a conversational CICS environment without restricting the number of terminals that can be in use. Terminal and journal tasks do not count towards the AMXT limit.

AMXT works to limit storage needs by reducing the number of tasks allocating and referencing storage. This directly reduces page faults. AMXT can also be used to restrict the size of the DSA, which can reduce paging, but also prevents unneeded storage compressions.

If AMXT is set too small, then AMXT induced lockouts could occur. AMXT causes CICS to stall when one transaction starts another transaction and then waits for that transaction to complete. If transactions are waiting on AMXT held transactions, then CICS processing will be delayed or totally stalled. If AMXT is set to a value larger than three or four, this problem usually does not occur. AMXT stalls are also prevented by setting AMXT close to, or larger than, the CMXT value for such transactions. CICS attempts to recover for AMXT stall conditions by temporarily increasing the AMXT value. The ICV interval time effects such stall recovery.

If AMXT is set too large, then it has no effect. In this case MXT will be the only limiting factor. If no AMXT waits are seen when CICS response is suffering from paging or storage waits, you should suspect the value is too small.

The CMXT value is used to limit the number of concurrent CICS transactions within the class defined by the TCLASS operand. Once the number of transactions within the specified class has been reached, CICS will not start additional transactions of that class. CMXT is used to force single threading within a limited number of transactions to ensure resource availability for other CICS work.

Use CMXT to limit CPU bound transactions. Use it also to limit transactions that monopolize the LSR pool through large numbers of browse requests. CMXT should not normally be used to limit conversational transactions, because very long delays can result. CMXT should be used to restrict the number of transactions using SQL services so that the number of SQL/DS links to CICS is not exceeded.

The CEMT INQUIRE command will show the number of transactions HELD due to the CMXT value. CICS shutdown statistics total CMXT waits by class. Most CICS performance monitors (including CICSPARS/VSE) offer online displays of CMXT waits. Any unexpected CMXT waits should be carefully analyzed.

11.5 CICS Storage Usage

CICS uses the partition GETVIS area, DSA (or program area), and System GETVIS area storage. CICS processing is limited by the size of these storage areas. DSA storage limits the number of transactions that can be executing at one time. GETVIS storage limits the number of files open at one time. Let us look at each area for storage use, performance issues, and storage management techniques. Figure 11.5 lists typical storage requirements for a small, medium, and large CICS system. These are guidelines only, and should not be used to reduce your current allocations without verifying your actual storage usage. The partition GETVIS values are for typical CICS applications and do not provide for unusual use like that encountered in various OEM products.

Storage Type	Small CICS	Medium CICS	Large CICS
Nucleus and Tables	730KB	1385KB	1575KB
DSA at Start	1285KB	2100KB	3100KB
Program Storage	700KB	950KB	1300KB
GETVIS	300KB	600KB	900KB

Figure 11.5 CICS Partition Sizes

11.5.1   GETVIS Area Size

CICS partition GETVIS space is used for VSAM buffers, system workspace, and by many OEM products. Running out of GETVIS will normally result in the failure of the CICS system. A slow but steady GETVIS "creep" has been the cause of the failure of many a CICS system. Sadly, VSE contains no tools to identify what components of CICS are using partition GETVIS space. Several performance monitors including Explore for VSE offer tools to track GETVIS usage.

The COBOL Programmer's Reference contains a list of COBOL features and verbs to avoid under CICS. These include STRING and UNSTRING. Use of COBOL features that use GETVIS will normally result in a gradual allocation of all available GETVIS. COBOL allocates but never frees GETVIS storage. If you experience a slow creep in GETVIS usage, the incorrect use of COBOL is a probable cause. Note that certain OEM accounting packages have had problems in this area, and should contact your vender if you suspect this in your environment.

One subtle way to lose partition GETVIS with COBOL programs is to compile CICS transactions with the STATE or FLOW options.

If SYSLST in the CICS partition is assigned to a PRT1 or 3800 type printer, then each time the COBOL transaction is entered, COBOL initialization opens the printer and VSE OPEN processing allocates a DTF extension within the partition GETVIS area. This DTF extension is never freed, and is not reused. Gradually much partition GETVIS is lost to printer DTF extensions. One quick fix to this problem is to define a dummy 1403 printer and use this as the POWER spooled SYSLST printer in your CICS partition. (1403 printers do not get DTF extensions allocated at OPEN time.)

Fragmentation of the partition GETVIS area is a long standing problem for CICS systems. Fragmentation occurs when the size of the total free area is adequate to satisfy a storage request, but the request fails because no single chunk of free storage is large enough. In VSE another kind of fragmentation occurs when free storage is available, but is reserved for another subpool than the one requested for the storage.

The VSE GETVIS console command can be used to monitor the amount of available GETVIS space, and the size of the largest free area. This command will also report the high water mark for GETVIS space. An over allocation of CICS GETVIS does not cause problems, and is desirable to prevent problems when the environment changes. This command and its output are discussed in Chapter 18, Tuning Specifications Summary.

11.5.2   DSA Size

The CICS DSA occupies the CICS partition program area storage not used by CICS itself for tables and CICS system programs. CICS manages DSA storage. DSA storage is used to hold application programs, maps, and to satisfy CICS dynamic storage needs. CICS uses the DSA until it is all consumed or allocation is within a user defined limit, at which point CICS performs a *storage compression* and releases all available blocks of storage. Because a storage compression is expensive, it is something to be avoided.

A too small DSA results in excessive storage compressions. A too large DSA causes increased paging. A CICS performance monitor is required to accurately tune the DSA size. However, the CICS storage compression count is a good indicator. If you are seeing more than one storage compress per half hour, you should increase your DSA size. In general, you should provide 3KB to the DSA for each 1KB of GETVIS as illustrated by Figure 11.6.

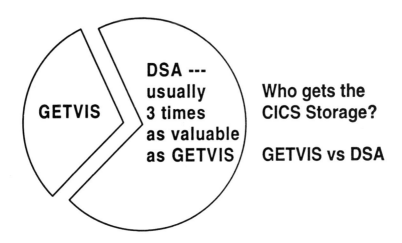

Figure 11.6 CICS DSA and GETVIS Allocation

The point at which a storage compression is performed may be controlled by specifying the Storage Cushion Size (SCS) operand of the SIT table. This defines a Short On Storage (SOS) limit. Whenever this limit is reached CICS will issue a DFH0506 CICS IS UNDER STRESS message and perform a storage compression. The number of times this occurs is also reported in the CICS shutdown statistics as "number of times storage cushion released." If a storage compression does not free enough storage, then the message is produced again, and CICS will stop attaching new tasks until the condition is corrected. This obviously affects CICS but can also seriously impact VTAM performance by causing messages to be queued within the VTAM partition. Thus the SOS condition is an indication of serious performance problems. You should specify an SCS value large enough to ensure that CICS can finish what is currently running when the condition arises, but small enough as a percentage of your available DSA that the condition does not occur often. If SOS conditions occur frequently, you need to look at increasing your DSA size.

If an SOS condition occurs, and CICS is unable to get out of this condition within the stall purge interval (your ICVS specification within the SIT), then CICS enters a *stall condition* state. This is only intended to occur as a result of a deadlock between a transaction that is waiting for storage and a transaction that is holding storage but also waiting on resources held by the first transaction. This is a serious condition that CICS takes serious steps to resolve.   CICS purges transaction marked as SPURGE=YES to release their storage and any resource locks they might hold to attempt to resolve the stall condition.   This is identified by an AKCP transaction abend code. If this does not allow CICS to continue, then CICS will hang, and must be manually canceled and restarted.

Short On Storage conditions that end with a stall and/or a CICS hang are a sign that your Storage Cushion size is too small. If the stall condition occurs at all, you must increase your Storage Cushion Size, and you should consider increasing your DSA size or reducing the number of resident programs.

11.5.3   Page Size

CICS manages storage in units of CICS pages. These are not the same as the VSE/ESA 4KB virtual storage page. Instead the CICS page is simply the increment by which CICS maps storage in a Page Allocation Map table. You may define a page size of 1KB, 2KB, or 4KB for the CICS page. The 1KB size is not documented, and is a little known but **very important** option. CICS rounds each program that is loaded to the nearest CICS page boundary. For this reason, if many small phases are being fetched by CICS, a significant amount of your DSA may be wasted due to fragmentation. You should consider reducing your CICS page size specification to reduce this fragmentation.

Resident programs are not aligned to a CICS page boundary. Instead, resident programs are packed together with no waste at startup time. CICS maps are often small, and have the largest amount of wasted space. You should review your phase load counts, and move the most frequently used, and smallest, programs to the resident area.

In one recent customer site, storage compressions were reduced from several hundred in a day to essentially none by merely changing the CICS page size. This eliminated the wild response times spikes which are the signature of storage compressions. So much storage was saved in this case that a number of additional programs and maps were also able to be defined as resident, with a further reduction in response time.

Of course, the CICS page size is not always the magic bullet. The smaller the page size, the more pages required for a given DSA size. The more pages CICS has to manage, the more CPU time is consumed in CICS storage management. Thus, CICS uses more CPU to handle small pages. If your system is CPU constrained, reducing the CICS page size is often not a good option.

11.5.4 SVA Usage

CICS makes only small demands on the System GETVIS area and the SVA. A small amount of System GETVIS area storage is used to anchor communications between partitions for Multiple Region Option (MRO). Additional system GETVIS space is used to create directory entries for CICS loaded PPT phases when CICS is run in a static partition. This system GETVIS space is not required for dynamic partition CICS usage.

Many CICS phases can optionally be loaded into the SVA. If you run MRO, your must load DFHCSEOT, DFHIRP, and DFHSCTE into the SVA. If you do not run MRO, you may remove these phases from your SVA for a small storage savings. In Appendix A of the IBM manual *CICS/VSE: System Definition and Operations GUIDE* is a detailed list of those CICS phases which may be loaded into the SVA. Figure 11.7 lists some phases more commonly loaded into the SVA.

11.6 Paging

Paging occurring within the CICS partition has a serious impact on terminal response time. This is a result of CICS single threading all page handling requests. A paging rate of less than 1 per second is optimum for CICS. From 1-to-5 pages per second is sometimes acceptable. From 5-to-10 pages per second is very noticeable, but may be tolerable. Anything over 10 pages per second will normally cripple CICS performance.

If your CICS response time suffers and you determine that your system is paging, look at paging first. The TPBAL parameter can be used to reduce the impact of paging on CICS. If paging impacts your CICS, you need to reduce the demand for real memory. This can be done external to CICS and internal to CICS.

Module	Size	Description
DFHCSEOT	0.5KB	IRC EOJ Cleanup Handler
DFHECID	66KB	Command Interpreter
DFHIRP	12KB	IRP Request Module
DFHSCTE	8	Subsystem Control Table
DFHSCP	6KB	Storage Control Program
DFHTMP	9.7KB	Table Management Program
DFHTSP	19KB	Temporary Storage Program
DFHXFP	20KB	Function Shipping Transformer
DFHXFX	6KB	MRO Function Shipping Fastpath

Figure 11.7 SVA Eligible CICS Phases

External real storage use is reduced by lowering the number of partitions active at the same time as CICS. Many shops defer large batch production work to the times that CICS is not operating to reduce paging (and other problems). You may want to reduce the number of available batch partitions. Accomplish this by altering your dynamic partition specifications, or by eliminating certain classes from the PSTART for static partitions. These techniques reduce real storage demand by funneling batch work through fewer partitions. This has been very effective for COBOL compiles.

Internal real storage use is reduced by altering the working set of CICS itself. A reduction in the size of the CICS DSA will usually reduce the amount of paging. However, care should be taken to not cause a large jump in CICS storage compressions by making the DSA too small. Switching to LSR in CICS will normally reduce the working set of CICS. In general, an initial LSR allocation of 25 percent (or less) of your prior total bufferspace is a good starting point. Large amounts of bufferspace for sequential files can increase the amount of real storage TFIXed by CICS, with a corresponding increase in paging. Switching from NSR to LSR will automatically correct this problem, especially where the total amount of VSAM bufferspace is reduced.

11.7   Program/Map Fetch Tuning

CICS fetches a number of phases from program libraries during execution. The order and length of CICS search chains can greatly impact the efficiency of CICS fetches. The size of the DSA also effects the frequency of program loads.

Two categories of phases are "programs" and "maps." A program is a phase intended to be executed. A "map" is a phase that contains a description of a terminal screen image. The principal difference from a performance standpoint is that maps are always fetched when needed, and programs are not.

Programs can be made resident in DSA by a specification on their PPT entry. A resident program is fetched only one time, at CICS startup. Even if a program is not declared resident, it can be reused once it has been loaded into the DSA, as long as CICS does not have to reclaim its storage. Although maps cannot be specified as resident, you can "lie" to CICS and declare MAPs to actually be resident programs. This is a useful option to reduce program fetches when DSA space is available.

11.7.1   DFHLOADR Subtask

CICS performs all application fetches from a separate task. This subtask is named DFHLOADR. Program fetches involve directory searches that can take a lot of time, require single threaded VSE system tasks, and can cause spikes in paging activity. A subtask is used so that long fetches do not delays or stop CICS dead in its tracks. If several transactions require program or map fetches at the same time, then the requests for the DFHLOADR subtask become queued up, and long transaction delays can be observed. Figure 11.8 illustrates how DFHLOADR is used to process program fetch requests.

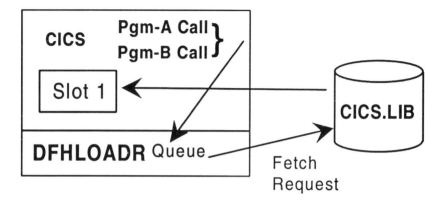

Figure 11.8 DFHLOADR Functions

11.7.2 LIBDEF SEARCH

All fetches performed by CICS can involve directory searches. The directory search proceeds through the directory names in your LIBDEF PHASE SEARCH chain until the desired phase is found. The fastest search occurs when the phase is found in the first library searched. Therefore, you should ensure that the most frequently loaded programs are in the first library. Many users do not have library search chains tuned for fetch performance, so this is an area worth checking into. Directory searches can be very slow. In fact, the number of I/Os required for a directory search often exceeds the number of I/Os required to read in a phase. Fortunately, CICS does not always require a full directory search.

The CICS PPT contains space for a directory entry. This directory entry is not large enough to contain the information required by the VSE fetch routine. Instead the PPT directory entry is used to save a pointer to a real directory entry built in the System GETVIS area. The System GETVIS directory entry is built by the fetch routine the first time directory information is accessed when sufficient System GETVIS free space is available.

You should ensure that your System GETVIS has at least 25 percent freespace at CICS startup. If sufficient freespace is not available, then CICS will need to perform a full directory search every time a program or map is loaded. If adequate System GETVIS is available, and the directory entry is built, then a full directory search is needed only the first time a program or map is fetched.

11.7.3   When is a MAP a PROGRAM?

All phases loaded by CICS are defined within the PPT. Phases may defined to be PROGRAMs or MAPs. Entries defined as MAPs can not be defined as resident. Entries defined to be PROGRAMs can be defined as resident. Resident entries do not need to be loaded each time they are used. For this reason, maps are often defined in the PPT as resident programs. This is effective as long as maps are not altered, or are reset for each usage.

You should monitor the number of times that each CICS phase is loaded, and consider making all high use phases resident. The author has seen CICS systems with more than 30 percent of the response time due to CICS program (and map) fetches. In one recent case, a transaction that required over three seconds to display a record was improved to a response time of less than a second by simply making the high use programs and maps resident.

11.7.4   Storage Compressions

A *Storage Compression* is a CICS internal function that scans DSA storage and frees areas that are not required. Storage compressions are expensive in terms of CPU time, their impact on working set, and because they are single threaded within CICS. Excessive storage compressions are usually associated with a too small DSA, or with too much demand upon DSA.

An inadequate DSA is corrected by increasing the size of the program area at CICS startup. This is accomplished by increasing the SIZE parameter on the CICS EXEC statement. Because increasing the program area reduces the available partition GETVIS, you may wish to alter the size of the partition. Alter the size of your CICS static partition by updating the ALLOC statement. If CICS is running in a dynamic partition, then the DTR$DYNC member is updated to increase the partition size. Increasing the size of the CICS DSA increases the CICS working set, and can increase paging if inadequate real memory is available.

If you are experiencing any paging in your CICS partition, you will not wish to increase the size of the DSA.

An alternative to increasing the DSA size is to reduce the amount of simultaneous demand upon the DSA. This is done by:

- Reducing the number or size of PPT entries declared resident. This increases the available DSA by the number of nonresident bytes. Note that resident programs are not aligned to a CICS page, while programs that are loaded are aligned. This means that a resident program usually requires less storage than one that is loaded.

- Reducing the max tasks, or class max tasks values. This saves DSA by reducing the effective level of CICS multitasking.

11.8   VSAM

VSAM is one of the most frequently used file types seen in CICS systems. It is a frequent source of CICS waits, but also one of the more easily corrected bottleneck sources. VSAM file structure and tuning is extensively discussed in a separate chapter, and we will concentrate only on CICS specific tuning options in this section.

CICS produces detailed VSAM statistics at shutdown time. The IBM supplied CSTT transaction may also be used while CICS is up to display this information. The IDCAMS LISTCAT command may also be used to display the catalog statistics for VSAM files. This information is only valid if the file is closed normally.

11.8.1   File Specifications for CICS

CICS file characteristics are defined within the *File Control Table* (FCT). The FCT is coded as a series of macros, assembled, and catalogued before CICS is started. The FCT phase is loaded by CICS initialization and the files defined within it are made available for application use. The FCT specification allows you to control a number of tuning parameters. These encompass when the file is opened, bufferspace, the number of concurrent requests, and LSR usage.

CICS files are opened either at CICS initialization time, or upon first access. Originally, CICS always opened all files at CICS startup. In a large CICS system with hundreds of files, this open processing could take ten minutes or more. The principal reason that *deferred open support* was added to CICS was to speedup CICS initialization.

Deferred opening of CICS files introduces some problems. Because file opens consume partition GETVIS, opens that are spread out during CICS processing can increase fragmentation of GETVIS. Also, "not enough memory" conditions may arise at any time during CICS processing. They can be difficult to predict, and can be almost impossible to test in a standalone environment.

11.8.2   Bufferspace

VSAM bufferspace is one of the most powerful tuning options available for VSAM under CICS. However, with only a few exceptions, VSAM under CICS is best managed via Local Shared Resources (LSR).

One of the exceptions, heavy sequential access, is where VSAM bufferspace is best used. VSAM LSR bufferspace is held from a start browse until browse mode is ended. Thus, a CICS transaction reading a large number of records in browse mode presents a challenge to LSR. Sequential mode access can result in most of the available LSR space being monopolized by a single file. If VSAM files that are accessed in this fashion are made part of the LSR pool, then wide swings in CICS performance can result. Such files are best left out of LSR, with a modest amount of dedicated VSAM bufferspace.

11.8.3   String Number — STRNO

The String Number (STRNO) parameter determines the number of concurrent VSAM requests. Although this is a VSAM option, its effect is typically only seen in connection with CICS so we discuss it here. The STRNO parameter also determines the maximum number of transactions that may be active at one time. If you run multiple transaction copies and have enabled this via CICS parameters then you need to ensure that the STRNO value will support the desired transaction activity. Add one to the STRNO value for each simultaneous read for update you expect to have in effect.

If you do not have sufficient strings available for a VSAM dataset, then CICS will experience waits as simultaneous accesses to the file occur. These string waits should be monitored, and are an important and inexpensive area to tune when CICS performance needs to be improved. Refer to the discussion of the CSTT command output in the LSR section for a discussion of how to perform string wait analysis.

11.8.4   LSR

LSR is an acronym for *Local Shared Resources*. As the name implies, LSR allows several VSAM files to share the same buffer resources. To use LSR with CICS, you define a pool of buffers and list the files that are to share the pool. CICS offers tools to determine whether you have enough VSAM buffers, and to assist in estimating how many to add.

All CICS users should be running with LSR for at least some VSAM files. If you are not currently using LSR for CICS, you should begin its use as one of your first tuning steps. If you are using LSR, you should look at its performance and tune it for high-use files. LSR is discussed in more detail in the VSAM chapter. Figure 11.9 illustrates how CICS files share buffers in an LSR pool.

LSR improves the efficiency of CICS VSAM processing. Switching to use LSR in CICS normally reduces the working set of CICS. In general, an initial LSR allocation of 25 percent (or less) of your old bufferspace is a good starting point. Use the LSR statistics displayed at CICS shutdown to tune your specifications.

Note that LSR was originally created as a virtual storage constraint relief option. This means that its use normally saves storage. The savings in CICS bufferspace can be added to available CICS DSA. This is done by increasing the CICS execute size parameter. LSR buffers are allocated from GETVIS. CICS DSA is allocated from the available problem program area.

CICS produces statistics on the effectiveness of LSR at shutdown time. You may also issue the CSTT SOR IEP1 FILE,DONE command at any time to get the current statistics displayed upon the system console. Figure 11.10 is an example of the LSR portion of the file statistics output. Note that the overall *waiting for string*

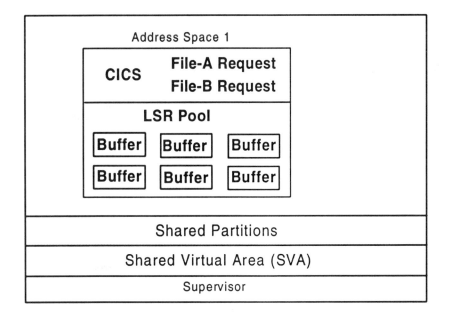

Figure 11.9 LSR Pool Use by CICS

counts are both zero. It is important to avoid string waits to the extent this is possible for good performance. The number of requests with waits is also reported at the file level. This can help in identifying methods of alleviating performance problems. In particular, you should look at the *highest number of requests waiting for a buffer at any one time* item. This is reported for each file and can be used to determine the number of extra buffers of each size that would be required to eliminate all buffer waits.

The output of the CSTT command is useful, but does not identify the causes of problems, and is difficult to use for realtime problem analysis. Various OEM performance monitors produce more detailed information on LSR than that offered by CICS. You may wish to check the information produced by your monitor.

11.9   Network Delays

VTAM network delays can be an important source of CICS waits. Let us illustrate the importance of VTAM with an example. We

```
********* VSAM SHARED RESOURCE STATISTICS *********

LSR POOL CREATED 13:19:24

  MAXIMUM KEY LENGTH                              24
  TOTAL NUMBER OF STRINGS                         18
  HIGHEST NUMBER OF REQUESTS WAITING FOR STRING    0
  TOTAL NUMBER OF REQUESTS WAITING FOR STRING      0
  MAX NUMBER OF CONCUR. ACT. FILE CONT. STRINGS    7

                      NUMBER
        BUFFER          OF
         SIZE         BUFFERS

          512           9
        1,024           9
        2,048           9
        4,096           9

                  DATA     INDEX    HIGHEST NUMBER OF
        FILE      BUFFER   BUFFER   REQUESTS WAITING FOR
        NAME      SIZE     SIZE     A BUFFER AT ANY ONE TIME

        DFHCSD    2048     1024              0
        IESTRFL   4096      512              0
        IESROUT   4096      512              0
```

Figure 11.10 VSAM LSR Statistics Example

will assume we have measured an average response time for a transaction of 2.5 seconds. A medium speed communications link used in this case might be 9600 baud. It takes over a second to simply transmit the data in a 1200-byte message at that speed. VTAM software delays, and control unit delays could easily add another second to the transmission time. In this example, we would see a total network delay equal to 80 percent of our response time. This is a typical contribution of network delays to the total response time where no other major bottlenecks exist. Obviously, any improvements in VTAM response will be of major benefit. And, since we described a "good" case in our example, any VTAM performance problems would worsen an already marginal situation. See the next chapter on tuning VTAM for specific actions you should take with respect to your network.

An excellent tool for gathering information on the exact location of network delays is the VTAM trace facility. This trace tracks messages processed by VTAM through various points. The individual trace entries include timestamps that allow you to identify the amount of delay in each segment of the network from CICS to a message destination.

VTAM buffer constraints are a common source of network delays. Use the D NET,BFRUSE command or the SMS trace facility to gather statistics on VTAM buffer waits. These problems are usually addressed by providing additional buffers or using pacing controls.

The IBMTEST command offers an easy way for anyone to check on their VTAM network performance. This command is issued to the VTAM network solicitor (not to CICS itself) at a terminal experiencing performance delays. Simply type IBMTEST, and ten messages will be issued directly from VTAM. If the reported delays are seen for these messages, then VTAM is the probable source of the problems. If no delays are seen, then CICS is the probable source of your problems.

11.10 Distributed Processing with CICS

Modern CICS networks are often *distributed systems*. A distributed system may involve multiple CICSs and/or multiple hardware systems. This may occur with several CICSs running on one system, or with CICS logical terminals implemented on Local Area Networks (LANs). It can also occur with several applications communicating between CICSs, or with the processing of a single large application distributed across several systems.

The availability of CICS/OS2 means that applications may now be distributed between your VSE/ESA host and a PC running CICS/OS2. In this mode *function shipping* and *transaction routing* may be used to either offload a portion of an application or the whole application to a workstation. We will also look at *Distributed Program Link* and *Distributed Transaction Processing* between VSE/ESA and workstations.

11.10.1 Intersystem Communications

CICS/VSE may communicate with CICSs running on other physical systems. The InterSystem Communications facility (called ISC) allows a transaction to be routed from the system upon which it is requested to another system upon which the transaction is implemented. This separate system may be another CICS/VSE or a different type of CICS system. The following may all communicate with CICS/VSE via ISC:

- CICS/MVS or CICS/ESA running on an MVS system

- CICS/VM running on a VM system

- CICS/VSE running on another VSE/ESA system

- CICS/OS2 running on a PC

Transaction routing is employed to get improved performance, or to run a transaction from a terminal attached to a CICS system that does not implement the transaction. Transaction routing can offer performance improvements when the network delay required to ship a transaction request is less than the time saved by running the request remotely. Two examples of the second type of transaction routing are, accessing of a DB2 transaction from a CICS/VSE system, or the running of a VSE SQL/DS database transaction from CICS/OS2. Figure 11.11 illustrates the routing of a transaction request from a VSE/ESA system to an MVS DB2 system.

Another alternative to routing a whole transaction to access a resource on a remote facility is to route only the request for the required function to the remote system. This is called *Function Shipping*. We will look at this next.

11.10.2 CICS/OS2 Function Shipping

Function shipping allows a request to access a CICS controlled resource to be automatically routed to another CICS system where it is processed. Thus, a CICS transaction running on CICS-A can access files owned by CICS-B. (See Figure 11.12.) Just as you

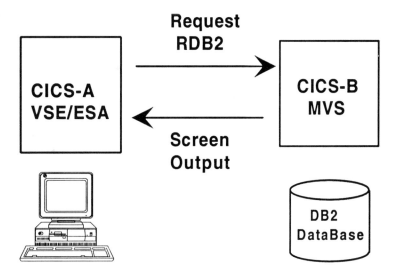

Figure 11.11 Transaction Routing from VSE to MVS

might employ function shipping to distribute portions of an application across several VSE/ESA systems, you can use ISC to split the work between your VSE/ESA system and one or more PCs running CICS/OS2.

The performance of a CICS application employing function shipping is dependant upon a number of factors. Let us briefly list the components of the distributed request response time, then look at each.

- Transmission time to send request

- Time waiting in queue on target CICS

- Request processing time

- Transmission time to return result

Certainly the transmission time is unique to distributed processing. It is also a straight "add-on" cost for the transaction since time spent doing data transmission is not overlapped with

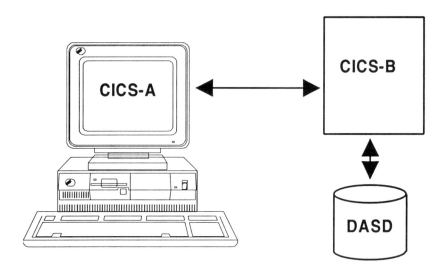

Figure 11.12 CICS/OS2 and CICS/VSE Communications

any other processing of the requesting application. The time in queue on the target CICS is usually small, but can become significant if the target CICS is busy. In this case, the request cannot be processed until the current application can be interrupted, and any higher priority CICS tasks are first serviced. The time to process the request may be less or more than it would be in a nondistributed environment. If the target system is much faster than the requesting system, it is possible for the request processing time to compensate for the transmission time. In fact, an actual performance improvement may be (rarely) seen.

11.10.3 CICS/OS2 Distributed Program Link

CICS/OS2 allows an application to issue an EXEC CICS LINK command to pass a request for processing by a separate CICS/OS2 or CICS/VSE system. This support is called *Distributed Program Link* (DPL). DPL ships the CICS COMAREA from the requesting OS2 system to the remote processing CICS. DPL in effect allows a CICS/OS2 program to employ LU6.2 distributed processing without need for LU6.2 programming.

DPL is a powerful means of providing workstation access to VSE/ESA SQL/DS databases, or to large VSAM files. It is also a way to utilize older macro level CICS programs that are unable to be ported to CICS/OS2. However, like transaction routing, and function shipping, DPL can introduce performance problems.

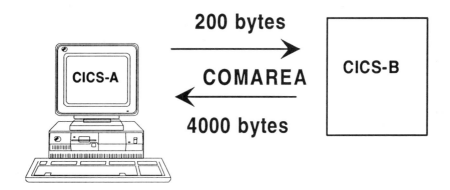

Figure 11.13 CICS/OS2 DPL Example

The CICS COMAREA is often the source of DPL performance problems. The CICS COMAREA can range in size up to 32KB. Data transmission of a large COMAREA can account for the bulk of the response time of a distributed application. CICS trims trailing hex zeroes (low values) from the COMAREA. For this reason, you should left justify any data sent within the COMAREA. If you send a 200-byte request, but expect to receive a 4000-byte response, the time to send the request is minimized if the 200 bytes are left justified within the 4000-byte COMAREA. Figure 11.13 illustrates the data transfers used by DPL.

11.10.4 Distributed Transaction Processing

Distributed Transaction Processing (DTP) allows a transaction on one system to initiate then communicate with a transaction on another system. DTP may be used by CICS/VSE to initiate a transaction on CICS/OS2, then to exchange information with the workstation transaction. DTP is an alternative to DPL when data owned by a remote CICS system is to be accessed from another system. Application programs employing DTP may use CICS commands to control an APPC conversation.

11.10.5 MRO

MRO is an acronym for Multiple Region Option. MRO allows the resources of a transaction to be split between several VSE partitions. For example, MRO allows the terminals used to access a transaction to be managed by one CICS partition while the program code is run in a second CICS partition. The Terminal Owning Region is called the TOR. The Application Owning Region is called the AOR.

   Figure 11.14 illustrates three CICS partitions communicating via MRO. Two of the partitions are in the same address space and the third CICS is in a separate address space. CICS-A and CICS-C share an address space, while CICS-B occupies another address space.

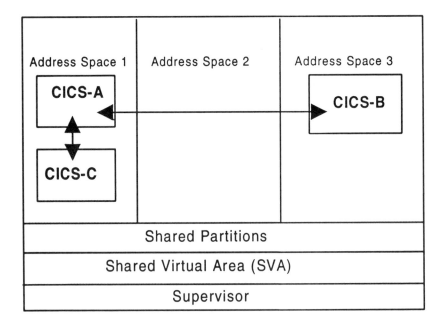

Figure 11.14 3 CICS Partitions Using MRO

   MRO is usually not a performance feature! MRO is much improved with VSE/ESA but is still to be avoided if at all possible. Benchmarks have shown MRO to increase CPU usage by 30 percent or more for function shipped transactions. However, MRO can still offer performance benefits.

When would you wish to run with MRO for *performance reasons*? MRO offers several possible solutions for a storage constrained CICS environment. Because work can be spread over multiple CICS partitions by MRO, each with its own resources, an online system can use over 16MB of memory when MRO is employed. If your CICS system is encountering excessive storage compressions, and all other tuning options have been exploited, then MRO can let you preserve a single CICS image while effectively doubling the available DSA. Note that if your system is CPU limited, MRO will not have the desired effect, and will probably impact response time.

MRO can also be used to simulate the effect of multiple LSR pools. This is accomplished by shipping file requests to a separate CICS partition that has its' own LSR pool. The total CICS transaction throughput can usually be improved by using MRO in this fashion. In fact, when large LSR pools are employed, less total CPU can be required for some cases. (This is unusual.)

If you choose to not run MRO, then you should review your SDL and remove any entries for DFHCSEOT, DFHIRP, and DFHSCTE. Removal of these phases can reduce the size of the shared area. MRO performance information is included in three areas in CSTT output. These are terminal, file, and link statistics.

Let us look at terminal statistics first. The Line ID section contains the characters "IRC" for all SEND/RECEIVE sessions, and "VTAM" for all IRC sessions. The Terminal ID section contains SEND or RECEIVE names as you defined them in your TCT TYPE=SYSTEM table entry (or via the CEDA SESSIONS SENDPFX/RECEIVEPFX keywords). For IRC, the "Transmission Errors" count is actually the number of times that the session was disconnected. Terminals defined as remote in a CICS do not have any statistics recorded.

File statistics information is unique only under the "Remote Data Sets" heading where the number of VSAM deletes is reported. The remaining statistics are reported as for any other file. The file statistics for intercommunication links are not separately recorded or reported.

The IRC/ISC link statistics reflect all local CICS activity with respect to function shipping. Transaction routing statistics show all remote plus local activity. The DFHCRP program is invoked every time a transaction request is routed to another partition. The mirror transaction is accounted for in the partition that it was routed to.

11.11 Journaling

The CICS journal file is an often overlooked source of CICS performance issues. Although this file is handled by a subtask of CICS, much internal CICS processing is single threaded, and significant CPU costs are associated with journaling. You should monitor the number and impact of the CICS journal I/O requests. Unfortunately, application changes are typically needed to reduce the impact of journaling upon CICS. However, you can and should take steps to tune the journal file like any other critical dataset in your system.

The DFHJRNLG subtask manages the journal file. A performance monitor that gathers statistics at the subtask level may be used to identify journaling performance issues. An analysis of waits of this subtask is a good place to start. Any non-ECB wait is of special interest. An ECB wait is used for communication between the CICS maintask and the subtask. Journaling statistics are also displayed at CICS shutdown time.

Two parameters that can have a large impact on journaling performance are the journal buffer size (BUFSIZE) and the journal buffer shift-up value (BUFSUV). The BUFSIZE value determines the size of the area available for storing journal records before they are written to the journal file. The BUFSUV value determines at which point a physical write occurs, and thus the size of the journal block that is written. In other words, BUFSUV actually functions like a buffer size, and the BUFSIZE value determines how many buffers. These two values can be confusing!

Determine the size of the journal records that will need to be written during a typical transaction and set BUFSUV to that value. Specify a BUFSIZE of at least two to three times this value. The intention is to prevent the buffer area from ever filling up completely. The journal control statistics include a "number of times buffer full" item which identifies how many time the BUFSIZE area was exhausted. If this value is significantly larger than zero, you should increase the BUFSIZE value.

11.12 CICS Trace

The CICS trace facility is expensive. For your production CICS, you can save up to 10 percent of your total CICS CPU usage by not running with trace. The trace is controlled by the CICS internal trace parameter in the SIT. Because the CICS trace can be required to diagnose complex application problems, it is desirable to be able to run with trace in a controlled environment. However, if possible, avoid running trace as a default in your production CICS environment.

Performance monitor and accounting packages can be responsible for a significant percentage of your CICS CPU time. Some performance monitors utilize the CICS trace facility to gather performance information. If your performance monitor offers options to control the number and/or frequency of traces that are enabled, you should investigate their use to reduce performance monitor overhead in your environment.

12

ICCF and the
Interactive Interface

ICCF/VSE provides an interactive computing environment for VSE and is used by many functions in the VSE/ESA Interactive Interface. ICCF is required to install VSE, and greatly simplifies ongoing VSE maintenance. ICCF is also often used as a program development workbench for applications programming. However, ICCF makes large demands upon system resources, and can also greatly impact the CICS system it runs with. In this chapter, we will look at ways to improve the performance of ICCF.

12.1 Cookbook for ICCF Tuning

The methods used to tune ICCF are very similar to those used to tune CICS. Because ICCF can make large demands on the system, the impact of ICCF on other work on your system should be considered before improving ICCF's share of that system.

- Use PRTYIO to favor scheduling ICCF I/O. This can be especially important with high DTSFILE activity.

- Do not run CICS production or heavy testing work on the ICCF CICS system.

- Set PRTY to run ICCF at a high priority. It should run right below VTAM, and above all batch partitions. Be aware that busy ICCF systems can make heavy demands on the CPU and impact all other work.

- Reduce ICCF paging. Use TPBAL, decrease the number of interactive partitions, restrict the size of the associated CICS system, and disallow online compiles.

12.2   CICS under ICCF

ICCF is started in a partition by executing DTSINIT. During initialization, ICCF creates an interactive partition environment by dividing the ICCF partition storage into a user designated number of logical partitions. CICS acts as the terminal interface for ICCF. CICS runs in an ICCF interactive partition as a subtask of the ICCF maintask. Therefore, CICS runs under the control of ICCF. This changes with VSE/ESA 1.3 where CICS owns the partition maintask and ICCF is attached as a subtask.   Figure 12.1 illustrates the layout of the ICCF ppartition.

ICCF uses CICS transactions to handle all foreground processing. Most ICCF user commands run in the foreground. This will be discussed later. Let us first look at the basic ICCF requirements imposed on its associated CICS and on VSE.

ICCF requires 20 bytes of TCT user area for its processing. You must ensure that TCTUAL includes enough space for your own usage plus the ICCF area. The 20 bytes for ICCF follow all other user storage. Use the ICCF TCTOFS parameter to specify the total number of bytes required. If your system uses 40 bytes of user area, then you must specify,

```
TCTUAL=60
TCTOFS=40
```

ICCF also requires a TIOAL specification. (This is the CICS terminal I/O area size.) Specify the maximum number of terminal input bytes. If the ICCF fullscreen editor is used, the value must be large enough for the maximum size of all modified lines. A suggested safe TIOAL value is your screen size. Thus, for a model 2 terminal you should specify a value of at least 1920 bytes and for a model 4 terminal you should specify a value of at least 3440 bytes.

GETVIS Area
Pseudo Part 3
Pseudo Part 2
Pseudo Part 1
CICS Pseudo Partition
ICCF Supervisor

Figure 12.1 ICCF Partition Layout

12.2.1   Partition and GETVIS Storage Usage

CICS GETVIS is not allocated from within the CICS interactive partition area. Instead, the CICS GETVIS requests are allocated from the actual partition GETVIS area. The other interactive partitions have their own emulated GETVIS areas and do not use the ICCF partition GETVIS area. ICCF makes additional demands on partition storage. When initially planning an ICCF partition you start with the requirements for CICS and add 128KB for ICCF, plus the storage to be allocated to the other interactive partitions. Typically, an additional 768KB to 1024KB will be required for these interactive partitions. The ICCF partition GETVIS area should be monitored to ensure that it is not gradually exhausted when ICCF remains active for extended periods.

ICCF makes additional demands on its partition GETVIS area. When initially planning an ICCF partition, you start with the requirement for CICS and add at least 200KB for ICCF. Remember to include space for any VSAM files opened by CICS. A small ICCF partition has been observed to use 600KB within its partition GETVIS area. If your ICCF CICS system runs anything besides

ICCF, then you will find your GETVIS area usage to be much higher.

Each interactive partition (except for the CICS interactive partition) has its own GETVIS area that is allocated within the interactive partition area. Each of these is totally separate, and is only used by a program running within that interactive partition. The size of each interactive partition GETVIS area is determined when it is defined.

12.2.2   CICS in an Interactive Partition

CICS is initialized in a special interactive partition created by ICCF. When CICS runs under ICCF, ICCF adds overhead to all CICS operating system requests. In general, it is bad to run a production CICS with ICCF because of this overhead. The CICS MRO feature is sometimes used to allow an ICCF system to use CICS resources. Figure 12.2 illustrates running ICCF under one CICS as an AOR (the MRO Application Owning Region) with the terminals owned by a separate production CICS (the MRO Terminal Owning Region).

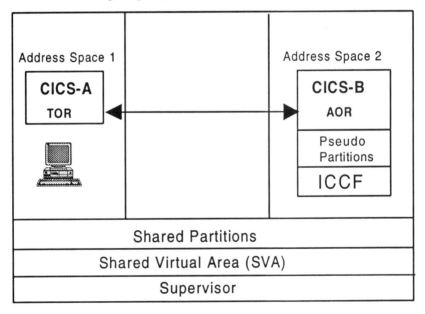

Figure 12.2 ICCF AOR CICS

Most users that run ICCF, run it with a test CICS or with a special CICS that only services ICCF. It may even be a bad idea to run your test CICS under ICCF, since a storage violation occurring during application testing could result in the loss of the entire ICCF system. A test CICS may also be separated from ICCF to allow the ICCF partition to be run at a high priority. Tuning ICCF processing is frequently a political issue because ICCF is often perceived by its users as slow, and as an impediment to application development. For this reason, ICCF is often run at a very high priority. When a test CICS is part of ICCF, it is hard to justify running ICCF at one of the highest priorities in your system.

The CICS run under ICCF can be small, especially when it is only used for ICCF terminal control. However, be careful to ensure that the CICS DSA size is adequate for ICCF's needs. The I$$x transactions run by ICCF require CICS resources and ICCF users will be single threaded if adequate resources are not available. It is never good to artificially constrain ICCF by employing CMXT or AMXT to restrict the number of simultaneous ICCF users.

12.3 Foreground Processing

Most user commands execute in the ICCF *foreground*. Foreground commands execute under the control of special CICS transactions that are supplied as part of ICCF. These users sign on to ICCF and are not easily identified using CICS commands via their ICCF user IDs. It is also difficult to determine the status of ICCF users from CICS for problem determination and tuning purposes.

A special ICCF command is provided to display the ICCF users that are logged onto the system. Use the /USERS command to display the current ICCF users. One line is displayed for each ICCF user. This line indicates the ID of each user, their status, and the identification of the terminal used to access ICCF. The status is displayed using a numeric code value.

The user ID displayed is the one used for sign on. If a user is in the process of signing onto ICCF, then a value of "****" is displayed. See Figure 12.3 for the ICCF user status values.

00	CM Command Mode
01	IN Input Mode
02	LS List Mode
04	ED Edit Mode
08	LS List Mode
16	EX Execution Mode
17	EX Execution Mode
18	SP Spool Mode
19	RD Conversational Read

Figure 12.3 Status Values for /USERS Command

12.4 Interactive Partitions

The ICCF interactive partitions are suballocations of the ICCF partition that simulate the VSE batch environment. A special interactive partition is used to run CICS under ICCF (this was changed in later VSE/ESA releases). All remaining interactive partitions are run under the control of a terminal session. They are initiated when a program is run by a terminal user. Interactive partitions are dynamically managed by ICCF, and are shared by all terminal users.

ICCF processing occurs in foreground mode or background mode. All ICCF fullscreen editor and system commands are executed as *foreground commands*. This means that these commands are performed by CICS, not in a separate ICCF pseudo partition. The ICCF copy of CICS runs all foreground commands in interactive partition 0 where CICS itself is running.

Background mode is used to run programs within the other interactive partitions. Interactive partitions are similar to normal VSE batch partitions. Each interactive partition has its own communications region, protect key, and partition GETVIS area. Interactive partition have classes, just as regular VSE batch partitions have classes. The interactive partition class may be used to select which job run in which partition. They are typically used to identify interactive partitions of a given size, or with a particular number of system work files.

ICCF supports up to thirtyfive interactive partitions plus one for its copy of CICS. You determine the number, size, and classes of interactive partitions via the PARTN parameter of the DTSOPTNS macro . You may choose to override this macro specification at ICCF startup time.

12.4.1 How Used?

Programs invoked under ICCF are run in interactive partitions. Whenever an explicit /RUN or /EXEC or /ENDRUN request is encountered, or a program name is referenced in an ICCF command file, an interactive partition is allocated and used to run the program. The interactive partition invocation request may be contained within an ICCF macro. Thus, user and IBM commands implemented by ICCF macros may use interactive partitions.

Common ICCF actions requiring interactive partition program execution include job submission, VSAM catalog information access, and VSE library member update. Various Interactive Interface panels also require an interactive partition for their processing.

Interactive partitions occupy ICCF partition storage and are dispatched by ICCF, not by the VSE supervisor. Foreground commands always have priority over all background execution of interactive partitions. The execution of the ICCF interactive partitions is *timesliced* by ICCF. ICCF timeslices using a clock to control the amount of time each task can run before control is taken and other tasks are given a share of the system. An interactive partition is given control by the ICCF dispatcher and runs until one of the following occurs:

- The program issues a read that is routed to the terminal. The task remains suspended until the read is satisfied by the terminal user.

- The supplied print buffer fills up or a /FORCE command is given. Here the output is displayed on the terminal before execution proceeds.

- The job terminates. Any remaining output is displayed on the terminal and the interactive partition is released.

- The task finishes its timeslice. In this case execution will be suspended until other interactive partitions have been serviced and the task is given a new timeslice. You control the ICCF timeslice values.

12.4.2 CPU Overhead

ICCF interactive partition execution carries the basic overhead of the program being used, plus additional ICCF specific overhead. This overhead comes from two main sources. The first is the internal ICCF spooler, and the second is the ICCF SVC screening code.

ICCF spools input and output for interactive partitions. Because the relatively inefficient ICCF library file (DTSFILE) is used for this spooling, the cost is higher than using POWER in a normal batch partition. In fact, if a large amount of printout is produced from within an interactive partition, all other processing within the ICCF partition slows visibly. This is a result of the CPU load and the large amount of DTSFILE I/O caused by spooling.

ICCF screens most SVCs issued from within interactive partitions. This is done to trap unit record I/O for the ICCF spooler, and to allow simulation of the interactive partition environment. This SVC screening process adds CPU overhead to all SVCs from interactive partitions. In general, CPU cost will increase about 10 percent as a result of running in an interactive partition rather than a VSE batch partition. Programs that perform mainly read and print operations are impacted much more than this. A simple display utility (LIBR member list) has been measured with more than 50 percent overhead due to ICCF processing.

12.4.3 /DISPLAY and /MAP Commands

It is sometimes desirable to display the status of the ICCF interactive partitions. The /DISPLAY command may be entered on the VSE system console to generate a display of the interactive partition status. The output to the console includes:

- The total number of request queue elements, and the number which are currently in use.

- The total number of interactive partitions, and the number which are currently being used.

- The total number of background tasks, and the number being used by interactive partitions.

The /DISPLAY command is used to produce a summary of the current interactive partition status. The /MAP command is used to display detailed information for each interactive partition. The output of this command is to the system console and includes the following:

- Partition number and identifier

- Virtual address of the interactive partition start

- Size of the interactive partition

- Interactive partition usage/user information

- Number of preallocated work files for the partition

- Scheduling class(es) of the interactive partition

12.4.4 /TIME Command

The /TIME command is used to change the timer value that controls dispatching of the ICCF high-priority task. This command is used to reduce the overhead of this task, so that performance measurements may be taken, or to do other timing critical work (such as running the SDAID program). The two formats of this command are:

```
/TIME {n}
/TIME RESET
```

Use the first form to set or change the timer value for the ICCF high-priority task. The value given is in minutes. Thus, /TIME 10 would change the timer so that the ICCF high-priority task would run only every ten minutes. You should request users to stop running background processes when you employ the /TIME command. This command locks out all such background processing at the next spooled terminal I/O request.

The second form of the command is used to restore the initial ICCF high-priority task timer value. This will allow current background processing to continue, and permit new productive use of interactive partitions. Use the /TIME RESET command after completing your performance measurement or other time critical work to restore normal ICCF functioning.

12.5   ICCF Storage Requirements

ICCF uses storage within the ICCF partition (real and virtual). ICCF also supports placing certain ICCF phases within the SVA. The ICCF partition is particularly sensitive to paging induced delays, so adequate real storage is key for acceptable performance.

The ICCF partition provides both program area storage and GETVIS area storage. Unlike many other VSE system facilities, ICCF makes relatively large demands upon the program area and relatively small demands upon the GETVIS area. The ICCF and CICS GETVIS area usage was discussed previously. Let us just note that a partition GETVIS allocation of 600KB is usually fine for an ICCF system that is not running additional CICS work.

12.5.1   Program Area Storage

ICCF should be executed with a relatively large size parameter to provide program area storage. The program area storage is used to load ICCF programs and to build the interactive partitions. The maximum size of an interactive partition is 9.9MB. A typical small ICCF system run by the author uses a size parameter of 5120K on the execute statement.

The interactive partitions are allocated from available program area storage. This includes interactive partition 0 which is required for CICS. ICCF must be run in a static partition, but may occupy its own address space. It is usually necessary to run ICCF in a separate address space to ensure that sufficient virtual storage is available to define all required interactive partitions.

CICS is executed in interactive partition 0. This interactive partition is usually defined at about 1.5MB. Additional storage may be required if more than ICCF is run by this CICS. One VSE/ESA system with a large number of ICCF foreground users specified 2.5MB for the CICS interactive partition.

12.5.2   SVA Usage

The following phases may be placed within the SVA. Doing so is optional. Placing these phases in the SVA improves ICCF performance and may slightly reduce the size of your interactive partitions. If all are placed in the SVA, the total storage required is only 40KB. On the other hand, if you need to reduce your SVA size, here are 40KB that are easy to save:

LINKNGO2	6.7KB
DTSCDUMP	8.4KB
DTSPROCS	9.5KB
DTSSBMT1	10.5KB
DTSXTRCT	0.4KB
DTSIPWR	4.0KB

12.6   Tuning DTSFILE

The ICCF library is maintained in the DTSFILE. This is a dataset that can occupy multiple extents managed by ICCF. The dataset is managed by ICCF as a number of libraries and as members within each library. The format of the DTSFILE is unique to ICCF, and not similar to that of VSE libraries.

A special utility is used to define, add, alter, and delete DTSFILE information. This is the DTSUTIL utility program. DTSUTIL may also be used to backup and restore DTSFILE library members. Most utility actions require standalone processing, and are run when the ICCF partition is not active. One important file maintenance operation is the periodic ICCF library reorganization. We will discuss this after a brief look at tuning the DTSFILE.

12.6.1   File Placement and Multiple Extents

If your only use ICCF for system programming functions such as operating system maintenance installation, the ICCF files may be placed wherever they fit. The default ICCF system provided with VSE/ESA is acceptable for many customers. If you use ICCF as an application development platform, you probably need to tune the default specifications for the ICCF files.

The ICCF DTSFILE can be a very high-use file. As such, it should be allocated away from all other high use datasets. Because ICCF often does a poor job of buffering itself, the DTSFILE is a good candidate for a caching control unit. Although DTSFILE I/O is often a major source of poor ICCF response time, you should not automatically assume it is the source of all performance problems. You should monitor the I/O counts for your DTSFILE to determine its usage and its performance costs in your own environment.

ICCF supports multiple extents for the DTSFILE. Because I/O can be overlapped for extents on separate DASD volumes, you should spread your DTSFILE allocation over several volumes. In general, it is better to allocate the DTSFILE over a number of volumes with other usage than to place it on a single dedicated DASD volume.

12.6.2   When to Reorganize

The DTSFILE space is managed by ICCF. Neither libraries or members within libraries need occupy sequential space. As the DTSFILE is used over an extended period of time, it becomes more and more fragmented. Fragmented members result in additional I/Os. These I/Os are also slowed by an increase in the number of nonzero seeks.

The DTSFILE can be reorganized with a backup and a restore. This reorganization should be periodically performed to avoid ICCF response time gradually getting worse and worse. A regular DTSFILE reorganization can easily be done as part of a weekly or monthly system backup. Refer to Figure 12.4 for an example of a DTSFILE reorganization done with a backup and a restore.

```
// JOB REORG DTSFILE USING TAPE
/* Backup DTSFILE to tape on SYS005
// TLBL DTSBKUP,'REORG ICCF'
// ASSGN SYS005,TAPE
// EXEC PROC=DTRICCF
// EXEC DTSUTIL
BACKUP
/*
/* Restore DTSFILE from tape on SYS005
*  Operator: Reply GO when message appears
// TLBL DTSRSTR,'REORG ICCF'
// ASSGN SYS004,SYS005
// EXEC PROC=DTRICCF
// EXEC DTSUTIL
RESTORE
/*
/&
```

Figure 12.4 DTSFILE REORG JCL

The output of the DTSFILE backup should be inspected to identify any problem areas. DTSFILE members have historically been prone to corruption, especially in conjunction with system abends while the ICCF system is operating. Lost (or *dead*) blocks are also recovered by a DTSFILE reorganization. Lost blocks result from VSE and ICCF abends.

HIFILE records are those records past the last member data within the DTSFILE area. After a reorganization, all free records are HIFILE records. ICCF processing of DTSFILE is good so long as HIFILE records are available. ICCF uses the contiguous HIFILE records first for all allocation requests, then it reuses deleted records. Deleted records are not contiguous. Members created using them are not contiguous and perform poorly. Thus, it does no good to reorganize the ICCF library file much before the HIFILE records are exhausted, but it is important to reorganize DTSFILE as close to that time as possible to prevent poor response time. The ICCF startup message **K088I** is produced to display the number of HIFILE records. You should monitor this message and schedule a reorganization as soon as possible whenever the number of HIFILE records is small. You should consider increasing the allocation of the ICCF library if very frequent DTSFILE reorganizations are required, or if the number of HIFILE records reaches zero before DTSFILE can be reorganized.

12.7   Interactive Interface, Source of Tuning Information

The Interactive Interface includes a number of displays of tuning related information. In this section we will look at several of the more useful displays. Examples of actual screen output are used to better illustrate the use of this information.

The Interactive Interface provides a snapshot of the current status of the resources it reports on. Some commands include "high-water marks" for resources. This output is of particular interest for system tuning.

The system status commands are all provided from the menu reached by the **3.6** *fastpath* from the main Interactive Interface menu (ICCF allows a series of menu selections to be performed as a single command). They are also available by selecting Operations (3), then the System Status entry (6) upon the Operations menu.

12.7.1   System Activity Display

The System Activity Display of the Interactive Interface offers a summary of the status of the whole VSE system plus an indication of the resource consumption of each partition. Detailed current resource usage information is provided for the System and for CICS at the top of the display. A single line is provided for each partition summarizing its status. This information is presented in descending priority sequence at the bottom of the display. See Figure 12.5 for an example of the content of this panel.

12.7.2   Storage Layout

The layout of storage within a single designated partition is displayed by this panel. The portion of the program area currently in use and the available program area storage is identified. The

```
IESADMDA              DISPLAY SYSTEM ACTIVITY          * SECONDS 09:20:18
*------------ SYSTEM ------------* *---------------- CICS --------------*
|CPU      :     0%   I/O/Sec:   2 |  |No. Tasks:     57  Per Sec    :  12 |
|Pages In :     2   Per Sec:    * |  |Active Tasks:   6  Suspended   :   0 |
|Pages Out:     1   Per Sec:    * |  |Most Active :   4  Pages Avail: 208 |
*--------------------------------* *------------------------------------*
Priority: X,W,V,U,T,S,C,E,Z,Y,BG=FA=F9=F8=F7=F6,FB,F5,F4,F2,F3,F1

 ID S JOB NAME  PHASE NAME  ELAPSED    CPU TIME   OVERHEAD    %CPU     I/O
 F1 S POWSTART   IPWPOWER  20:18:09     11.48       1.06             22,360
 F3 5 VTAMSTRT   ISTINCVT  20:17:53      9.46       2.31              3,724
 F2 4 CICSICCF   DTSINIT   00:02:56      4.84        .31              6,575
*F4 4 JCLSCHED   JCLSCHED  20:17:52     47.64      11.84             86,818
 F5 4 <=WAITING FOR WORK=>               .00        .00
 FB 3 <=WAITING FOR WORK=>               .03        .00                 32
 F6 2 <=WAITING FOR WORK=>               .00        .01
 F7 5 <=WAITING FOR WORK=>               .03        .00                 31
 F8 5 EXP/VTAM   EXPVMAIN  20:17:51     45.78      11.44                649
 F9 3 <=WAITING FOR WORK=>               .03        .00                 31
 FA 3 <=WAITING FOR WORK=>               .03        .00                 31
 BG 1 <=WAITING FOR WORK=>               .00        .01
```

Figure 12.5 Activity Display

status of the partition GETVIS area is also displayed. The current available and high water mark values for your CICS Partition GETVIS Area is of particular interest. See Figure 12.6 for an example of the content of this panel.

```
IESADMPM                DISPLAY STORAGE LAYOUT

Partition ID..... F2      Enter the desired partition ID

                    PARTITION: F2        |K-Byte Byte |K-Byte |K-Byte|
*------* X'600000' -----------------------*------------*-------*------*
|      |                                  |            |       |      |
|EXEC- |            LOADED (PROGRAM SIZE) |  5106    0 |       |      |
|SIZE  |                                  |            | 5120  |      |
|      | X'AFC8D7' -----------------------*------------*       |      |
|      |            AVAILABLE             |   13   808 |       |      |
*======* X'B00000' =======================*============*=======*======*
|      |                K-Byte Byte |                          | 7168 |
|      |     HIGH WATER MARK:  580    0 |                       |      |
|      |               USED:   559  768 |  2032    0 |          |      |
|GETVIS|               FREE:  1472  256 |            | 2048  |         |
|      | LARGEST FREE BLOCK:  1469  512 |                       |      |
|      | * X'CF0000' -----------------------*------------*       |      |
|      |            CONTROL AREA          |   16    0 |        |      |
*------* X'CFFFFF' -----------------------*------------*-------*------*
```

Figure 12.6 Partition Storage Layout

12.7.3   Shared Virtual Area Layout

The layout of the Shared Virtual Area (SVA) is provided by the display in Figure 12.7. The sizes of the System Directory List (SDL), Virtual Library Area (VLA), System GETVIS Area, System Label Area (SLA), and V-POOL are each reported. The current available and high-water mark values for the System GETVIS Area are of particular interest.

```
IESADMSVA                    SHARED VIRTUAL AREA LAYOUT

                    SHARED VIRTUAL AREA (SVA)      |K-Byte Byte |K-Byte |K-Byte|
  * X'085000' -------------------------------*------------*-------*------*
  |                 SYSTEM DIRECTORY LIST (SDL)   |   28    0 |       |      |
  * X'08C000' -------------------------------*------------* 2104 |      |
  |                 VIRTUAL LIBRARY AREA (VLA)     | 2076    0 |       |      |
  |                      FREE:   396    735       |          |       |      |
  * X'293000' -------------------------------*------------*-------*      |
  |                 CONTROL AREA                   |   40    0 |       |      |
  * X'29D000' -------------------------------*------------*       |      |
  |                 SYSTEM GETVIS   K-Byte Byte   |          |       | 4524 |
  |                 HIGH WATER MARK:  1296    0   |          | 2056 |      |
  |                          USED:    929  368   | 2016    0 |       |      |
  |                 FREE (RESERVED):  1086  656 (72)|        |       |      |
  |                 LARGEST FREE BLOCK:  830  128 |          |       |      |
  * X'495000' -------------------------------*------------*-------*      |
  |                 SYSTEM LABEL AREA (SLA)        |  108    0 |       |      |
  * X'4B0000' -------------------------------*------------* 364 |      |
  |                 V-POOL                         |  256    0 |       |      |
  * X'4EFFFF' -------------------------------*------------*-------*------*
```

Figure 12.7 Shared Virtual Area Layout

12.7.4   Channel and Device Activity

The Interactive Interface also provides for an I/O device status display. The Display Channel and Device Activity menu entry produces the display in Figure 12.8 below. Note that this display includes I/O counts by job, by partition, and by device. The total I/O requests for channel and control unit can be used to judge whether or not your I/O load is well balanced.

In a MODE=370 or MODE=VM system these numbers represent physical unit I/O counts and do not show the effects of channel switching (if any). For MODE=ESA, the numbers reported are the

```
IESADMSIOS        DISPLAY CHANNEL AND DEVICE ACTVITY

DEVICE ADDRESS RANGE FROM: 120 TO: 200

DEVICE     PART     JOB        CHANNEL I/O    CONTROL UNIT    DEVICE I/O
           ID       NAME       REQUESTS       I/O REQUESTS    REQUESTS

  12D      F8     EXP/VTAM       110986         109920            23
  12E      F4     JCLSCHED       110986         109920         84635
  143      F2     CICSICCF       110986           1005           991
           F8     EXP/VTAM       110986           1005            14
  1DF      F3     VTAMSTRT       110986             61             61
```

Figure 12.8 Channel and Device Activity Display

sum of the I/Os to the device, where the channel and control unit counts are not meaningful except to indicate the total volume of I/O requests processed.

12.8 Tuning ICCF Processing

Although we are usually concerned with reducing the impact of ICCF on the rest of VSE processing, we sometimes find ourselves wanting to improve ICCF performance. ICCF tuning techniques often improve one aspect of performance as perceived by the ICCF user, and impact another. We must first determine what aspect of ICCF performance we wish to tune. We can usually tune only one of the following items at a time:

1. Terminal response time
2. Interactive processing

12.8.1 Terminal Response Time

ICCF terminal response time is influenced by the usual factors we see in other online systems, plus several that are unique to the ICCF environment. The primary sources of response time issues for ICCF are:

1. *NBUFS/CISIZE values.* These often have a large effect on foreground processing because most delays in command

processing are caused by I/O. The more buffers that are defined, the less I/O required for command processing.

2. *User Profile values.* The *size and number of libraries* are major factors in response time. Many small libraries will always perform better than a few large libraries. ICCF is affected by directory search time. This is often seen when a number of ICCF macros are used as commands. You should specify a reasonable value for the maximum size of a library member. IBM suggests a value in the range of 500 to 1000 to reduce the cost of editing and copying members. The number of user profile records should be kept as small as possible. Unused records should be deleted. It is suggested that you have well under 300 user profiles if at all possible. Frequently used profiles should be kept near the front of the list, as ICCF sequentially searches the user profile records.

3. *Library Considerations.* The number of members in each directory should be kept as small as possible. ICCF employs slow sequential directory searches. IBM suggests that you define the maximum number of entries in a directory as less than 300. This obliges users to delete old/unused members, or to use multiple libraries rather than creating a single very large library. Active directories should employ the FREESPACE option. Specify this option on the ADD LIBRARY command to ensure that directory entries are kept in the same area of the DTSFILE, even when entries are volatile or defined after the last reorganization of the DTSFILE. Of course, frequent reorganizations of DTSFILE are also recommended. You should monitor the ICCF startup K088I message. When the number of HIFILE records gets close to zero, a reorganization should be scheduled as soon as possible. If reorganizations occur too frequently, you should increase the size of the DTSFILE so that HIFILE records are always available. ICCF response time visibly deteriorates as soon as this value reaches zero.

4. *Line Configuration.* The usual network tuning considerations apply to the ICCF system. It is especially important that you reduce the number of ICCF terminals that are multi-dropped on a single line. Faster line speeds

are better. A minimum value of 4800 baud is important to prevent large delays for full screen writes by the edit and display commands.

12.8.2 Interactive Partition Response Time

Interactive partitions are used to run normal VSE batch programs under the control of ICCF. ICCF provides its own miniature spooling system for the interactive partitions. Tuning of interactive partitions is dependent upon a number of factors. Some factors are program related, some are ICCF related. Let us look at the most common factors for Interactive Partition performance.

1. *Program used.* The usual VSE batch compilers can perform poorly when run Interactively. These batch compilers (with the exception of VS BASIC) employ work files. Work file I/O is the usual cause of delays for Interactive compilers. If you have a choice of an *in core* compiler (a compiler that uses virtual storage rather than work files), you should use it under ICCF. You can also reduce the amount of work file I/O by giving additional virtual storage to compilers frequently run under ICCF. The ICCF System Program Table contains an entry for each compiler. Use the DTSM2 macro to specify additional storage for those compilers with problems. If you are using the COBOL compiler, you will also have to catalog a CBL options statement to specify a larger BUFSIZE value before COBOL will make use of any additional storage.

2. *Interactive Contention.* When several Interactive jobs are run at the same time, or if a lot of foreground work is being run by ICCF, then Interactive partitions will perform poorly. When such contention occurs, you should move less critical work to VSE batch partitions. All except the very smallest VSE batch compiles ALWAYS use far less resources than Interactive compiles. Well tuned SAM managed VSAM workfiles will result in fast batch VSE compiles, much faster than all except the very smallest ICCF interactive compiles. A large buffer size is the most important parameter for tuning VSAM workfiles.

12.9   ICCF Subtasks

ICCF employs a number of subtasks to accomplish its mission. These tasks are listed below along with a brief description of the functions they perform. Any analysis of the performance of ICCF must include an analysis of the waits associated with each of these subtasks.

- **DTSCHIGH** is the high priority task. It runs at a higher priority than the other ICCF subtasks. DTSCHIGH manages emulation of system services that must be serialized. It also performs resource management for ICCF time slicing. DTSCHIGH waits impact all of ICCF.

- **DTSNTFY** is the notification subtask. It routes notify messages to users.

- **DTSCOPCM** is the operator communications subtask. It handles the ICCF console commands (the "/" commands).

- **DTSCICS** is the name of the ICCF subtask where CICS is run. This is a key task whose waits impact all of ICCF.

- **DFHSKP** and **DFHLOADR** are attached by CICS. They serve their usual function of offloading CICS processing.

12.10 ICCF and VSE/ESA 1.3

ICCF will not receive much additional functionality in the future. The direction for VSE interactive will be to expand via Client Server applications. However, several significant ICCF changes were made with VSE/ESA 1.3. Previously, ICCF was executed as the maintask within a partition, and it started CICS as a subtask within an interactive partition. This meant that CICS was unavailable unless ICCF was operational. And, CICS would fail if ICCF failed. As a result, most ICCF users could not afford to run ICCF with their production CICS system. CICS and ICCF storage was separately managed, which meant that excess storage needed to be allocated to each so that problems could be avoided.

With VSE/ICCF and VSE/ESA 1.3, CICS is the maintask, and ICCF runs under the control of CICS. In fact, ICCF may be started and stopped without impacting CICS operations. CICS transactions are provided to initiate and terminate ICCF processing. ICCF allocates all of its storage for code and interactive partitions from the CICS partition GETVIS area. This simplifies CICS storage management since the separate ICCF area is gone and only the CICS DSA and partition GETVIS areas need be tuned.

13

VTAM

VTAM is an acronym for Virtual Telecommunications Access Method. VTAM is the primary VSE remote device access method. VTAM is also used to access local terminals and PC LANs in many VSE shops. This chapter discusses tuning VTAM at the Version 3 level for VSE/ESA. However, much of the information is applicable to prior VTAM releases.

VTAM is an important consideration in our tuning task for many reasons. It requires large amounts of virtual and real storage. It must be run at a high priority, and can consume a significant fraction of the CPU. It can do large numbers of I/Os. And VTAM is supplied with defaults that do not fit the needs of most VSE environments.

VTAM has many configuration parameters. It operates at several software and hardware levels, each of which can effect performance. As a result, tuning VTAM can be a complex task. VTAM configuration is not well understood. Seemingly simple changes can have large effects. Therefore, many shops have adopted a hands-off policy towards VTAM. This is a mistake because VTAM delays are often the largest single factor in the response time of an online system.

In this section we will discuss the major elements of VTAM performance. We will develop correct parameter values for your environment. And we will look at safe ways to verify changes before they are made. We will see the importance of changing only one parameter at a time in minimizing the introduction of problems. We can always "unchange" the one parameter if a problem occurs.

This chapter assumes some basic familiarity with VTAM terminology. For the new VSE user, we will look at the structure of VTAM, how you describe your network to VTAM, and how the NCP is generated, all from only a performance standpoint. The IBM manual *IBM VSE/Enterprise Systems Architecture: Networking Support* (SC33-6508) is an excellent source of information on VTAM basics plus a simple guide for defining the network to VSE.

The IBM manual *VTAM Network Implementation Guide* (SC31-6404) contains a chapter titled "Tuning VTAM for Your Environment." This is a source of additional VTAM tuning guidelines. However, the buffer pool specifications and other values provided in this book are generally superior to those in the IBM manual.

ACF/VTAM 3.3 also includes a storage estimates diskette. This can be a valuable tool in determining the resource requirements for your VTAM and the correct partition size to define.

13.1 VTAM Tuning Cookbook

This section lists some common tuning considerations for VTAM.

- VTAM buffer pool specifications should be reviewed using TNSTAT data, and adjusted to reduce pool expansions.

- VTAM delay parameters are a frequently overlooked source of network performance problems.

- VTAM should be run in the private area to maximize available storage. No performance penalty is incurred by running VTAM in private.

- VTAM should be the highest priority batch partition. It can still be a POWER controlled partition but should run at a higher priority than POWER. This is accomplished by specifying NCP on the POWER PSTART command.

- Eliminating paging for the VTAM partition is critical.

13.2 Overview of VTAM

VTAM operates at several software and hardware levels. We will look briefly at these levels, and at what impact each has upon performance. We will look at the VTAM partition, the user application partition, and the operating system software components.

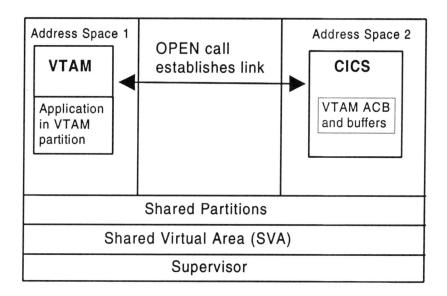

Figure 13.1 VTAM Overview

VTAM runs in a partition in VSE as illustrated in Figure 13.1. It consumes CPU time, uses large amounts of virtual storage, and performs many I/Os in the VTAM partition. This portion of VTAM is the one most users think of as being the real "VTAM." The VTAM partition serves as an interface between your application and the hardware for which VTAM manages the communications. VTAM is accessed from an application. Generally, each application occupies its own partition. The application establishes a connection to VTAM by issuing an OPEN. It then makes requests of VTAM. These requests are performed partially in the VTAM partition and partially in the application partition. Resources are required in both partitions. CICS is an example of a VTAM application that occupies its own partition.

VTAM processing also involves code that runs as part of the operating system. This code allows VTAM early access to I/O status information, provides communications services across partitions, and ensures that VTAM cleanup is performed as applications terminate. Little tuning can be done to reduce the impact of this portion of VTAM, but it is important to be aware of this level's system requirements because they can impact system stability, in addition to performance.

13.3   VTAM Initialization

VTAM is started by executing the phase ISTINCVT in the VTAM partition. Initialization parameters can be provided in VSE library members. Many parameters can be altered via operator commands after VTAM initialization, but it is good to have correct values provided automatically to reduce errors. Initialization is controlled by the VTAM *startup parameters*. The source library member ATCSTR00.B and other ATCSTRxx.B members contain the VTAM startup parameters. See Figure 13.2 for an example of these relationships. The operator may specify the suffix to be used for the VTAM startup members via the LIST=xx option.

The VTAM *configuration list* contains the names of all network major nodes to be activated. The ATCCONxx.B members contain configuration lists. The startup parameter CONFIG=xx specifies the suffix of the ATCCONxx.B member used to initialize VTAM. (The default member name is ATCCON00.B.) The entries in the *configuration list* member name various network configuration source library members that are to be processed.

The source members of type "B" whose names begin with "VTM" are all VTAM *network configuration members*. Default members are supplied in IJSYSRS.SYSLIB, but the actual members used by VTAM are typically in the PRD2.CONFIG sublibrary. These are the members named in the configuration list. Any members not explicitly named are not processed.

Many fetches are performed during VTAM startup. As many as 4000 I/Os have been observed during VTAM startup. Make the VTAM startup library the first library in the search chain to reduce startup time. Library fetches are also greatly impacted by other activity on the same disk as the library. VTAM starts up much faster if it is not competing with the initialization of other partitions vying for the same library.

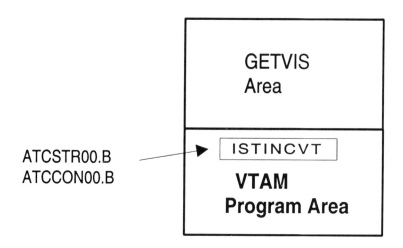

EXEC ISTINCVT,SIZE=ISTINCVT

Figure 13.2 VTAM Initialization

The remainder of this section VTAM parameter organization in more detail and may be skipped by the experienced VTAM user. If you are familiar with the VTAM configuration members, resume reading at the "Altering VTAM Parameters" section . Additional information may be found in the IBM manual *VTAM Resource Definition Reference.*

13.3.1   Startup Parameters

The VTAM *Startup Parameters* define many performance related items. These parameters are held in a library member whose name is of the form ATCSTRxx.B.   (The default member name is ATCSTR00.B and is supplied in the PRD2.COMM sublibrary.) The various VTAM buffer pools are defined within the startup parameters, as is the name of the VTAM Configuration List.

The startup parameter member ATCSTR00.B is processed first, then modified by any addition startup member specified.   The ATCSTR00.B member is always processed first by VTAM, even if

```
SSCPID=1,
SSCPNAME=SSCP01,
NETID=VTAM1,
HOSTSA=1,
HOSTPU=NODE01,
CONFIG=00,
LIST=00,
NOPROMPT,
IOINT=0,
SGALIMIT=0,
APBUF=(16,,,51),
BSBUF=(28,,,1),
CRPLBUF=(60,,,1),
LFBUF=70,288,,11),
LPBUF=(12,,,6),
SFBUF=(20,,,20),
VFBUF=102400,
VPBUF=446464,
WPBUF=(30,,,20),
XDBUF=(6,,,1)
```

Figure 13.3 Startup Parameters in ATCSTR00.B

you code a LIST=xx operand on the EXEC statement, or if the operator supplies an alternate member. If an ATCSTR00.B member is not found, an error message will be issued at VTAM startup.

All startup parameter changes first should be tested in an alternate member, then copied to the usual ATCSTRxx member only after VTAM has run for a period of time. You may code an EXEC statement parameter of LIST=xx to determine what ATCSTRxx member is used to start VTAM. The operator may also override the default member name via the LIST=xx option.

You may select the default list of ATCSTR00.B and include in that list an option of LIST=yy. If this is done, the ATCSTRyy.B list is merged with the current list. This allows a baseline set of options to be customized for the needs of a specific domain. The merge feature can also be used to more easily test changes you make to improve VTAM performance.

Some of the Startup Parameters important to performance are briefly described here. The Buffer Pool specifications will be discussed in detail in a later section.

IOINT The IOINT option enables request timeout messages. You specify as "IOINT=n" where "n" is the number of seconds before a message is issued. If omitted, the default is "IOINT=180." Code "IOINT=0" to disable this option.

SGALIMIT The SGALIMIT option is used to limit the amount of System GETVIS Area storage VTAM may use. Code as "SGALIMIT=0" if no limit is desired, otherwise code "SGALIMIT=nK" to restrict SGA usage to "n" kilo-bytes. "n" is rounded upward to the next page boundary.

TNSTAT The TNSTAT option enables tuning statistics. You specify as "TNSTAT,CNSL,TIME=n" to enable gathering of tuning statistics. Statistics will be computed every "n" minutes. The default "TIME=" value is 60 minutes. Statistics will be written to the trace file. The "CNSL" option causes the statistics to be also displayed on the console. If this option is omitted, the default is "NOCNSL." This causes output to be only written to the trace file.

13.3.2 Configuration List

The VTAM *configuration list* contains the names of members defining the major nodes that must be activated for the network to operate. The configuration list is held in a member whose name is of the form ATCCONxx.B, usually in the PRD2.CONFIG sublibrary. The suffix "xx" is taken from the CONFIG=xx entry in the startup parameters member, with a default value of "00." Refer to Figure 13.4 for an example of the IBM supplied configuration list.

The configuration list contains the names of additional library members that provide configuration information. The default ATCCON00.B member (provided by IBM with VSE) starts the applications before the terminals.

```
Col10                                    Col72
VTMAPPL,                                    X
VTMSNA,                                     X
VTMNSNA,                                    X
VTMPATH,                                    X
VTMCA1,                                     X
VTMCA2,                                     X
VTMCA3,                                     X
VTMCTCA,                                    X
VTMCRDM,                                    X
VTMCDRS,                                    X
VTMSW1
```

Figure 13.4 ATCCON00.B Member

The full list of possible parameters that may be used in the VTAM configuration list follows:

1. Path table
2. NCP and cross domain link
3. Local (non-SNA) terminals
4. Applications
5. Cross domain resource manager
6. Cross domain resources

As indicated previously, the default configuration member defines the applications first. The applications are defined within the VTMAPPL.B member. This is followed by SNA control unit definitions, then by non-SNA control unit definitions. The VTMSNA.B member defines the SNA control units and associated terminals. The term non-SNA control unit includes any local terminals under VTAM's control. The VTMNSNA.B member defines the local and non-SNA terminals.

A VTAM domain is essentially a single host computer system running VTAM plus the NCP controllers and SNA controllers driven by that VTAM. Multiple VTAM domains involve multiple host systems, each with its own copy of VTAM. Multiple domain systems are often connected via Channel-To-Channel Adapters (CTCAs) for improved performance. The VTAM CTCAs are defined within the VTMCTCA.B member.

13.3.3 Altering VTAM Parameters

Many people have acquired a distaste for modifying VTAM startup parameters. This is a result of past problems, such as VTAM failing to come up, or VTAM hanging once a load is placed upon the system. VTAM uses large amounts of storage and is sensitive to inadequate storage. VTAM will sometimes hang or abend when it runs out of storage, and will run poorly even when it does not fail.

For these reasons, it is crucial that correct procedures be used in altering VTAM parameters. First, only change one value at a time, unless you KNOW exactly what effect will be achieved. Second, be familiar with how much storage remains after VTAM initializes on your system, and how much is required to run it under a full load. The D NET, BFRUSE command can be used on your unmodified system, then on your updated system to determine if a significant increase in storage occurred, or if a large loss of storage resulted from your change. This command should be used shortly after VTAM initializes, and later once it has been fully loaded. The storage used and storage available numbers at initialization will assist you in determining if it is safe to run the new VTAM. The values under load will tell you whether an increase in storage is needed before future changes are made.

Because changes do not always work as intended, it is a good idea to save the unaltered VTAM parameters before making any changes. This is known as the *Do not go where you can not get back from* rule. Keep good records of all changes made, the desired affect of each change, and the actual results of each change. These records will assist you in improving the safety and accuracy of future changes.

The sections titled "Storage Usage" and "Buffer Pool Specification" explore the characteristics behind VTAM behavior, and discuss various techniques that permit VTAM to operate even when started with too little storage.

13.3.4   NCP Generation

VTAM requires a *Network Control Program* (called an NCP) to be run within 3725 and 3745 control units.   The NCP handles communications between the host processor and SNA devices.   (See

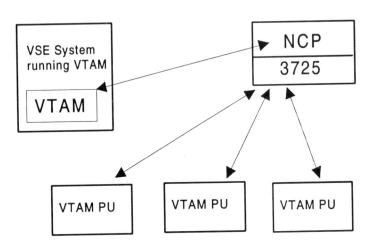

Figure 13.5 VTAM NCP in Relation to VTAM

Figure 13.5.)   The NCP definition is comprised of a description of the links, physical devices, and logical devices to be interfaced.   The NCP definition is processed by the System Support Program (SSP) on the VSE/ESA host system, and the actual NCP is built as a phase (usually in the PRD2.CONFIG sublibrary) or as a sequential file.   The phase or file contains the control program image for the 3725 or 3745 control unit.   This phase is downloaded to the control unit by VTAM.   If you use the phase option to load the NCP, then you must have enough available space in the program area of the VTAM partition for the largest NCP phase.   You can save this VTAM partition storage by using only the sequential file load method.   Several NCP's may be defined, each with its own name.

The remainder of this section describes the NCP definition in more detail.   The description of the link contains a variety of information.   Each link has a unique name.   It indicates whether the link is on a leased or switched line.   The address of the link on the control unit is also defined.   The data mode tells NCP to communicate in half-duplex (HDX) or full-duplex (FDX) mode. The SPEED definition identifies the transmission rate of the link.

The physical unit definition describes a physical device attached to a link. The subsystem group definition identifies the device as a display/printer system or as an intelligent system. The physical unit type defines the device number and model information. The SDLC station address is the hexadecimal byte value associated with this device and must be unique within a link. The identification block and identification number are IDs that are used to tag message traffic by the NCP. You provide SDLC token ring parameters to describe devices attached via a token ring LAN.

The logical unit definition describes the path through which a user accesses the VTAM network. The logical unit specification includes the device name, the local address, and the VTAM/CICS parameters. The device name is a generic name of a given set of device characteristics. The local address is a port number for a 3270 terminal, or a label assigned within an intelligent system.

13.4 Storage Usage

VTAM requires large amounts of virtual and real storage. Real memory is consumed both through explicit specification, and because most VTAM virtual storage is frequently accessed. VTAM uses storage for the following:

- VTAM buffer pools
- VTAM program phases
- Tables for major and minor nodes
- SSCP tables for routing capabilities
- SSCP tables for sessions
- Temporary work space for operator commands, and session create/destroy request processing

The amount of storage required depends on the number of sessions required by application programs, and on the number of major nodes defined. VTAM also sometimes uses storage assigned to application programs to process VTAM requests made by the applications.

Many methods exist to control the amount of storage used by VTAM. Many of these may be specified as part of VTAM startup parameters and also altered to some degree while VTAM is active. These are summarized in the following list:

- Start options for number of buffers in a pool.

- SGALIMIT to limit the amount of System GETVIS Area use.

- MAXBFRU operand. This may be coded on the LINE definition for a major node channel attachment, the NCPHOST definition, and the local SNA PU definition. This specification limits the number of buffers to be used in each area.

- SONLIM start option used to limit the amount of fixed storage. The default is too large if you pre-allocate most of your buffers. If you do not perform much buffer pool expansion, the SONLIM value should be specified smaller than the 60 percent default.

IBM provides a diskette that may be used to determine VTAM storage requirements. This is the *VTAM Storage Estimates* program diskette. This PC program may be used to determine the size parameter for the execution of ISTINCVT, the total size for the partition, and thus the amount of partition GETVIS required for a particular VTAM configuration. It is also useful in estimating the amount of System GETVIS Area storage needed by VTAM. This program is a helpful tool for estimating your storage requirements. However, some of the estimates it produces are larger than will be actually required for typical systems. You should review the buffer status of your running VTAM system to determine if some storage can be reclaimed.

13.5   Buffer Pool Tuning

VTAM requires buffers for all data that it processes. VTAM buffers are grouped together to form *buffer pools*. A buffer pool is simply a set of buffers, usually reserved for a single purpose. VTAM uses a number of different types of buffer pools (listed in Figure 13.6). The space in these pools is dynamically allocated and deallocated as needed for VTAM control blocks, channel programs for data transfer, and for the actual I/O buffers.

Buffer Name	Buffer Purpose
APBUF	Fixed common storage
BSBUF	Session information
CRPLBUF	Copied RPLs
LFBUF	I/O buffers for all data transfers
LPBUF	Scheduling and Audit trail control blocks
SFBUF	LU control blocks
SPBUF	LMPEO send buffer
VFBUF	VTAM fixed control blocks
VPBUF	VTAM pageable control blocks
WPBUF	Application program LU session information
XDBUF	VTAM initialization I/O buffer

Figure 13.6 VTAM Buffer Pool Names

VTAM is able to continue even when a buffer pool is exhausted. The VTAM feature that makes this feasible is called *buffer pool expansion*. Expanding a buffer pool requires significant amounts of CPU time. Tuning buffer pools affects both CPU time and storage. Too large a buffer pool specification may waste storage, but save CPU time that would otherwise be required for frequent expansion. With proper tuning, you can reach a balance between your initial buffer pool size and the CPU cost of expansion.

A VTAM network is comprised of many elements. These include the central processor, communications controllers, cluster controllers, and intelligent peripheral nodes. The various network elements can be viewed as a series of storage spaces. One aspect of tuning VTAM buffer spaces is balancing storage needs across all of the network elements. As data flows through the VTAM network, storage is required in each element. If one element presents a performance bottleneck, the whole network suffers. And, if VTAM pushes data out of the CPU into the network faster than the network can accept it, performance also suffers.

13.5.1   Types of Buffer Pool Allocation

VTAM uses two type of buffer pool allocation. These are Static and Dynamic allocations. Static allocation is performed at VTAM startup time. Dynamic allocations occur after VTAM is running based upon current buffer needs that cannot be satisfied by the static allocation amount. If dynamic allocation is not enabled, then VTAM will either abnormally terminate or hang if the static buffer allocation is exhausted. For this reason, you should permit dynamic allocation in your environment.

VTAM allows you to define certain buffer pools to be fixed in real memory. If you need high performance, and you have some infrequently used buffer pools, you may wish to define these as fixed. In general, VTAM buffers are referenced frequently enough that they stay in real memory, so it is not necessary to explicitly specify a pool to be fixed.

13.5.2   Overriding Buffer Pool Values

VTAM has both fixed and pageable buffer pools for data buffering. Additional buffer pools are required for the VTAM control blocks used to track all inbound and outbound data. You specify the size and characteristics of each buffer pool during VTAM startup. The ATCSTR00.B member contains the VTAM startup parameters. The name of this member may be altered via the LIST=xx startup operator option. During VTAM startup you specify the following parameters for each buffer pool:

- **baseno** is the number of buffers in each pool. This value should be a page multiple. VTAM does not pad the value to fill a page, and any extra space is wasted. You should choose the *baseno* value to minimize this page level fragmentation.

- **bufsize** is the size in bytes of each buffer in the buffer pool. This operand is only available for LFBUF, and should always be an even number of bytes. The value specified should be

equal to the average PIU size usually encountered. It should
also be chosen to fill out a page, to avoid waste. Note that
each LFBUF buffer has a 70-byte prefix, and that this prefix
is added to your specification by VTAM. Do not include the 70
bytes when you code *bufsize*, but do account for it when
determining the number of buffers that will fit within a page.

- **slowpt** is the slowdown point for the pool, i.e., the threshold
for when VTAM will no longer accept new requests for service.
This is a number of buffers. When the number of buffers
available falls below this value, VTAM will only accept priority
requests. Buffers required to read data in response to an
ATTN are priority requests. Nonpriority requests are queued
or rejected with a return code if they cannot be queued.
Buffers requested to write to the network are nonpriority
requests. If you have a small number of channel attached
devices, slowpt should be specified as the sum of their
MAXBFRU values.

- **xpanpt** is the expansion point for the pool, i.e., the threshold
for when expansion will be performed. This value must be
larger than the slowdown point value. If not, VTAM will force
it to be one larger than the slowdown point. The xpanpt value
should be chosen so that xpanpt minus slowpt provides
sufficient buffers to handle the largest request usually
encountered. If this is not done, significant network delays
can be caused during each buffer pool expansion.

- **xpanno** is the number of buffers to add during expansion.
Specify zero to disable expansion. The default is one, which
results in the minimum storage use, and the worst CPU
performance if expansion occurs frequently. VTAM rounds
this value up to fill a page with buffers. Because any
remaining space is wasted, you should choose *xpanno* to
minimize page level fragmentation.

- **xpanlim** is the expansion limit for the buffer pool. This
operand is only available for LFBUF. Specify *xpanlim* in units
of 1024 bytes (number of "KB").

Each of these values is a number of buffers. You express both
the expansion point and the slowdown point as a count of buffers

that are not currently in use. Whenever the number of free buffers
falls below the *slowdown point* (slowpt), then VTAM limits access
to the buffer pool by not accepting new requests. Whenever the
number of free buffers falls below the *expansion point* (xpanpt),
then VTAM adds more buffers in the increment specified by the
expansion number (xpanno). Refer to Figure 13.7 for the IBM
supplied default buffer pool specifications.

```
Col1                                          Col72
APBUF=(16,,,51),                                *
BSBUF=(28,,,1),                                 *
CRPLBUF=(60,,,1),                               *
LFBUF=(70,288,,11),                             *
LPBUF=(54,,,6),                                 *
SFBUF=(153,,,20),                               *
SPBUF=(210,,,32),                               *
VFBUF=262144,                                   *
VPBUF=1048576,                                  *
WPBUF=(100,,,20),                               *
XDBUF=(6,,,1)
```

Figure 13.7 ATCSTR00 Buffer Pool Definitions

13.5.3   Buffer Pool Expansion

As we have seen, buffer pool expansion occurs for short storage
conditions when enabled, and can be expensive. We want to enable
expansion, but we also want to specify enough initial buffers so that
VTAM does not perform expansion very often. We enable
expansion to prevent VTAM hangs or abends when buffers are
exhausted. We specify enough initial buffers to reduce the CPU
overhead of frequent expansions.

Use the D NET,BFRUSE command to determine the number of
buffers required for normal processing. CURR TOTAL minus
CURR AVAIL gives the number of buffers currently in use.
Compute this value at several points during realistic daily

processing, and use the average as your initial number of buffers. Specify the expansion amount as one page. This is the most efficient use of storage. Determine the expansion number by dividing the buffer size into 4096. VTAM will obtain additional buffers through expansion, but this should occur infrequently enough that performance is not greatly impacted. If excessive expansion and contraction are still a problem, change the expansion number to the number of buffers that fit in two pages. This may occur for the LPBUF and CRPLBUF areas.

Buffer expansion consumes CPU time, and also slows VTAM. This occurs when buffer expansion is required but takes so long that buffers are not available when needed. If you see message IST561I STORAGE UNAVAILABLE then you need to address this problem. This is done by increasing the buffer pool expansion number, or by increasing the *baseno* value to prevent expansion. Increase the expansion number in increments of the number of buffers that fit in a page.

In environments where large numbers of sessions come up at one time, you may find it desirable to preallocate enough WPBUF and CRPLBUF buffers to handle the total demand. This occurs when a VARY LOGON operator command is used to start a number of sessions at one time. In this case, the average number of buffers computed after startup time could be inadequate.

13.5.4   Buffer Pools in Depth

The following summarizes each of the VSE buffer pool types, its use, type of storage, and performance recommendations. When calculating storage requirements, remember that buffers do not cross page boundaries. The LFBUF pool is one of the most critical for VSE VTAM performance.

APBUF   Used to provide fixed common storage. The default of sixteen 60-byte buffers is normally adequate. APBUF is used for the allocation of NCBs and DCBs for channel attached devices. You should always allow expansion of APBUF. Expansion should occur rarely, but must be allowed.

BSBUF   Manages session information.   Set base to the
               average number of concurrent boundary type 2.1 LU
               sessions.

CRPLBUF   Copied RPL pool in virtual storage. One buffer for
               each application program request, until the
               operation is completed.

LFBUF   Used for input/output data. Every PIU that enters
               or leaves VTAM does so through one of these
               buffers. Fourteen (14) buffers fit in a page. You
               should define the LFBUF *bufsz* value the same as
               the UNITSZ parameter. *baseno* should be specified
               as a little larger than the number of small
               applications. *slowpt* should be coded the same as
               MAXBFRU. *xpanpt-slowpt* should be enough buffers
               for the largest commonly encountered request. Set
               xpanpt to MAXBFRU*2+1.

LPBUF   Pageable SGA buffers used for scheduling and audit
               trail. One buffer is needed for each active VTAM
               session. The defaults are normally adequate. Two
               buffers fit in a page. Set *xpanno* to 4 or larger for 2-
               page expansion.

SFBUF   LU control blocks. One fixed SGA storage buffer is
               required for each active application program.

SPBUF   A buffer is required for each concurrent LMPEO
               send (Large Message Processing Enhancement
               Option). It is used when a message exceeds a
               session's RU size and is split into several buffers.

VFBUF   Used for all remaining VTAM fixed control blocks.
               The VFBUF pool occupies real storage. 40KB is the
               minimum storage size required. 100KB is a more
               reasonable value for the VFBUF area.

VPBUF   Used for all remaining VTAM pageable control
               blocks. The default (and minimum) value for VSE is
               256KB (262144 bytes). A value of 1MB is more
               typical of an actual specification. Refer to the IBM

manual *Network Program Products Storage Estimates* to determine the exact size required for your configuration.

WPBUF   One buffer is required for each application program LU session. The default is normally adequate. Note that WPBUF CURR TOTAL minus CURR AVAIL is the number of LU to LU (user) sessions.

XDBUF   Used for physical I/O to VTAM peripheral nodes to activate a connection. One example is the initial XID exchange.

13.5.5 LFBUF Thrashing

Thrashing occurs when expansion of the LFBUF pool is quickly followed by a buffer pool contraction. This is a problem because expansion consumes CPU time, and because VTAM requests become queued up during expansion. Thrashing is identified by observing large numbers of expansions where the size of the buffer pool does not greatly increase. (Equation 7 below gives the condition for expansion that does not involve thrashing.)

$$TimesExp \times ExpIncr \approx MaxTotal$$

Equation 7 Condition for Expansion without Thrashing

During a buffer pool expansion, VTAM flags that congestion is occurring. Congestion is a problem that results in network delays. This is not a serious problem during normal buffer pool expansion, because expansion does not occur frequently. Once expansion is completed the congestion problem is eliminated. When the LFBUF buffer pool is thrashing, the congestion indication is false, and serious network degradation is the result.

Thrashing is prevented by increasing the *baseno* value, or by adjusting the *xpanno* value to include an extra page of buffers. Whenever real and virtual storage availability permits, the *baseno* value should be increased to cover the usual CURR TOTAL buffer value. If your network contains many (forty or more) local PU 2 devices, then your only option to prevent LFBUF thrashing is to increase the *baseno* value. This commonly occurs for 3174 token ring gateway configurations.

To control thrashing, you must be able to control the *contpt* (contraction point) parameter.   Unfortunately, no specification exists for this parameter.   VTAM computes the *contpt* value using the following formula:

$$CONTPT=(2*EXPINCR)+XPANPT$$

Equation 8 CONTPT Computation

Notice that VTAM uses EXP INCR and not your *xpanno* value. You should specify your *xpanno* value such that no page alignment is required and so that EXP INCR is equal to *xpanno*. *contpt* is displayed as CONT THRESHOLD on the BFRUSE display output, but is only available if the buffer pool is currently in expansion. Whenever the number of available buffers reaches the *contpt* value, then buffer pool contraction will be performed.   We force a *contpt* value to be used that eliminates or reduces the probability of thrashing.

Care should be taken before trying to adopt VM or MVS tuning recommendations for a VSE VTAM system.   For VSE systems, you should specify *slowpt* the same as MAXBFRU.   On a VM or an MVS system you should code *slowpt* as zero.   This is a result of the different uses of the LFBUF area between these different operating systems.

13.5.6   LFBUF BUFSIZE Selection

Choosing the correct LFBUF buffer size value can improve VTAM performance and storage utilization.   All message data passes through the LFBUF pool.   Knowledge of the distribution of messages sizes is required for selecting a good buffer size.   VTAM buffer trace data can be used to determine the sizes of messages encountered and to estimate their relative frequency.

You have several objectives in selecting the buffer size value. You want a value small enough to ensure storage efficiency.   A value that is large wastes storage for all small messages.   At the same time, you want a large buffer size for I/O efficiency.   Messages that fit in one large buffer would require multiple small buffers. You want to ensure that your selected buffer size fits well into a page, as any unusable fragment within the page is simply wasted. Remember to include the buffer prefix of 70 bytes, and to round to the nearest doubleword (8-byte boundary).

The average message size is almost always a poor value to use. This is illustrated with a simple example. Let us assume that our traffic is made up of 50 percent 300-byte messages and 50 percent 700-byte messages. The average is 500 bytes. If we code 500 bytes, VTAM actually uses 576 (500 plus the 70-byte prefix rounded up to the next 8-byte boundary). Each 300-byte message uses one of these buffers, and wastes 200 bytes. Each 700-byte message uses two of these buffers, and wastes 300 bytes. Messages cannot share buffers, so excess space is tied up and wasted for the duration of an I/O.

A better buffer size to use for the above example would be 350 bytes. We will fit nine buffers per page (each buffer will be 350 plus 70 rounded up to a total of 424 bytes). The small messages will still require one buffer and the large messages will still require two buffers each. However, we will waste much less space per buffer. We could increase the buffer size to fully utilize the page, but if this space was never used because of our actual message sizes, this would not alter our space utilization at the buffer level

You should always use a trace rather than guess what message sizes to use and how many of each size should be provided. Note that any applications employing *definite response* (DR protocol) have messages you may not be aware of. For each message sent, the DR application is given a tiny 29 byte message saying that the previous message was received. These messages can account for 50% of your message traffic! If DR protocol is being used, you must consider the 29 byte messages in determining your buffer utilization, and in forecasting the number of buffers required. This is also a good reason to reevaluate the use of DR protocol.

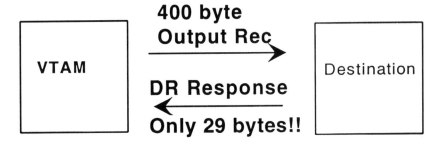

Figure 13.8 LFBUF Utilization and DR

13.5.7   D NET,BFRUSE Output Explained

The D NET, BFRUSE command is one of the native VTAM ways to get tuning information on the status of the various VTAM buffer pools. The output consists of one set of IST920I through IST924I messages for each buffer pool. These statistics are followed by current and maximum storage requirements for SGA and private storage.

Let us look at sample console output from this command, and see what we can determine about VTAM performance. Figure 13.9 contains sample output for the LFBUF pool, plus the storage statistics.

```
IST097I DISPLAY ACCEPTED
IST350I DISPLAY TYPE = BUFFER POOL DATA
IST920I LF      BUFF SIZE   00343       EXP INCREMENT    00027
IST921I         TIMES EXP   0000000248  EXP/CONT THRESH 00003/*N/A*
IST922I         CURR TOTAL  0000000064  CURR AVAILABLE   0000000049
IST923I         MAX TOTAL   0000000428  MAX USED         0000000016
IST924I --------------------------------------------------------------
IST449I SGALIMIT = NO LIMIT, CURRENT = 0000359K, MAXIMUM = 0000359K
IST790I MAXIMUM SGA USED = 0000359K
IST595I IRNLIMIT = NO LIMIT, CURRENT = 0000000K, MAXIMUM = 0000000K
IST981I VTAM PRIVATE: CURRENT = 0001342K, MAXIMUM USED = 1342K
IST314I END
```

Figure 13.9 LFBUF BFRUSE Statistics

The IST920I through IST924I messages are repeated once for each type of buffer pool. The most important value displayed is the count of buffer pool expansions. This is the "TIMES EXP" item in the IST921I message output. If the buffer pool experiences any appreciable number of expansions, then you should consider a larger initial allocation. If you do not think you can afford allocating the space initially, you should consider increasing the expansion *xpanno* value to reduce the number of expansions that are required to reach the "MAX USED" buffer count.

The "MAX TOTAL" item in the IST923I message is the largest number of buffers ever allocated, including any due to buffer pool expansion. The "MAX USED" item in the IST923I message output is the number of buffers required to prevent any expansion of the buffer pool. The "CURR TOTAL" and "CURR AVAILABLE" items in the IST922I message are the current allocated and available counts. These numbers do not reflect any expansion buffers that were later reclaimed.

Note that the LFBUF BUFF SIZE value displayed may be incorrect. Most VTAM releases have incorrectly computed the actual buffer size for the display. Old VTAM used a prefix of 55 bytes, and the BUF SIZE value displayed was computed incorrectly using that value rather than the correct prefix size of 70 bytes. You should always take your specified LFBUF BUFF SIZE value and add 70 bytes then round up to a doubleword to determine your actual buffer space requirement.

13.5.8   MAXBFRU Parameters

Use the MAXBFRU parameter to define the number of buffers VTAM is to allocate for an NCP, a SNA physical unit, or a CTCA. This parameter is coded on the NCP host definition statement to define the number of buffers VTAM is to allocate for the NCP. The MAXBFRU parameter may be coded on the SNA major node physical unit definition statement to specify the number of buffers VTAM is to reserve to receive data from that PU. Code the MAXBFRU parameter on the channel-attachment major node LINE definition statement to specify the number of 4K pages VTAM is to allocate for data transfers across CTCAs connecting VTAM systems.

This parameter specifies the number of VTAM buffers to be used for each data transfer from NCP. It is also the number of buffers that must be available to perform a data transfer. You must always specify MAXBFRU as smaller than the *baseno* value for the LFBUF pool. You should define the IOBUF *bufsz* value the same as the UNITSZ parameter.

The MAXBFRU parameter is a tool that allows you to reserve resources to ensure that a critical path is serviced. It may also be used to detune a less important path to ensure that VTAM is available for higher priority work. The MAXBFRU parameters are also a tool that may be used to control the total bufferspace required by VTAM.

The MAXBFRU value should be increased when the TNSTAT RDATN count is observed to be large. Refer to the VTAM I/O tuning section for information on getting TNSTAT information. If MAXBFRU is increased then you may also need to increase the LFBUF *baseno* value.

13.5.9   UNITSZ Parameter

The UNITSZ parameter specifies the size of the VTAM I/O buffers. Use this value to determine the amount of data that can be transferred in a single request. You should specify the LFBUF *bufsize* value to be the same as your UNITSZ value. VTAM does not enforce this, and it needs to be manually done by you, each time that you alter the UNITSZ specification. Figure 13.10 illustrates the relationship of UNITSZ to message size.

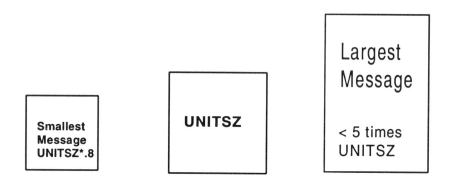

Figure 13.10 UNITSZ Specification

If storage is not at a premium, then the best performance can be gained by setting UNITSZ to the size of the largest message usually transferred by your network. For terminal networks, the inbound messages are usually small, and the outbound messages are much larger. Inbound messages from a terminal are normally restricted to the modified data on a screen. Outbound messages are usually complete screens. If you do not have a tool that enables you to determine the size of your outbound messages, 20 percent over your screen data size is a good estimate.

When storage is constrained, a different procedure should be used to select UNITSZ. If your inbound message and outbound messages are usually of the same length, then you should specify UNITSZ equal to your message length. If your inbound messages are not the same length as your outbound messages, then you should code UNITSZ to be a little larger than the smaller message. You should ensure that UNITSZ is not so small that more than five to seven buffers would be needed to transfer the larger message. Another way to express this is that UNITSZ should be larger than the smaller message but not less than 15 percent of the larger message size.

13.5.10 INBFRS Specification

The INBFRS parameter is coded on the host definition statement. It specifies the number of buffers used by NCP to receive data from the host. The suggested value is such that typical messages fit within a single buffer. If multiple messages are queued at a single time, then the value should be large enough to hold all messages.

If NCP storage is constrained, then enough storage to hold the typical message must be reserved, or outbound delays may be encountered. If you determine that outbound traffic is the source of most of your network delays, then the INBFRS value must be increased to enable NCP to run more efficiently.

13.5.11 Storage Management Trace

The VTAM storage management (SMS) trace collects information on VTAM's buffer usage, including what buffers are used in what pools, plus the number of buffer expansions and contractions. The Storage Management trace is enabled via the command TRACE TYPE=SMS,ID=VTAMBUF. The information that is produced is similar to that of the D NET,BFRUSE command, but is available for subsequent processing by a program.

An SMS trace allows the chronology of storage usage to be viewed. All storage accesses are captured, in sequence, with the type and size of each storage request. This information allows you to identify *what* was happening when VTAM used more storage than anticipated.

Note that an SMS trace is expensive and should not be used except to analyze a performance problem's cause in a controlled environment. Response time numbers generated while the SMS trace is active should not be used because the trace usually greatly impacts VTAM thruput.

13.6   GETVIS and SVA

VTAM uses large amounts of GETVIS storage. It uses both System
GETVIS and partition GETVIS area storage. In this section we
look at why and when VTAM uses GETVIS storage. We are
interested in the steps we can take to control its use. System
GETVIS area storage is especially important as its usage increases
the size of the shared area, and correspondingly reduces the size of
the private area. VTAM also uses SVA storage. This is the first
area we will look at.

13.6.1   SVA Usage

Several VTAM modules are required to be placed in the SVA prior
to VTAM initialization. The $SVAVTM load list is used by
VSE/ESA to load these phases into the SVA. The $SVAVTM4 load
list is used by the VSE/SP 4.1.2 Release. These SVA resident
modules permit an application program to survive an abend of the
VTAM partition. Refer to Figure 13.11 for the effect of a load list.

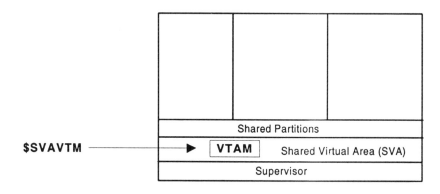

Figure 13.11 $SVAVTM Load List

13.6.2   System GETVIS Usage

When VTAM runs in a private partition, various information must
be in the shared area. VTAM places control blocks and code in the

System GETVIS area of VSE for this purpose. Observations of VTAM systems show that system storage typically ranges from 300KB to 500KB or more. Thus, System GETVIS usage is a significant factor for VTAM tuning.

Because any storage that is part of the System GETVIS area reduces the size of the private area, you may find it desirable to tradeoff a reduction in VTAM storage use with an increase in the size of the private area. You should be aware of when and why VTAM uses System GETVIS area storage. The prior section on buffer pools identified those pools allocated from the System GETVIS area.

VTAM refers to System Getvis Area memory as *SGA* storage. The SGALIMIT parameter is used to specify the maximum amount of SGA storage that VTAM can use. SGALIMIT is a VTAM start option, and may also be altered while VTAM is running. The maximum amount of SGA used since VTAM was initialized may be displayed via the D NET,BFRUSE command. If the SGALIMIT value is reached, the results can be unpredictable. Observed results can include the following:

• VTAM is unable to create new messages.

• VTAM cannot expand SGA buffers (including LPBUF, SFBUF, WPBUF). This may impact performance with no indication.

• VTAM may hang.

This last possibility needs to be avoided. The SGALIMIT value must be altered in connection with other VTAM buffer control values to ensure that nothing *bad* can happen. Because the VSE/ESA operating system will not function when SGA storage is exhausted, the VTAM SGALIMIT value should always be specified.

13.6.3 Partition GETVIS Usage

VTAM maintains all information that is not accessed by both the VTAM partition and the application partition in its partition. This includes the physical I/O buffers (LFBUF storage) used for all VTAM data transfers. VTAM requires both pageable and fixable storage in the partition area.

One way to control VTAM is to reduce the amount of available partition GETVIS storage. VTAM does not attempt to use more GETVIS than is provided. However, VTAM performance generally suffers whenever it is constrained by partition GETVIS. VTAM should not be restricted by GETVIS unless you intend to delay network processing so that additional batch capacity is available.

VSE/ESA permits VTAM to run in the private area, and total virtual storage is not usually a limiting factor for the VTAM GETVIS area size. Running VTAM in the private area does not impact performance. If real storage constraints do not result in paging, overallocate the VTAM partition GETVIS area. This provides ample space to tune buffer pool sizes.

VTAM is able to use partition GETVIS space for all of its partition storage needs. The best way to start VTAM is via the following EXEC statement:

```
// EXEC PGM=ISTINCVT,SIZE=ISTINCVT
```

All available partition storage is allocated as partition GETVIS area. VTAM will use partition GETVIS space to load the remainder of the VTAM programs at startup. Any extra program area storage is not used by VTAM. When VTAM is started in this fashion, it is impossible to over allocate the program area.

13.7   VTAM I/O Tuning

VTAM uses channel programs to read and write all data passed by it to, or received by it from the outside world. Each read request issued by your application may involve multiple read operations on the part of VTAM. The amount of data passed by each individual read operation is dependent on the number of buffers used for a read channel program, and the size of each buffer.

In order to tune VTAM I/O operations, you must first gather tuning statistics. For VSE systems, this is done by specifying the TNSTAT start option (NOTNSTAT is the default). Tuning statistics are written to the trace file, and optionally may be displayed upon the operator console. If you want the statistics displayed at the operator console, then you should code TNSTAT,CNSL. You should periodically gather tuning statistics from your VTAM system. This is done to establish baseline values, so that trends can be observed before performance is impacted. You should also gather tuning statistics after each change to VTAM parameters. This will assist you in determining whether or not the desired effect has been achieved. A sample report for an SNA controller can be seen in Figure 13.12.

```
IST440I    TIME = 07431380    DATE = 91142      ID = 0D0-L
IST441I    DLRMAX = 1         CHWR = 178      CHRD = 135
IST442I    ATTN = 31          RDATN = 0       IPIU = 196
IST443I    OPIU = 180         RDBUF = 196    SLODN = 0
```

Figure 13.12 Tuning Statistics for SNA Control Unit

Let us look at each of the key data items included in the TNSTAT report.

ATTN   Number of times an attention interrupt caused a channel program to be issued. RDATN is included in this count.

CHRD   Read channel programs issued.

CHWR   Write channel programs issued.

DLRMAX   Maximum number of Dump-load-restart requests seen at one time. If this exceeds your DLRTCB specification, increase DLRTCB to at least equal DLRMAX to reduce waits within VTAM.

IPIU   Number of inbound PIUs received from this controller.

OPIU   Number of outbound PIUs sent to this controller.

RDATN   Number of attention interrupts included in the ending status of a prior read. The number of times VTAM completes a read, only to find that a new read is immediately required. A large **RDATN** value indicates that MAXBFRU should be increased.

RDBUF   Total number of input bytes used for read operations.

SLODN   VTAM maintains a count of the number of times a slowdown condition has occurred. This count is reported as the SLODN value. Any nonzero value is indicative of a potentially serious performance problem.

13.7.1 Coattailing

Coattailing is the process whereby VTAM transfers multiple messages in a single I/O operation. This occurs for reads when multiple messages are read without intervening attention interrupts, and by a single request. For write requests, coattailing occurs when VTAM is able to output multiple PIUs with a single I/O. Coattailing also occurs when inbound and outbound traffic happen simultaneously. In each of these cases CPU time is saved within the operating system, and within the VTAM partition. Coattailing is illustrated by Figure 13.13.

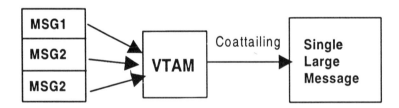

Figure 13.13 Write Coattailing

Coattailing can slow down response time if VTAM holds outbound PIUs for too long. Coattailing is directed by having VTAM wait until enough messages are available to exceed a count or if a timer is used to delay the start of a transfer. Of course, a small delay timer can actually improve response time by ensuring that VTAM does not tie up an I/O path with a single PIU when other PIUs will shortly be queued. A performance objective is to use coattailing to save CPU time for VTAM without negatively impacting response time.

Let us look at how VTAM accomplishes coattailing. VTAM batches PIUs into a single transfer until one of the following occurs:

- The channel delay time expires. This is controlled by the DELAY parameter at the device level. Different values may be specified for different channel attached devices. A suggested value is 0.2 seconds. This is small enough to not visibly impact response time, but large enough to ensure coattailing occurs once the I/O rate reaches fifteen (15) requests per second. Larger values increase the amount of coattailing at lower I/O rates but also may visibly affect response time.

- The PIU queue reaches its limit. The QDPTH tuning statistic is the number of PIUs transferred during the channel delay interval multiplied by 75 percent.

- A virtual route pacing request is seen.

- An attention interrupt from an NCP or SNA controller occurs.

- Data at transmission priority 2 is seen.

13.7.2   Tuning Using TNSTAT Data

Look at your TNSTAT output to determine the amount of coattailing that is occurring for individual control units. Divide the number of channel program requests by the number of PIUs to determine the average number of messages processed in a single I/O request. Compare CHRD to IPIU to determine inbound buffering and coattailing. If the ratio of IPIU divided by CHRD is larger than one, then significant input buffering is being performed. Compare CHWR to OPIU to determine outbound buffering and coattailing. If the ratio of OPIU divided by CHWR is larger than one, then significant output buffering is occurring.

$$IPIU/CHRD>1 \Rightarrow inputCoatTailing$$

Equation 9 Input Coattailing Efficiency

$$OPIU/CHWR > 1 \Rightarrow OutputCoattailing$$

Equation 10 Output Coattailing Efficiency

The RDBUF value is an indication of how efficiently you are using the available input buffer space. Divide RDBUF by IPIU to estimate your average message size. It is desirable for an integral number of messages to fit in each buffer. If the buffer size is larger than the space needed for the average number of messages read in a single request, then your bufferspace is under utilized. The RDATN value gives an indication of how much additional inbound coattailing might be possible by increasing the size and/or number of input buffers.

The SLODN value is the number of times the control unit entered slowdown mode. For NCP, this is the number of times the CWALL buffer threshold was exceeded. A nonzero value indicates that response time was impacted. Any significant value indicates a problem that may be corrected by increasing the number of buffers.

13.7.3   Line and PU Performance

The performance of a line can be affected by capacity limits and by a number of parameters. A line that is at capacity is a performance bottleneck that can only be removed by changing the line. Thus, a fully loaded 9600 baud line will need to be upgraded. Note that a line is considered to be fully loaded at less than 100% utilization. A 9600 baud line is nominally capable of transferring over 1000 characters per second, but is at capacity well below that point. In general, a line is good for 60 percent of its theoretical bandwidth. Queuing theory models show that significant traffic delays begin over 60 percent utilization.

The parameters influencing the performance of lines and physical units include MAXDATA, MAXOUT, PASSLIM, PAUSE, RETRIES, and SERVLIM. We will briefly discuss each of these parameters.

MAXDATA determines the number of bytes per PIU or PIU segment that are sent to the device. This value is dependent on the type of device. MAXDATA should be similar to the INBFRS value.

MAXOUT is the maximum number of PIU's that can be transferred before the PIU must respond. Too small a value increases overhead similar to the way pacing does. Too large a value impacts transfers to other PU's on the same line.

PASSLIM specifies the maximum number of PIU's that can be sent before going to the next PIU on the line. Too large a value impacts other PU's on the line. Too small a value can greatly impact thruput.

PAUSE determines the minimum time that each entry can be serviced. Too small a value causes increased NCP overhead. Too large a value impacts other PIU's on the same line.

RETRIES defines the maximum number of retries and the time spent in retry for each line. Too small a value can cause a unit to be removed from service even though its error could have been recovered. Too large a value impacts all other PIU's on the same line when error recovery is required. This is an often overlooked parameter. If you encounter many errors, you should review the RETRIES specification.

SERVLIM specifies how many passes NCP should make through the service table before performing special services. This value is not usually critical.

13.7.4 LU Performance

In this section we will briefly look at several of the factors affecting LU performance. We will discuss the BATCH, PACING, and VPACING parameters.

BATCH determines the raw priority of an LU. All LU's specified as BATCH=NO will be allowed to send data before any specified as BATCH=YES. Specify BATCH=YES when a delay would not negatively impact LU performance, and could help it, or when the device is of less importance.

PACING controls transfers from NCP to LU's. PACING determines how long the LU can hold a line. Specify the number of PIU's that can be sent before the LU must respond with a pacing indicator. PACING is used to prevent a busy PU from swamping all other LU's. One example of where you will want to use pacing is a PC file transfer. PC file transfers can totally monopolize a line for the duration of a transfer. Specify pacing to ensure other LU's receive their fair share.

VPACING is the parameter controlling pacing from VTAM to NCP. It is required to prevent transfers to a slow device from occupying most available NCP buffers. When multiple NCP's are present in a transmission path, VPACING may be required to prevent swamping the whole path.

13.7.5   Control Unit Performance

Individual control units can also be tuned. This is done at the VTAM level, and also at the control unit level. The MAXBFRU option discussed above is one example of a VTAM option related to the performance of an individual control unit.

The SLODN value in the TNSTAT output for a SNA control unit is an important indication of a bottleneck that needs to be addressed. A nonzero value indicates that NCP in the control unit ran out of buffers. The MAXBFRU values needs to be increased. This is the preferred tuning option. An alternative is to use session pacing to restrict the amount of data VTAM sends to the control unit at one time. Lower pacing values limit the number of PIUs sent at one time to the controller by VTAM.

VTAM determines the size of the RU used to transfer the NCP phase to, or the static dump from a 3720 or 3745 control unit. The default size is 512 bytes. For VM, you may code the NCPBUFSZ parameter as either 1024 or 2048 to improve the performance of these requests. VTAM also determines the size of an RU for a dynamic dump. VTAM always attempt to use 2048 bytes, if that fails it will fall back to a 256-byte size. You may ensure that dynamic dumps can use the 2KB size by verifying that all of the following are true:

- The SSP supports the 2KB size
- NCP supports the 2KB size
- The lines between VTAM and NCP support the 2KB size

13.8   Network Delay Sources

The term "Network Delay Sources" refers to all waits that occur outside the mainframe where VTAM is running. It includes front end processor delays, line delays, and delays occurring within nodes (including end user terminals).

An excellent tool for gathering information on the exact location of network delays is the VTAM trace facility. This trace tracks messages processed by VTAM through various points. The individual trace entries include timestamps that allow you to identify the amount of delay as a message flows through each segment of the network from an application to its destination.

Front-end processor delays are typically caused by too few NCP buffers or by a nonfailing mismatch in buffer sizes between VTAM and the NCP. Although some mismatches in buffer sizes result in a hard failure that is quickly noticed and corrected, some merely result in slower thruput than would be predicted. Many NCP performance problems result from running out of NCP storage or CPU cycles. The 3725 and 3745 control units are CPUs and can easily exhaust their local resources. When NCP delays are encountered you should check the following areas:

- Transmission group threshold
- Link session priority
- Buffer sizes
- Delay option (for data transmitted between NCP and VTAM)
- Pause settings
- Pacing options (for example: adaptive session pacing)

Delays within end-user devices occur for a variety of reasons. One recent example in a southeastern state involved a particularly poorly written LU 6.2 interface running on a PC. Several small changes to the PC interface code improved performance by a factor of almost five times.

The choice of 3270 board or SNA interface card for a PC can greatly affect thruput. You must also take care which emulation software you choose. For example, it is unwise to run IRMA for Windows on a 16MHz SX machine with only 2 Meg of memory. The standard DOS E78 emulation ran twice as fast on that same SX processor.

Also, how you configure your emulation software on the PC affects end-user device performance. Choosing all available options for the Attachmate emulation software increases memory usage and impacts performance with no benefit for the unused options.

An often overlooked source of VTAM network delays is a marginal component encountering a higher percentage of hardware errors than normal. A major performance problem in one shop was caused by a failing channel interface card that generated 900 errors in an hour. This problem was discovered only after attempts to tune all of the "obvious" delay sources failed.

One tool that can assist in identifying network components with problems is the IOINT start option. This option is coded as "IOINT=n" where "n" is the number of seconds VTAM will wait for a response to a request before issuing a message. Code "IOINT=0" to disable this feature. If omitted, the default is "IOINT=180." The minimum value is "IOINT=60." Any smaller non-zero value is rounded up to 60 seconds.

13.8.1   What is Response Time?

VTAM networks are often judged using response time numbers. Before we leap to the conclusion that response time is all VTAM, we should take a closer look at what response time is, and at its components. Response time is usually defined as the user perceived delay between making a request, and the request completion. For terminal systems this is the delay from pressing the ENTER key to seeing the output. This *response time* is made up of several components:

- Internal Application Time
- Input Delay Time
- Network Transit Time
- Terminal Display Time

Internal Application time is the amount of time spent within the application. This information is usually available from your CICS performance monitor, or other application tools. The Internal Application time can be the largest single portion of response time. This often occurs for SQL/DS applications, where a single SQL request can take anywhere from a few seconds to many minutes to perform.

The *Input Delay Time* is the time required for the input message to become available for processing. It is dependent on the poll delay, data line speed, and input message size. Because input messages are small, the most important factor to tune is the polling delay. Faster lines offer little benefit for small input messages.

Network Transit Time is the amount of time required to transfer the data through the network. It is equal to the VTAM reported Network Delay Time minus the Terminal Display time. The Network Delay time is easily determined for applications employing Definite Response.

Terminal Display Time is the time required to display the message on the output device. It is determined by the output message size, and by the data line speed. Output messages tend to be much larger than input messages and are the primary factor in determining a good data line speed. If output message traffic is such that the data line is heavily utilized then large sporadic delays will be encountered, especially when a wide range of message sizes is seen. This often occurs once line utilization exceeds 50 percent.

$$RT = IAT + IDT + NTT + TDT$$

Equation 11 Response Time Components

13.8.2   IBMTEST Command

IBMTEST is a "poor man's" VTAM diagnostic tool. When someone complains that CICS response time is poor, this command may be used to quickly determine whether the delay is in VTAM or in an application such as CICS.

The IBMTEST command may be entered at any terminal to the network solicitor (your VTAM terminal startup screen) to test for VTAM and network delays. When VTAM sees the IBMTEST command it responds by writing message number 11 (defined in the USSTAB) ten times. By observing the speed of writing this message you can estimate your VTAM and network performance. If these messages are written quickly, but CICS response time is poor, then CICS (rather than VTAM) is the probable cause of the performance problem. If the messages are written slowly, then the probable cause of the performance problem is VTAM.

The IBMTEST command can be used periodically to take the temperature of your VTAM network. This can enable you to identify problem areas before your users do. Of course, a network performance monitor is the preferred tool to exactly identify problem sources.

13.9   Priority/VTAM Waits

The priority of the VTAM partition is critical. In general, VTAM should be the highest priority partition or second after POWER.

Remember that any VTAM delays are translated into incremental delays for all VTAM services users. The VTAM partition should always have a higher priority than the application program partitions it services. VTAM can still be a POWER controlled partition while it has a higher priority than POWER; simply include the NPC parameter on the PSTART command for the VTAM partition.

The best procedure to follow in tuning VTAM is to monitor the sources of all delays in VTAM processing, and to address them in the following sequence:

1. Eliminate delays in VTAM partition being dispatched. Adjusting the priority of the VTAM partition falls here.

2. Reduce or eliminate VTAM internal waits for resources. VTAM internal buffer waits are in this category.

3. Reduce delays within the network. The NCP buffers are included within this group.

13.10 Paging

VTAM is affected by paging as is everything that runs under VSE. However, several factors make VTAM more often a cause of heavy paging than a victim of it. Most critical VTAM storage is fixed in real memory and does not encounter page faults. VTAM's variable demands upon real storage can cause heavy paging, as can the TFIX requests associated with I/O operations.

One easily controlled user of VTAM real storage is buffer pool expansion. Buffer pool expansion and contraction requires more real storage than a system not using this feature. Since expansion and contraction also require significant CPU, they should be reduced. Note that VTAM can hang or abend if a critical buffer pool is exhausted and it is unable to perform expansion.

Most VTAM pageable areas are referenced frequently enough that they stay in real storage. In a lightly loaded VTAM system, certain control blocks or buffers may become paged out, with resulting page requests when they are next referenced. This is normally not a concern since it only occurs in little used VTAM systems.

13.11 Running VTAM in Private

For VSE/ESA, VTAM is delivered running in a private address space. It should be left in private. Do not change VTAM to run in the shared area. The small amount of CPU time saved is more than compensated for by the reduction in the size of the maximum private area. Running VTAM in the shared area requires increasing SPSIZE by 3 megabytes, and thus reduces the maximum size of each private partition by 3MB. The reduction in the size of the private area typically impacts your ability to tune CICS and other large applications such as SQL/DS.

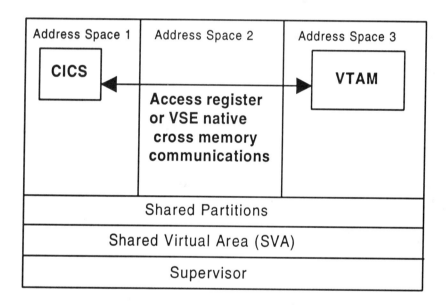

Figure 13.14 Running VTAM in Private

If you do choose to run VTAM in the shared area, it is critical that you check your buffer usage and adjust the size of all shared buffers. Refer to the section on VTAM buffer pool requirements above. Regardless of where VTAM is run, the following types of buffers are always allocated from the shared area:

CRPLBUF, LPBUF, SFBUF, WPBUF

The defaults for these buffers shipped with VSE/ESA 1.1 are typically too large. About 150K of shared area may be saved by a reduction to the corrected default values used with VSE/ESA 1.2. The VTAM 3.3 storage estimates diskette is a valuable tool available for your use in determining VTAM resource requirements.

13.12 LAN Considerations

Many VSE customers are attaching Local Area Networks (LANs) of PCs to their VSE systems using VTAM. LANs can represent a significant percentage of your total VTAM network load, and must be considered when performing resource allocation. The first rule is a simple one; a LAN is not a single device. A LAN is actually as many devices as PCs attached to the Local Area Network, and perhaps even more. If you treat a LAN as so many local devices, you will take a step in the right direction. However, LANs do not behave exactly the same as many "standard" VTAM local connections and have their own set of tuning tips and techniques.

Figure 13.15 below illustrates a small LAN of five nodes attached via a server to a 3174 owned by one system. The LAN is accessible to a second system attached via a CTCA. Activity on any one LAN node will impact the other LAN nodes as well, and may even effect the host systems. For example, a file transfer running from a System A application to any node could cripple the performance of the other four LAN nodes, plus impact all other System A to System B communications. Even something as simple as the submission of a large job or the transmission of a printout to a LAN node could have the same effect as the file transfer.

LFBUF thrashing is one area where special considerations apply. Thrashing is prevented by increasing the *baseno* value, or by adjusting the *xpanno* value to include an extra page of buffers. You should not count on the *xpanno* parameter for controlling thrashing for a token ring LAN. If your network contains many (40 or more) local PU 2 devices, then your only option to prevent LFBUF thrashing is to increase the *baseno* value. This problem commonly occurs for 3174 token ring gateway configurations.

File transfer operations also affect resource allocation for LAN attached devices. We frequently estimate message traffic based on the applications being used, the average user "think" time, and similar factors. A single file transfer can generate more message traffic than several days of typical application usage! A file

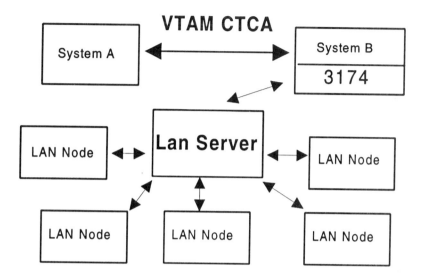

Figure 13.15 LAN Connections

transfer can also employ message sizes that were not anticipated when your buffer size specification was made. If file transfers are a part of your LAN use, you should perform measurements during a typical file transfer to choose better buffer size, *baseno*, and *xpanno* values.

When file transfer operations occur frequently, then sporadic cases of long response time can be seen. These are caused by buffer exhaustion, line capacity over utilization, LAN server congestion, etc. If a single function (such as a file transfer) uses most of the available buffers, than all other users will wait, and **very** long delays can be seen. If a file transfer uses a large percentage of the available line bandwidth, then all other network activity will be seen to slow down. When a file transfer swamps the LAN server then large sporadic delays will be common. Alleviating one of these bottlenecks will often have little effect as another area of contention surfaces when the first is corrected. In this case, leave the first performance fix in place, and continue tuning until improved performance is observed.

Chapter

14

DASD Sharing Tuning

This chapter presents tuning issues specific to the *Shared DASD environment* (controlled by the DASDSHR IPL parameter). Although DASDSHR environment issues are briefly discussed with each relevant VSE component, they are also gathered together in this chapter, and additional detail on tuning the shared DASD environment is included.

If you are not running a Shared DASD environment, this chapter does not apply to your shop. If DASDSHR=NO is specified, or you do not define any DASD with the ,SHR parameter on the IPL ADD statement, then you are not running a DASDSHR environment. If you are considering running DASDSHR=YES, read this chapter first in order to understand the costs of the shared DASD environment.

14.1 Cookbook for Tuning Shared DASD

- Do not run DASDSHR=YES unless needed.

- Use a dedicated volume on a dedicated path for the best lock file performance. Do not put high use files with the lock file.

- Do not specify ,SHR for a DASD unless it is actually shared. If not used at the same time, the DASD may not need to be ADDed with the ,SHR parameter.

- Do not share libraries unless needed. Avoid updating sharing libraries if at all possible.

- Consider POWER PNET as a better performing alternative to the use of shared POWER spool.

- Consider the use of a product to improve the efficiency of the VSE lock manager. Two such products are VM/Magic and Extend/VSE.

14.2 Lock File

VSE incorporates a central resource *lock manager*. All VSE components use *resource enqueues* to protect operating system resources from simultaneous access and update. The lock manager is responsible for tracking these enqueues. Resources enqueued include system control blocks, programs, and DASD based resources. In a nonshared environment, all lock information is maintained in storage resident control blocks. This *lock table* information is dynamically allocated from within the System GETVIS area.

In a Shared DASD environment any lock information about shared DASD resources must be available across CPUs. The lock manager writes such information into a special file called the *lock file*. The lock file is the source of all performance issues encountered in a DASDSHR=YES environment. Figure 14.1 illustrates the use of the external lock file in a DASDSHR=YES environment.

14.2.1 Placement

The VSE lock file is one of the highest use files in a VSE system. This file should be placed on a low use DASD, and care should be taken to ensure that the path to that DASD is not heavily loaded. Also, other heavy use files should be placed on other channel paths rather than that for the lock file.

The lock file cannot take advantage of multiple channel paths. It is critical that its one path be a low use path. When more than two VSE systems share the same DASD, they also share the same

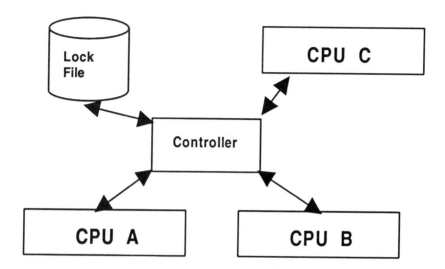

Figure 14.1 VSE Lock File

lock file. Each additional VSE system adds lock file I/O requests.

In a VM environment, the lock file can be placed on a small minidisk containing only that file. This option is only available when all VSE systems sharing the same lock file all run under the same VM system. If a mixed VM and VSE DASD sharing environment is used, then the lock file must occupy a real DASD.

14.2.2 Hardware Reserve

The VSE lock manager uses the DASD RESERVE/RELEASE commands to serialize access to the VSE lock file. This is the only DASD volume for which hardware RESERVE/RELEASE is used by VSE/SP and VSE/ESA. This is important because the hardware RESERVE/RELEASE facility severely impacts performance wherever it is used.

To understand this performance issue, let us look at what the hardware RESERVE facility does. The RESERVE command is issued for a DASD volume and locks the entire volume from access by all other CPUs until a RELEASE command is issued. Note that the volume level lockout stays in effect until a corresponding RELEASE command is issued by the originating CPU. This means that using RESERVE to lockout access to a small file actually locks

ALL access to ALL files on the designated volume. This is another reason why the user must be very careful where they place the lock file. Because of the large number of accesses to the lock file, the lock file volume will be unavailable for other CPUs to access a high percentage of the time.

Some disk and tape managers employ hardware reserve for their catalogs. It is critical that tape and disk manager catalogs not be placed on the same volume as the VSE lock file. A serious performance impact can occur if both of these high use files are accidently defined on the same volume.

14.3   Use of ,SHR

VSE does not unconditionally use the lock file for all lock requests. In general, lock requests for memory resident resources are never reflected in the lock file. Also, lock requests for DASD resources are not always reflected in the lock file. Only locks for resources on DASD designated as shared are written in the lock file. You designate DASD as shared via the ,SHR parameter of the IPL ADD statement.

If ,SHR is present, then all locks for that DASD are also entered into the lock file. If ,SHR is not present, then no locks for that DASD are entered into the lock file. If a DASD is really being shared (is being accessed at the same time by multiple systems), then the ,SHR parameter must be specified.

If a DASD is not shared, then it should not include the ,SHR parameter. If a DASD contains information used by several systems, and you know that this information is never used at the same time, then the DASD may not need to be specified with the ,SHR parameter. For example, if one system runs a production CICS that updates VSAM files, and these VSAM files are accessed by another system when CICS is down, then the DASD containing these VSAM files need not be ,SHR.

14.4   Tuning Different Types of Shared VSE Data

The general rule for tuning shared files is to not share anything unless it is necessary that it be shared. VSE file sharing overhead is associated with the ,SHR parameter of a DASD volume. This means that files that are not shared should be defined upon DASD without the ,SHR parameter. Thus, pools of VSAM workspace should be defined local to each CPU, as should system workfiles and log files.

We will look at the characteristics of a number of types of VSE files in detail in the remainder of this section. We look at why files are shared, how often lock file requests occur, the relative cost of the lock file I/Os, and alternatives to the use of shared DASD for each type of file.

14.4.1 POWER Sharing

Shared POWER is one of the common reasons that DASD is shared. This is done to allow jobs submitted on one system to be run in available partitions of another system. It is also used to create printed matter on one system, and to output it to a printer on another system. Shared POWER also facilitates central management of a group of shared VSE systems.

POWER sharing can be somewhat expensive. When POWER RJE (PNET) can be used to accomplish the same objectives, it should be considered as an alternative to shared POWER. PNET is attractive when small amounts of data are transferred between POWER systems. If large reports must be routed between systems, PNET is usually not a good choice.

Even if the QFILE is shared between VSE system, the POWER account file does not need to be shared. The cost of shared POWER can be reduced by not sharing the account file. Most job accounting software allows multiple POWER account files to be merged. Therefore a shared POWER account file is not a requirement for combined reporting of accounting information.

14.4.2 Shared VSAM Catalogs, Datasets

VSAM catalogs and datasets can be shared across systems. A shared VSAM catalog allows easy access and update across systems to all files within that catalog. Shared VSAM also allows the user to implement a shared pool of DASD space across systems. SAM managed VSAM allows work files to occupy shared space across

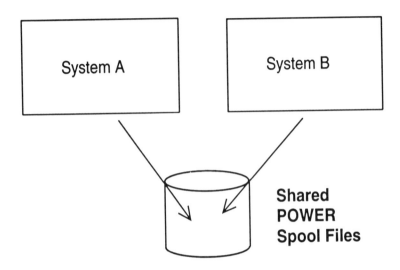

Figure 14.2 POWER Sharing

systems. This can result in less total space than if separate pools were maintained for each system.

In general, the VSAM catalog should be shared if any catalog updates will occur at the same time on both systems. If catalog updates will not occur simultaneously, then the DASD should not be defined as shared. The cost of sharing a VSAM catalog is not high unless a large amount of file definitions, alterations, or deletions occur. If this type of catalog activity occurs often, then the number of I/Os to process a shared VSAM catalog can easily be double the I/Os for the unshared case. For this reason, shared SAM managed VSAM workspace is usually undesirable.

One simple tuning technique is to define separate user catalogs for each system in a shared DASD environment. These catalogs should not be shared. This allows all DASD owned by these catalogs to be defined without ,SHR and avoids the large lock file overhead. The use of separate user catalogs also reduces contention between the systems.

VSAM files should never be shared across systems. At this time, share option 4 is not supported across most VSE systems. Even where this option is supported, its performance can be unacceptable, and the additional lock file load impacts all other VSE lock file users.

With VSE/VSAM in VSE/ESA 1.2, share option 4 across CPUs is now supported, but should be used carefully, and its performance evaluated against the need to share the file for update on multiple processors. Share option 4 across CPUs results in several lock file I/Os for each update request. This performance impact is usually too large for most applications to tolerate.

14.4.3 Shared Libraries

VSE libraries may be shared across systems. All functions are available in a DASDSHR environment. Performance of updates is severely impacted. For example, cataloging a library member can require ten times as much I/O if the library is defined as ,SHR.

The performance cost of shared libraries is a result of the way the librarian performs locks. Each time a new block or group of blocks is allocated, the librarian locks the library. In a nonshared environment, these locks occur within processor tables and do not visibly impact performance. In a shared environment, these lock requests require far more I/O requests than the actual allocate does. Because the lock occurs at the library level, access to anything within the same library (even in different directories) is impacted.

Similar performance problems occur for directory updates. In the case of directory updates, the lock requests are at the directory level. These serialize write accesses within the same directory, but do not delay accesses of other directories.

A library is shared if the first extent of the library is defined on a DASD with the ,SHR parameter. If a library is updated by multiple systems at the same time, then it must be defined as shared. If a library is not updated on multiple systems, then it is not required that the DASD be defined as shared.

The best way to tune libraries is to *not share them*. If you must share libraries, then ensuring these libraries are not fragmented is even more important than in a non-shared environment. Unfortunately, it is usually more difficult to reorganize a library in a shared environment. The librarian will not delete a library that is LIBDEFed or being shared between two or more processors.

14.4.4 Shared VTOCs

If the Volume Table of Contents (VTOC) of a DASD will be updated by multiple systems then the DASD must be defined with the ,SHR parameter. If you can ensure that VTOC updates do not occur on multiple systems at the same time, then you do not need to define the DASD as shared.

If a DASD is defined as shared then all VTOC updates are serialized via lock requests. This means that twice as many I/Os will be required for many VTOC operations on a shared DASD. This is the basic minimum overhead of shared DASD. Any access method or user specific lock file overhead is added to the VTOC overhead.

You should consider restricting file creation and deletion to a single system per DASD to allow defining DASD as unshared. One way to accomplish this objective is to reserve DASD for specific systems. This allows the DASD to be defined as unshared, and also improves performance by reducing contention between systems. When DASD is used by only a single system, no other systems should include the definition of the disk. Omitting the definition ensures that accidental sharing is impossible.

If you do not define a DASD as shared but actually do update the VTOC on two systems at the same time, serious problems can result. You can lose the VTOC entry for a file, or in certain cases can even define two files occupying the same DASD space. Frequent volume backups are desirable in a shared DASD environment. The risk of accidental file damage is eliminated by defining all unshared DASD only on the system that owns them. If you must define the DASD on several systems, it usually should be defined as shared.

15

Tuning VSE Utilities

This chapter looks at tuning considerations for various VSE system utilities, plus certain other frequently encountered programs. The IBM manual *VSE/ESA: System Utilities* (SC33-6517) is a reference for many of the IBM supplied VSE system basic utilities.

15.1 General

Tuning utility programs is no different from tuning regular applications. We discuss certain programs here and include specific tuning actions to save you time in developing these rules empirically. In general, if a program is frequently used, consumes large amounts of resources when it is used, or is a known bottleneck during a key production period, it is worth special attention. Many utilities fall into one of these groups.

15.2 Sort

The SORT utility is used to read one or more input files and place the records into an other than current sequence. SORT utilities offer a merge option which allows multiple input files, already in a desired sequence, to be merged into a single large file in the same sequence. Sort utilities support tape or disk input, and tape or disk output. They also require intermediate work files.

Sort utilities have two basic sections. The first phase reads the input file(s) and builds strings of sorted records. The second phase merges the strings, and is called the internal merge phase. The last merge step of the second phase usually writes the output file, or passes the output back to the calling program for internal or "own code" sorts. The number of merge passes is a major factor in determining how long a sort will take. The amount of storage available to the sort utility determines the number of merge passes.

SORT makes use of program area workspace. It can efficiently use large amounts of virtual storage. If your environment does not encounter paging problems you should consider running with as large a SIZE parameter as possible. Small increases in size value result in very large savings in elapsed execution time. Increasing the size of the intermediate sorted strings produced by the input phase of a sort reduces the number of internal merge passes.

Sort I/O is fairly efficient with little room for tuning by the user. You may wish to review the installation options of your sort package for any product specific special buffering options for this portion of the sort process. CASORT and SYNCSORT are examples of SORT products with a variety of tuning options of their own.

The intermediate portion of the sort is where the bulk of the work for a sort operation takes place. In this step, the data is merged within the intermediate work files. You should define work files spread over volumes with different paths. The more work files. the better for sort operations. You should allocate up to one work file per available path, with a minimum of three work files.

The SORT program can be invoked from within an application program. COBOL includes an extensive facility allowing you to develop applications that read the input for SORT, and also handle output of the final sorted data. When a program invokes SORT, a pass at the data can often be eliminated. For this reason, many programs invoke sort. However, SORT uses optimized I/O handling that results in faster standalone sorts. Standalone sorts have access to all partition resources, not just what is left over by a COBOL application. Separate SORT steps have been seen to finish in one tenth of the time of a SORT called by COBOL. Of course, all COBOL invoked SORTs are not bad, and testing is needed to determine what SORT option is best in a specific environment.

15.3 COBOL and Other Compilers

The COBOL compiler translates COBOL source programs into machine language. COBOL reads a card image source program, optionally merges in program source from one or more VSE source libraries, and outputs a text file.

The work files used by COBOL include IJSYS01, IJSYS02, IJSYS03, and IJSYS04. The first two files are the most important and should be placed on the fastest DASD when possible. These files are good candidates for SAM managed VSAM.

COBOL uses program area virtual storage for workspace. A suggested SIZE= value is a minimum of SIZE=256KB. No dynamic GETVIS storage beyond that required for SAM managed VSAM is used. COBOL II can make use of large amounts of virtual storage resulting in improved performance in a non-storage constrained environment.

COBOL compiles are frequently *very* CPU intensive. Thus, it is a good idea to run them in a low-priority partition. The compiler also can have a fairly large working set for large programs. It is a good idea to run it in reduced virtual storage when it is run at a low priority. This will reduce wide swings in paging that could occur when a COBOL compile is restarted after waiting for the CPU to become available.

The CBL BUFSIZE option allows you to determine the size of the compiler buffers. COBOL was designed to run in partitions far smaller than those typically encountered in a VSE/ESA system. Its default buffers are smaller than optimum. Refer to your COBOL manual and select a larger BUFSIZE value appropriate to your environment.

Care should be taken with the LIBDEF SOURCE SEARCH chain to ensure that COBOL does not have to search through many directories when expanding COPY statements. Although the librarian SPI uses several buffers, the number of I/Os spent reading VSE library directories can be a significant percentage of the total COBOL I/Os.

15.4 Assembler

The assembler is used to translate Basic Assembly Language (BAL) programs into machine language and produce a text file. The name

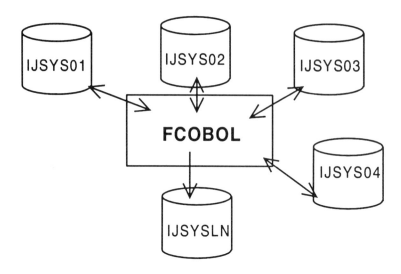

Figure 15.1 Compiler Work Files

of the assembler program is ASSEMBLY. Refer to Figure 15.2 for
an illustration of the functioning of the ASSEMBLY program.

The input to the assembler is a card image file. Additional input
can be provided from VSE libraries as copy members and as
macros. The assembler uses three work files. These are IJSYS01,
IJSYS02, and IJSYS03.

Care should be taken with the LIBDEF SOURCE SEARCH chain
to ensure the assembler does not have to search through directories
with no data of interest. Although the assembler optimizes macro
accesses, the total number of I/Os spent reading VSE library
directories is often a significant percent of the total required for an
assembly.

The work files should be defined on three different DASD devices
if possible. These files can be very efficient when defined as SAM
managed VSAM files. You should specify a large bufferspace for
the IJSYS01 and IJSYS02 files.

The assembler uses program area storage for workspace.
Therefore, it should be executed with an explicit size parameter.
A suggested value is SIZE=256KB as a minimum. No dynamic
usage of GETVIS is made except for SAM managed VSAM files.

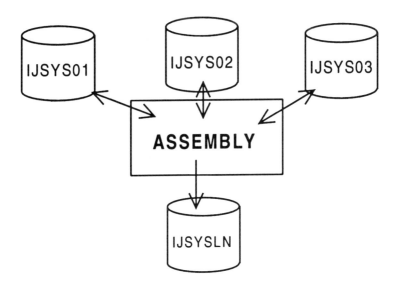

Figure 15.2 Assembler Work Files

15.5 Linkage Editor

The linkage editor is used to combine the output of a compiler or
assembler with IBM and vendor provided text files to build an
executable phase. As such, the linkage editor is one of the more
frequently used programs in many shops. Refer to Figure 15.3 for
an illustration of the LNKEDT program and its work files.

The input to the linkage editor is read from SYSIPT by job
control and written to the IJSYSLN file. The linkage editor makes
use of one work file named IJSYS01. The linkage editor also reads
text input from libraries and writes an executable phase into a
library.

Normally the amount of I/O to IJSYS01 is too small to be of
much concern. Also, the amount of I/O to IJSYSLN is usually
small. However, both of these files can be important to
performance. The amount of time required to initialize, create, and
delete them is often a major percent of the entire linkedit process.
You should employ options provided by your disk manager (or SAM
managed VSAM) to optimize the management of these files. Goal

System's FLEE product handles the linkage edit process in an especially efficient fashion. The CA/Dynam disk manager can also be used to manage the linkage edit work files in virtual storage, with a large savings.

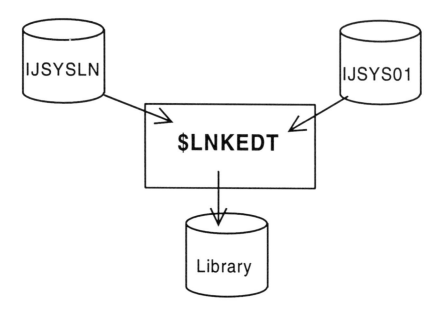

Figure 15.3 $LNKEDT Work Files

15.6 LIBR

The LIBR utility is the batch interface used to define, catalog, alter, and delete VSE libraries, sublibraries, and directories. The program name is LIBR and the utility is provided in the IJSYSRS.SYSLIB library.

The most important tuning option available for LIBR is virtual storage. LIBR will take advantage of additional partition GETVIS space for buffers. You should ensure that LIBR is run with at least 256KB of GETVIS space. This is done by always supplying a SIZE= parameter on the execute statement for LIBR.

15.7 IDCAMS

IDCAMS is the VSAM batch utility. It is used to define catalogs, VSAM data spaces, and VSAM files. IDCAMS is also a general purpose VSAM file move utility, and will move data from sequential to VSAM or from VSAM to sequential files. IDCAMS is often encountered as part of production jobstreams.

The IDCAMS program is best executed with a SIZE=IDCAMS parameter because it uses GETVIS storage for its processing. IDCAMS makes no use of program area storage, and any additional program storage allocated to it is wasted. The SIZE=AUTO option should be avoided because many larger programs with the same first four characters are present in IJSYSRS.SYSLIB along with the IDCAMS phase.

IDCAMS uses normal VSAM processing for any VSAM files it accesses. You may employ normal VSAM tuning options for these VSAM files, and IDCAMS can benefit as would any other program. Note that special IDCAMS buffering options are also provided to improve the performance of files read or written by IDCAMS.

15.8 FASTCOPY and FCOPY

The FASTCOPY program is a standalone volume-level disk-copy utility. It permits the entire contents of a DASD to be copied to tape or to another DASD of the same type. Standard labeled tapes are supported by FASTCOPY. The utility operates in two basic modes. It will copy all datasets listed in the VTOC, or perform a full volume copy where each track is read and copied without regard to any VTOC indication as to the track belonging to a dataset.

The FCOPY form of the utility may be executed in a partition under the control of VSE, while the FASTCOPY utility may be run in a standalone mode where it is IPLed. The VSE partition mode uses a program name of FCOPY (FCOPYFB for FBA DASD). See Figure 15.4 for a CKD utility example jobstream. The FCOPY utility allows single datasets to be copied in addition to whole volumes. (Whole volume is the only option for the standalone form of the utility.) The standalone mode may be used to restore a system residence volume that has been corrupted, or when a usable VSE system is not available. When operated in the standalone mode, FASTCOPY receives its commands from the system console. The FASTCOPY program may be customized via the CUSTABLE to reduce the number of messages, or to eliminate totally, this console traffic.

IBM supports the **OPTIMIZE** parameter for FCOPY and FCOPYFB to allow performance tuning of the fast copy utility. This option is supported for ECKD and FBA DASD and for those CKD DASD that implement *Read Full Track*. The Read Full TTrack command directs the control unit to read all records on a track. The effect of the OPTIMIZE parameter is different for each type of DASD. In all cases, this parameter is coded as OPTIMIZE=n, where "n" is a number (the default is 1).

For CKD DASD, the OPTIMIZE value determines the number of tracks of data read with a single I/O request. This also effects the size of the buffer used for the request, so additional storage is required for larger values. A value of OPTIMIZE=3 or OPTIMIZE=4 is suggested for the best possible performance. Note that additional real memory is required to support the larger buffers used by larger OPTIMIZE parameter values. Refer to Figure 15.4 for an example of how to invoke FCOPY with the OPTIMIZE parameter.

```
// JOB FCOPY
/* Example of FCOPY with OPTIMIZE parameter
// ASSGN SYS004,1C2    Input DASD
// ASSGN SYS005,284    Output TAPE
// EXEC FCOPY
DUMP VOLUME NOREWIND OPTIMIZE=3
/*
/&
```

Figure 15.4 CKD FCOPY Example

With the OPTIMIZE parameter, *bigger is not always better*. If you have DASD caching control units the best option is usually OPTIMIZE=1. When an OPTIMIZE value of two or greater is coded than cache load is disabled by FCOPY. Note that the OPTIMIZE parameter has no effect unless the DASD control unit supports the READ TRACK command.

For FBA DASD, the OPTIMIZE value determines the size of the tape buffer to be used. The default value of OPTIMIZE=1 results in a small buffer of 16KB to be used. For a backup operation, larger optimize values reduce the number of reels of tape required, reduce wear and tear of the tape drive, and improve the performance of the request. The value specified determines the number of 16KB buffers that are to be used. The maximum value supported is 24, however performance does not improve beyond a value of OPTIMIZE=4. See Figure 15.5 for the effects of suggested OPTIMIZE values.

OPTIMIZE Value	CKD	FBA
1	2 track buffers	1 16KB buffer
2	4 track buffers	2 16KB buffers
3	6 track buffers	3 16KB buffers
4	10 track buffers	4 16KB buffers

Figure 15.5 FASTCOPY OPTIMIZE Values

The standalone version of FASTCOPY supports the OPTIMIZE parameter only for FBA DASD. In the standalone mode this parameter is essentially the same as described for FCOPYFB. You are encouraged to run with a value of OPTIMIZE=3 or larger for the best possible performance of the standalone utility.

15.9 DITTO Utility

The DITTO utility provides a number of commands to process data from cards, disk, diskette, and magnetic tape. DITTO may be run online with ICCF, under VM/CMS, or in batch. Batch mode execution is supported for both static and dynamic partitions. The DITTO program has storage requirements varying from 200KB to about 350KB depending upon the function selected. Data transfer operations may require two 64KB buffers (or 128KB) in addition to the listed program storage requirements. If VSAM files are processed by DITTO, then any VSAM GETVIS storage is in addition to these requirements. The DITTO utility phases all have names of the form DTOMODxx.

16

Tuning VSE in a VM Environment

VSE is often run as a guest in a VM environment. This chapter discusses special considerations for tuning VSE systems running under VM. In this book our treatment is fairly basic. Advanced users, or users interested in tuning VM for other than VSE guests, are encouraged to reference Savit's book *VM and CMS: Performance and Fine Tuning*.

Historically, VSE was run under VM because of real hardware and virtual storage constraints. VSE/ESA has eliminated most of these constraints to the point where VSE/ESA often makes better use of available hardware than VM can. However, customers still employ VM for other reasons. These include separating test and production systems for stability reasons, exploiting certain VM scheduling options, the use of CMS as a program development environment, and the use of VM as an additional production platform.

VSE can be run under VM in two basic modes. The first is MODE=VM|VMESA where VSE knows it is running under VM, and all unneeded supervisor code is eliminated for functions performed by VM. The second is MODE=ESA where a full functioned VSE/ESA system is present with no knowledge of VM and where no real advantage is taken of VM being present. Note that when we talk about VM in this chapter we are referring to VM/XA or VM/ESA. VSE/ESA cannot run in ESA mode under the older VM/SP or VM/HPO systems. It can be run in 370 mode.

Note that VM is never a performance option. That is, you never choose to run VSE under VM for performance reasons. Once a choice has been made to run VSE under VM, your interest is in reducing the cost of doing so. VSE/ESA in particular will always run much faster without VM, and removing a production VSE system from VM is the ultimate VM tuning option.

16.1   MODE=VM and MODE=VMESA Tuning

In a MODE=VM or MODE=VMESA system, the supervisor does not include much code related to page handling, and the I/O scheduling path is streamlined. Additional interfaces from VSE to VM facilities are also provided.

These VM cognizant modes are the most efficient available for VSE under VM. Unfortunately, they are also the most restrictive. In a VM aware system, only a single 16MB address space is supported for VSE. All partitions must be defined within one address space.

MODE=VM systems make excellent performing test VSE systems. If you run VSE under VM for testing purposes, you should attempt to fit such test systems into the MODE=VM environment, even if that means running several test systems.

16.1.1   CP Overhead Reduction

The MODE=VM|VMESA environment results in a reduction in CP overhead for several reasons:

- VSE eliminates privileged instructions that are not required.

- VSE does not page itself, but still overlaps paging.

- The VSE I/O scheduler lets VM do all the work.

Additional steps may be taken by the user to further reduce the overhead of such systems. One easy step is to reduce the number of times VSE is pre-empted by increasing its VM scheduling priority. This is desirable for production VSE guests anytime, and may also be desirable for high use testing systems. For VM/SP based systems, SET FAVOR is suggested. For VM/XA and VM/ESA systems, the QUICKDSP option is usually very effective.

16.1.2   I/O Scheduling

In a MODE=VM environment, VSE relies on VM to handle the whole I/O scheduling task. VSE passes its I/O requests directly to VM without determining what path to use, or whether or not a path is available.

VM allows a single DASD volume to be defined as a number of VM minidisks, each of which looks to VSE like a separate (but small) DASD volume. VM minidisks increase CPU overhead because all disk addresses must be translated by VM from the simulated minidisk address to the correct cylinder on the real DASD.

One important tuning option under VM is to define the VSE lock file on a small dedicated minidisk. This is only possible if all VSE systems run under the **same** copy of VM. VM employs virtual device reserve/release support that allows the lock file to occupy the same volume as other VSE data without the hardware lockout. Of course, if the VSE lock file is heavily used, be careful to not place it on the same physical volume as other high use datasets.

16.1.3   Paging

In a MODE=VM environment, VSE does no paging for itself. All paging is done by VM. All VM paging is communicated to VSE via a pseudo page fault interrupt. VSE supports the pseudo page fault interrupt to place a task into a page wait, and to continue execution of other tasks. VSE/ESA performs a SET PAGEX ON command at IPL time to request signaling of these pseudo page faults.

Paging overhead is still an important factor under VM, and should be avoided whenever possible. One way to reduce the impact of paging on VSE is to allocate real memory to the VSE system. The best approach is to run in V=R (real) mode. When insufficient real memory is available, you should consider reserving real memory for the VSE system. An additional action you may wish to consider is to lock most of the VSE supervisor into VM memory. This eliminates supervisor paging which suspends all VSE processing.

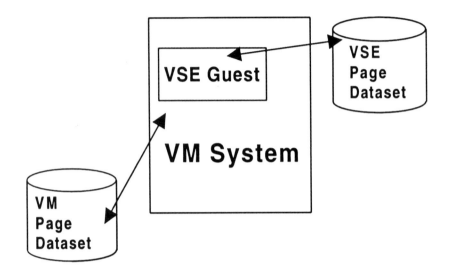

Figure 16.1 Double Paging with VM

16.1.4   16 Meg Maximum Size

The major restriction encountered in MODE=VM systems is that the VSE system is only 16MB. This means that all partitions, including the large POWER, VTAM, and database management partitions, must be mapped within a single 16MB address space.

Often the only option available for MODE=VM systems is to run additional systems to spread the desired partitions across several 16MB address spaces. If this is done, avoid the use of DASD sharing, or minimize the high performance cost of this option.

Many users have discovered that a single MODE=ESA system often will outperform a number of MODE=VM systems, especially when DASD sharing can be eliminated by merging the MODE=VM systems into a single VSE/ESA system. We will look at the performance of MODE=ESA systems next.

16.2 MODE=ESA, MODE=370 Performance

Running VSE under VM without MODE=VM eliminates the VM handshake logic, and causes VSE supervisor code to be executed that is not required under VM. Both of these result in performance problems. In this section we look at various performance costs that are effected by running VSE under VM.

16.2.1 CP Overhead Problems

When VSE is run in MODE=ESA|370 under VM, all normal VSE supervisor functions are performed. This results in a number of privileged operations being executed that would be eliminated for MODE=VM. In fact, running a MODE=ESA system under VM is similar to running an MVS system under VM. Unless such a VSE is run with dedicated resources, an increase of up to 40 percent or more of the total CPU cost can be seen.

The VM overhead can be reduced by running the guest as V=R or V=F. Unfortunately, this requires dedicated real memory, and is not as efficient as running the VSE system in a hardware managed logical partition (LPAR). If you have the I/O subsystem to support running VSE in an LPAR, this is preferred to running VSE under VM.

16.2.2 Paging

In MODE=ESA|370 under VM, double paging may occur. This is a result of VSE handling paging within its virtual machine that is viewed as real storage by VSE, but is actually virtual storage being paged by VM. This overhead may be eliminated by running VSE in a V=R or V=F area or by locking all of the VSE virtual machine.

The cost of double paging may be reduced by using SET RESERVE to reduce the number of page frames that VM can remove from the VSE guest. VM paging increases VM CPU overhead and can reduce the amount of work that VSE can perform. VM paging reduction is often the number one action that can be performed to improve VSE performance under VM.

16.2.3   I/O Scheduling

The performance of VSE I/O scheduling is always superior or equal to VM scheduling. It has a smaller path length, and does a better job of driving devices to saturation than VM does. Most importantly of all, VSE gives you the option of favoring I/O for your critical jobs.

You should consider eliminating the use of minidisks for your production VSE systems. The additional VM CPU overhead elongates all I/Os and reduces your maximum device utilization. Dedicated devices have a much reduced path length within VM. VM overhead can be almost eliminated by using dedicated devices with a preferred guest.

Note that the absolute best way to reduce all performance problems is to not run a VSE production system under VM at all. If possible, you should use LPAR mode to separate your VSE production totally from VM. This is the best overall performance, and improves the reliability of your system by allowing VSE to run even after VM fails.

16.3   Cost of VM Spooling

VM spooling is relatively expensive and is harder to operate than VSE spooling. If double spooling must be done, then you are encouraged to reduce unit record access via POWER chained I/Os. This takes advantage of POWER's efficient channel programs to reduce the number of times VM takes control for spooling, and thus greatly reduces the VM CPU spooling overhead.

If at all possible, you should not use VM to spool printer devices. There are several reasons why. VM offers relatively poor printer control facilities, and is particularly weak in the area of page oriented restarts. VSE also offers a number of functions not available in VM such as direct spooling to tape, flexible spool file backup and restore, and automatic queuing of multiple printouts produced by a single VSE partition. Operators are easily confused by the two quite different spooling systems when both VM and VSE spooling is used. Use of VM to spool printers is also inefficient and greatly increases the CP overhead.

Note that it is generally not desirable to bypass POWER and spool directly to VM. The VM spooling overhead is far greater than the cost of POWER spooling. POWER's operator friendliness, performance, and flexibility make it the spooling system of choice.

16.4   VM and VSE DASD

When VSE is run under VM, all of its DASD are known to VM. You may define VSE DASD as either full volumes or as minidisks. A VM minidisk is a portion of a DASD volume that is treated as a smaller sized DASD unit. Minidisks are allocated as an integral number of cylinders. They are formatted with their own volume ID and VTOC.

VM does not support duplicate volume IDs for the full volumes under its control. This presents a problem when multiple VSE systems are run under VM control, and a shared SYSRES volume is not being used. The standard VSE DOSRES and SYSWK1 volume IDs must be changed to prevent duplication, or these volumes must be fitted onto minidisks. Changing the standard volume IDs can be cumbersome because VSE documentation and examples all use these names. VM minidisks work well when the VSE DASD is not shared under VM, and standard names are desired. Each minidisk is defined to VM within the directory entry of the machine that owns that DASD space. The standard VSE ICKDSF utility may be used to format minidisks for use by VSE once they have been defined to VM.

16.5   VM and PR/SM

The PR/SM facility allows you to run up to six preferred guests under VM, or split your processor into as many as seven logical machines. PR/SM support is only available with VM/XA or V/ESA. PR/SM offers two very different ways to run both VM and VSE/ESA with little performance degradation. These are Multiple Preferred Guest support and Logical Partition (or LPAR) support. Let us look at each of these options.

16.5.1   Preferred Guest

Running an operating system like VSE/ESA under VM normally incurs substantial processor overhead. This is a result of VM simulating many of the privileged machine instructions, and the need for VM to manage a second level of virtual storage. VSE/ESA in ESA mode uses many such privileged instructions, and also makes heavy use of virtual storage for dynamic partitions and the static partition address spaces.

The VM Multiple Preferred Guest support with PR/SM allows processor real memory to be reserved for VM guests in order to eliminate essentially all of the virtual storage management overhead of VM. (See Figure 16.2.) On a uniprocessor, you may designate one V=R guest and up to five V=F guests, or you may have no V=R guest and up to six V=F guests. All V=R and V=F guests receive the benefit of a dramatic reduction in VM processor overhead associated with virtual storage management functions. With VM/ESA on a multiple CPU processor, up to 14 different V=F guests may be run if enough real storage is available.

VM/ESA or VM/XA		
VSE/ESA Test	VSE/ESA Batch Production	VSE/ESA Online

Figure 16.2 VM Running Multiple Preferred Guests

Of course, these benefits do not come without an associated cost. Each preferred guest has dedicated memory resources, just as though it were running outside of the control of VM. In fact, running a VSE system as a preferred guest removes that guest's real memory from the control of VM. This is the source of the performance improvement.

All V=R and V=F guests are still run under VM control, with their I/O requests managed by VM. They are allowed to access both full volume DASD and VM minidisk DASD. If large amounts of I/O are done by these guests, they will still experience degradation due to VM processing of their I/O requests. And, V=F guests are lost in the event of a VM failure. Let us now look at LPAR mode. It offers a mechanism to reduce this overhead, and allows VSE to survive a VM failure.

16.5.2 LPAR Mode

PR/SM also supports *Logical Partition* mode, which we will also refer to using the acronym, LPAR mode. Each logical partition is a separate logical processor, with its own real memory, CPU, and I/O facilities. (See Figure 16.3 for an example.) PR/SM supports up to seven partitions on a uniprocessor system, and up to 14 partitions on a multiple processor system. LPAR mode is the best performing option for multiple VSE/ESA systems on a single processor.

Each partition has dedicated real memory and I/O, but shares the processor. LPAR mode includes powerful processor resource sharing capabilities. You can give an LPAR an absolute share of the processor, or a variable share with a cap, or use a priority based processor sharing method. Currently, LPAR offers a much better processor control facility than VM. VM cannot set a maximum limit on a guest's use of the CPU, while LPAR can. VM also does a relatively poor job of dispatching a small number of resource intensive VSE or MVS systems compared to LPAR mode. On the other hand, VM is the best tool to manage a large number of interactive users. Also, with LPAR, you often cannot share the I/O devices without additional hardware.

VSE/ESA may be run in one logical partition, while VM is run in a separate logical partition. In this case, VSE/ESA is not aware of VM, and VM is not aware of VSE/ESA. Thus, VSE/ESA incurs no overhead associated with running on the same machine as VM. However, VSE/ESA run with an LPAR separate from VM does not have access to VM minidisks, and all data transfer must be via shared real devices or by a communications channel. And, LPAR mode adds its own overhead to each logical partition. This overhead is processor model dependent and also varies based on what each partition is doing. The initial implementation of LPAR mode had high overhead, but most of these issues have been resolved with newer versions of microcode. LPAR mode is normally

ES/9000 Running 3 LPARs		
VM/ESA with VSE/ESA Test Guest	VSE/ESA Batch Production	VSE/ESA Online

Figure 16.3 LPAR Example with VM and VSE/ESA

less overhead for a VSE/ESA system than running that guest under VM. You should monitor the cost of LPAR mode carefully to ensure it is acceptable in your environment.

17

Hardware Tuning

In this chapter we will in some detail look at the tuning of hardware used by VSE. We are interesting in hardware features that VSE is able to exploit. We are also interested in hardware configuration options that effect VSE performance. We will also look more closely at tuning paging than we have to this point.

Hardware tuning includes both changes to the hardware configuration, and the use of various VSE parameters and options that are directly related to hardware management. This chapter looks at these area, and also includes information on various hardware capacities that can be useful for tuning.

17.1 Cookbook for I/O Tuning

- DASD device utilization should be less than 30 percent.

- DASD XA channel utilization should be less than 75 percent. 370 DASD channel utilization should be less than 40 percent.

- Four channel paths to one controller are far better than two paths to each of two controllers.

- Moving from 3380 to 3390 DASD typically offers a 20 percent I/O throughput improvement.

- Caching control units can offer immediate and dramatic I/O service time improvements.

- Separate high-use system files from each other and from busy application files.

- CPU utilization of 100 percent is not bad, unless you cannot get your work done. 100 percent CPU is a tuning target.

17.2   Tuning CPU Usage

When CPU is the limiting factor in your VSE system, you have accomplished the main goal in VSE tuning. Of course, we still wish to use the CPU efficiently and not waste CPU time. Your first objective in running a VSE system is to eliminate all bottlenecks except for CPU. Only when CPU is the limiting factor can you take full advantage of faster processors. When CPU is not a limiting factor, a faster CPU will not usually help you in a cost effective fashion. Once CPU is a limiting factor we can upgrade our processor to get more work accomplished. However, often we can do things to postpone upgrading to a faster processor.

Two areas of tuning exist when you are limited by CPU. You can reduce the amount of CPU required, or you can ensure that the CPU is used first by the most critical tasks within your system.

17.2.1   Reducing CPU Usage

In this section we will look at a number of tuning features that can have the effect of increasing the amount of CPU used for a given process. If we are CPU constrained, we may wish to moderate our use of these features.

- LSR is an important tuning option. Used effectively, it can reduce CPU consumption, and save large numbers of I/O requests. However, too large an LSR pool wastes CPU. This is a result of a *large system effect* when many LSR buffers are provided. Large system effects occur when CPU costs grow non-linearly. The CPU cost of searching LSR buffers increases in a non-linear fashion. When many nonproductive buffer searches occur, significant CPU elongation is observed.

- CICS MRO is very expensive in VSE. In fact, benchmarks have shown increases in CPU for MRO transactions of more than 30 percent compared to the same transaction run without MRO.

- Multiprogramming task switches in VSE are expensive. A batch job run at the same time as CICS is being used will encounter a large increase in CPU cost because of these interruptions. Whenever possible, you should defer large batch production work to periods when CICS is not operational or is being lightly used. This is not to say that multiprogramming of VSE batch work is *bad*. However, if you are CPU constrained, a reduction in multiprocessing can result in better CICS response time.

- The reduction of VM overhead should be reviewed in all VM environments. You should consider use of V=R, or eliminate VM altogether for LPAR mode. Refer to the separate tuning VM chapter for details.

17.2.2 Managing CPU Usage

The term *managing CPU usage* refers to making more CPU time available for critical work, and less for work not as critical. It also refers to giving immediate access to applications that need little CPU time, because they are I/O bound. The VSE PRTY command is one of the easiest tools available to allocate CPU to your critical tasks. You should also review running noncritical work when online systems are down.

The *PRTY* Job Control Command is used to define the priorities of the static partitions, and the priorities of the classes of dynamic partitions. The format of this command is **PRTY part|class**. Specify one or more partition IDs or dynamic partition classes separated by commas. Specify the lowest priority partition first, followed by the next lowest priority partition, and ending with the highest priority partition. If all valid partition IDs and classes are not specified, then any not named assume a priority less than the lowest specified, within the same priority sequence that they previously had. Thus, if the current priority had F6 below F7 and a new priority statement **PRTY BG,F1** was encountered then the new priority sequence would be F6,F7,BG,F1.

The user may separate partition IDs and classes with commas or with equal signs. Commas indicate a strict priority sequence, while equal signs indicates partitions of equal priority, that are to be balanced partitions. Balanced partitions have their priority periodically switched such that each partition within a group has an equal share of the system with all other partitions within the group. Thus, **PRTY BG=F6=F7,F1** specifies that F1 has the highest priority, and that BG, F6, and F7 have an equal priority below that of F1, and that these three partitions will have their priorities altered to ensure an equal share of the system. VSE supports only one group of balanced partitions.

The keywords EQUAL and BELOW may be included at the end of a list of partition IDs or classes to place the partition IDs within an existing priority sequence. For example, **PRTY F4,F5,BELOW,N** would place F4 and F5 just below the dynamic class N within the current priority list.

No keyword ABOVE is needed since the default is to place all named partitions and classes above any previously listed. Thus, coding **PRTY Q,F1** will ensure that partition F1 is the highest priority partition and that the dynamic partitions of class Q are immediately lower than F1.

17.3   I/O

In this section we will look at tuning the VSE I/O subsystem. We are interested in both the hardware configuration, and the software options that affect how VSE drives the hardware. We begin with a description of how I/O is scheduled, and what kinds of delays are encountered. Most of our discussion is directed towards DASD I/O, because disk I/O is the source of many VSE bottlenecks.

17.3.1   Device Service Time and Queuing Delays

Each device type has its own characteristics that determine the amount of time a typical I/O request will take. This standard I/O time is called the *device service time*. If a device is available when an I/O request is made, the request will be processed in the device service time value. However, many I/Os occur in an environment with multiprogramming, and therefore with contention. Whenever the requested device is busy, the I/O request will be delayed. We will refer to this as the *queuing delay time.*

The device service time varies based upon device model, type of I/O request, and number of bytes transferred. The device service time for DASD includes the time spent positioning the arm to the data (seek time) plus the time spent transferring the data. The channel is disconnected during the time spent positioning. Positioning time includes the seek time and the rotational delay (or latency) to locate the start of the data. The channel is reconnected for the data transfer. If the channel is unavailable, then the data transfer must wait for a complete rotation of the disk. This adds twice the latency time. Figure 17.1 below lists average device service times for several different models of modern DASD.

Device Type	Avg. Seek	Device Service Time
3350	n/a	21
3380-A	16	16.8
3380-E	17	15.4
3380-J	12	14.1
3380-K	15	15.1
3390-1	10	11.2
3390-2	12.5	12.0

Figure 17.1 Device Service Times

If unrelated I/O requests are being considered then the distribution of queue delay times will be exponential (also called a Poisson distribution). The queuing delay is the amount of time that an I/O request will have to wait before it can be initiated due to a prior request or several requests in progress or waiting. The expected value of the queuing delay can be computed as:

$$T_1 = \frac{dst * \%Busy}{1 - \%Busy}$$

Equation 12 Queuing Delay

In the equation, *dst* is the average device service time. *%Busy* is the amount of time the device is busy. Thus, for a 3380J with a typical device service time of 14ms and a device busy of 60 percent we would expect to find a queuing delay time of (14ms*.6)/(1-.6) or 21ms. The queuing delay time is larger than the device service time because the device is usually busy and the queue depth is usually nonzero for this case. For the same device at 10 percent utilization we find that the queuing delay time has decreased to 14ms*.1)/(1-.1) or 1.26ms. This small value is a result of the device usually being available. A maximum device utilization of 30 percent is a good guideline for acceptable performance (a queue delay of about 1/2 service time).

Of course, when I/O requests are related and contention does not occur, then the average queuing delay is different. Sequential I/O and paging I/O on dedicated volumes are both potential examples of this effect. Uncontended sequential I/O requests will have a queuing delay equal to the device service time. Paging I/O requests frequently encounter little paging interference at the device level, and will experience much smaller queuing delays than predicted.

17.3.2   Latency and Transfer Time

The *latency* of a DASD I/O is the time required to locate the start of the data upon the desired track. The device latency is half a single rotation, because on average half of a track must be searched to locate the position of the data. The channel is not connected during the latency time. The *transfer time* (see Equation 13) is the time required to transfer the data once it has been located. The channel must be connected during the time data is transferred.

$$TransferTime = \frac{RotationalDelay}{RecordsPerTrack}$$

Equation 13 Transfer time computation

The transfer time is easily estimated given the rotational delay and the number of blocks that are stored on a track (note, this is an approximation that is only valid for large physical records or when multiple physical records are read with one I/O).

We simply treat the transfer time as the fraction of a track occupied by the data. Thus, for 3380 DASD we determine the transfer time to be 1/10 of the rotation time or about 1.7 milliseconds. Figure 17.2 below summarizes rotational delay and latency values for several types of DASD. All times are in milliseconds.

Device	Rotation Time in ms	Latency
3350	16.67	8.33
3375	20.20	10.10
3380	16.56	8.28
3390	14.08	7.04

Figure 17.2 DASD Rotational Delay and Latency Values

17.3.3 I/O Delay Sources

Everyone is aware that I/O requests take time, and that the requestor of the I/O usually has to wait for the completion of the I/O operation. Most people are not aware of the number of different ways that an I/O requestor can wait. Let us look at each of the places that a delay in processing, and therefore a wait, can occur.

1. An application program issues SVC 0. A page fault within SVC 0 processing is about the only source of delay.

2. The supervisor allocates Channel Queue entry for I/O. If no channel queue entry is available, then the SVC 0 is delayed until one becomes free.

3. The virtual I/O request is translated to a real request. Copy buffers are required, and real storage may be required. The request can wait for copy blocks to become available. The SVC 0 can wait for real memory to be free so that the areas covered by the I/O can be TFIXed into memory.

4. The supervisor communicates the I/O to the hardware. In 370 mode, the supervisor delays issuing a request while a device is busy, or unavailable due to a busy path.

5. The I/O subsystem hardware executes the I/O. The I/O request takes time to complete. This is the only delay most people think of as being part of an I/O request.

6. A completion interrupt is received and processed. The interrupt can be delayed if the operating system is running with interrupts disabled. Because the I/O interrupt path is not short, a separate delay is added to the time for the I/O just in processing the interrupt.

7. The application program is told of completion. The I/O is posted as complete. If other higher priority work is currently executing, then the I/O requestor is delayed until the processor becomes available.

We have seen that an I/O can require more time than is needed to actually access and transfer the data. VSE/ESA in ESA mode reduces the impact of several non-I/O wait components. The delay to issue the request to the hardware is smaller, because the I/O is queued within the I/O subsystem, rather than within supervisor tables. Fewer interrupts are required, which reduces the amount of time with interrupts disabled.

17.4 I/O Tuning Options

In this section we will look at the effects of various I/O configuration and tuning options. We will look at the effects of multiple channel paths, and of the FASTTR software option. We will look at how to exploit caching DASD control units in another section.

17.4.1   Multiple Paths to Devices

An I/O transfer occupies a path to a device. This path leads from the processor to a control unit, and from the control unit to the device. If any portion of the path from the processor to a device is busy, then an I/O request must wait for the path to become available. One or more channels may be used to connect a single control unit to the processor. When a control unit has only a single device attached to it, or a channel is not used by many control units, then a single path may be adequate. However, multiple devices are frequently attached to a single control unit, and multiple control units are attached to a single channel. Whenever several devices on a single controller can be busy at the same time, it is desirable to have multiple channel paths.

VSE in 370 mode communicates the I/O request to the hardware via a Start I/O Fast instruction (SIOF). These old VSE/SP and VSE/ESA 370 mode systems support only two paths to a control unit. This support is called channel switching (CHANSW). In a channel switching environment, a path is allocated to an I/O request at the time the I/O is started. The path originally allocated is the only one that may be used within this I/O request. This 370 mode I/O results in excessive waits for I/O even when channels have a relatively low percentage utilization.

VSE/ESA supports XA mode I/O by issuing a Start Subchannel (SSCH) instruction after an I/O is queued to the channel queue. This newer ESA or XA mode support allows for up to four channel paths to new control units. The name of this hardware is the Dynamic Channel Subsystem. An I/O request is not limited to a single path, but instead may be started on any available path (Dynamic Path Selection), transfer data on a second path and finally complete on yet another path (Dynamic Path Reconnection). Dynamic Path Reconnection is only available for those devices that support it (3880 and 3990 control units). XA mode I/O allows a channel to be run at close to saturation before substantial I/O degradation is seen. See Figure 17.3 for a diagram of the XA I/O flow.

It is important to note that a single control unit with four channel paths is far better than two control units each with two paths. This is a result of much larger queuing delays for the same channel utilization when only two channel paths are provided. Modeling and benchmarks have shown that RPS reconnect failures

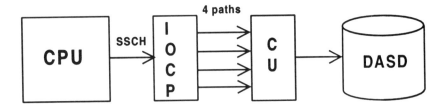

Figure 17.3 XA I/O Subsystem Flow

are essentially nonexistent for 3990 controllers with four channel paths.

17.4.2 Is FASTTR a Performance Option?

The FASTTR option enables or disables the CCW translation lookaside processing. In most environments, it is not an option that should be enabled. Let us look at what the FASTTR option is supposed to do, then look at why this option may impact performance rather than improve it.

VSE uses significant CPU cycles in translating the virtual addresses in channel programs to real addresses, and in locking all storage used for I/O into real memory. In fact, VSE generates a whole new channel program for each I/O request. FASTTR allows VSE to save the translated channel program, and to attempt to reuse this channel program when the same I/O request is repeated at a future time.

OPTION FASTTR is used to enable or disable the fast translate feature. You may specify this as a system wide option in the BG ASI IPL procedure. The default supervisors supplied by IBM come with the FASTTR feature enabled, so the only normal action you would take would be to explicitly disable it. FASTTR should not be used in your environment unless it is known to be beneficial.

The FASTTR option results in a large increase in the working set of applications. This is a result of leaving I/O buffers locked into real memory past the completion of the I/O. If a program is I/O bound, this can be beneficial. For programs that perform a lot of processing, it can increase paging. If your system experiences excessive paging, and you are using FASTTR, you should disable the FASTTR option.

FASTTR should not be used when channel programs are dynamically built. Such channel programs cannot typically be reused, and FASTTR just increases overhead. Thus, FASTTR is not effective for VSAM nor VTAM I/O. It is also ineffective for VSE librarian I/O, and most database system I/O requests. If a large percentage of your application I/O is to VSAM datasets, or to a database, then you should not use FASTTR. It will be of limited effectiveness and could even result in a net slowdown due to its CPU cost.

The use of FASTTR will almost always require you to increase your SYS BUFSIZE specification. You should monitor CCW translation buffer waits whenever FASTTR is being used. If you are doing any appreciable amount of paging then you can not afford the additional real storage, and should not run with FASTTR enabled.

17.5 DASD File Placement

Different disk files have different access patterns, and different activity levels. For these reasons, you should analyze your files, and spread them among available DASD to maximize your total throughput, and to optimize your key production work. Your performance monitor should gather both I/O counts by dataset, and the number plus length of non-zero seek requests. Your objective is to distribute the number of I/O requests as evenly as possible, while improving the average seek distance. Remember, you do not want to make seek distances any worse than they already are!

One simple rule that is often overlooked has to do with VTOC placement. The VTOC on a non-SYSRES DASD should be placed as close to the center of the disk volume as possible. This reduces the average seek distance from the VTOC to the datasets accessed through the VTOC. For SYSRES DASD, you have little choice, since the VTOC must be placed someplace in the free area following the main IJSYSRS extent, and often will be past the half way point.

You should also analyze high-use system datasets for preferential treatment. This is suggested because certain system datasets are single threaded and impact the performance of the whole VSE system, rather than the performance of a single task. The VSE lock file, POWER queue file, and high use libraries are all in this group.

Next you should analyze key application files. Your database files, and any high-use VSAM catalogs or files are in this group.

Application response time often determines user perception of system performance. When this is the case, it is important that key application files are tuned early, and often.

17.6 Cache Support

VSE/ESA supports the IBM 3990 caching control unit. Caching control units are a very important tuning option for VSE/ESA. This is especially true for the VSE lock file, VSAM catalogs and files that are frequently read, and it may be important for your POWER queue file as well. Figure 17.4 illustrates a caching control unit.

If you do not currently have caching control units, you should consider their benefits for your environment when you next upgrade your I/O configuration. DASD cache control units offer immediate performance improvements with little tuning effort.

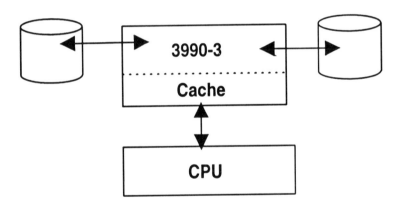

Figure 17.4 DASD Cache Control Unit

17.6.1 AR CACHE Command

The Attention routine CACHE command is used to enable caching at the control unit (3990) or the drive (3380/3390) level. VSE only supports Read Only Caching and Basic Write Caching. The

CACHE command accepts the FAST and NVS parameters, but these parameters are not supported by VSE/ESA prior to Version 1.2.1. VSE/ESA defaults to CACHE ON at IPL time for all cache devices. The following forms of the command may be used:

CACHE UNIT=cuu,ON
Enable Read-Only and Basic Write caching for the designated unit.

CACHE SUBSYS=cuu,ON
Enable Read Only and Basic Write caching for the 3990 subsystem at address cuu. All drives on this subsystem will be cached.

CACHE UNIT | SUBSYS=cuu,STATUS
The STATUS operand results in a display of the status of the designated unit or subsystem. If the unit or subsystem is not cached, a message "NON-CACHED CONTROL UNIT" is produced.

CACHE UNIT | SUBSYS=cuu,REPORT
The REPORT operand results in a display of performance information of the designated unit or subsystem. This information can be used to determine the effectiveness of caching one unit over another unit.

17.6.2   What Files Should be Cached?

The following general guidelines identify the files that benefit the most from cache support:

- Files with a high read-to-write ratio that have a high EXCP rate.

- High-use VSAM indices, especially those where the index and data components are separated.

- High-use libraries.

- High-use VSAM catalogs.

- High-use system datasets such as lock file, label area, POWER queue file. (Note: do NOT cache page datasets.)

Where you can perform tuning by allocating additional buffers, and can afford these buffers, you should use buffers to tune. Caching is most effective where other tuning options do not exist. The system lock file is a classic example of a file where very large improvements have been seen from caching. Another such example is VSAM catalogs in an active SAM managed VSAM environment.

Most VSAM files are best tuned using VSAM bufferspace. One exception is a very large VSAM index, where you cannot afford enough bufferspace to get benefits. If you choose to employ caching for a VSAM index, then you should not specify a large index bufferspace. Doing so will reduce the effectiveness of the cache. In other words, if VSAM bufferspace gives you a large benefit, DASD cache will not give you much more and should not be used.

VSE Page datasets should not be cached. The VSE page handler selects pages to be written using a Least Recently Used (LRU) algorithm. Page I/Os that write data that will not be needed soon (or perhaps ever) are a poorly performing choice for caching.

17.7   Paging

VSE/ESA is a virtual storage system. As such it is designed to page. However, VSE/ESA does not page efficiently, and it is important to minimize paging, and to ensure that what paging is done occurs as fast as possible. Your first tuning option to reduce paging is to change your application work mix, or to add real memory. Assuming you cannot do either of these, or if you still have paging problems after tuning, this section will help improve the performance of your paging I/O requests.

The TPBAL option reduces an application's working set that is impacting a key transaction processing system. This is accomplished by not dispatching lower priority partitions, and thus slows these partitions down. Of course, if a partition is not being dispatched, its working set cannot impact the higher priority work. This is the purpose of TPBAL.

VSE paging is even more of a problem in a VM environment. Refer to the chapter on VM Tuning if you run VSE under VM. If possible, your objective under VM is to eliminate or reduce double paging, then to improve the performance of all remaining paging. In general, VSE performs its own paging better than double paging under VM. The preferred option is to run your VSE system as V=R or V=F under VM. If this is not feasible, you should lock or reserve pages to reduce VM paging.

17.7.1 Number/Placement of Page Datasets

In this section we will look at how to choose the number of page datasets, and where they should be placed. If your system does not encounter page delays, then this section does not apply to you. Paging at less than four requests per second usually does not require page dataset tuning. If you encounter an appreciable amount of paging, you will wish to spread this paging across several page datasets. VSE/ESA supports as many as 15 page dataset extents.

You should never define multiple page datasets on the same volume. You should define no more than one page dataset on each channel path to your DASD. You should also place page datasets on the lowest use DASD on each channel. Even if you do little paging, you want what paging you have to get done as quickly as possible.

You should avoid placing paging datasets on the same volume as other key system datasets. Paging files should not be mixed with the lock file, console hardcopy file, nor the recorder file. VSE system I/O is priority I/O, and should not be allowed to interfere with other system I/O. The I/O for these files is key to the throughput of the whole VSE system. Any conflicts will generally impact the whole system.

17.8 DASD Capacities

VSE supports a variety of different DASD types, each with its own characteristics. The capacity of DASD is the amount of data that can be stored on a given device type. The capacity varies for different block sizes. We will use a 4KB block size and look at the capacity of the various VSE supported DASD types. A 4KB size is important because it is the size of a page dataset block, a common VSAM physical block size, the size of a SQL/DS DBSPACE data block, and is commonly used for other types of datasets as well.

Figure 17.5 below lists the capacity of most commonly encountered VSE/ESA DASD.

DASD Type	Cyls	Tracks / Cylinder	Megabytes per Cylinder	Megabytes per Volume
3350	555	30	0.4687	260.12
3375	959	12	0.3749	359.53
3380 E	885	15	0.5858	518.43
3380 J	1770	15	0.5858	1036.87
3380 K	2655	15	0.5858	1555.3
3390 A	1113	15	1.6999	1892
3390 B	2226	15	1.6999	3784

Figure 17.5 DASD Capacity Using 4KB Blocks

17.9   3390 DASD Benchmark

Recent debate over the actual limits of VSE/ESA I/O led to a new benchmark.   The purpose of this benchmark was to identify whether or not channels running in XA I/O mode would experience performance degradation at high channel utilization levels.

A standard IBM utility was chosen to facilitate recreation of test results. Running full pack formats with the ICKDSF utility was selected. The tests were run on an ES/9021-340. The DASD tested were 3390 volumes on a 3990 control unit with four paths. A single format was run in a standalone mode, then four identical formats were run concurrently against four different volumes. The results are summarized in Figure 17.6. Note that at 85 percent channel utilization we experience batch elongation of less than 5 percent for each concurrent format. Although this is an artificial example, it indicates that the XA I/O subsystem is capable of running channels at 85 percent with little performance impact. In contrast, an attempt to run 370 mode channels above 50 percent busy has been frequently seen to result in 100 percent elongation (even more in some perverse cases).

Number of Formats	Elapsed Time	% Chan Busy
1	35 Min	22%
4	37 Min	85%

Figure 17.6 ICKDSF 3390 Format Benchmark

18

Tuning Specifications Summary

This chapter discusses how the VSE/ESA system is configured and controlled during the Sysgen process, the IPL, system initialization, and lastly during execution. The parameters and commands used to configure and control VSE are covered in an overview form. Specific information on usage of these commands occurs throughout this book. The information is included here to list all applicable options in one location and for reference purposes.

18.1 SYSGEN Parameters

This section discusses the supervisor generation process. The discussion is for the VSE/ESA system supervisor, and not for earlier levels of VSE which are not covered.

In general, it is not necessary to reassemble a VSE supervisor as part of the performance tuning process. This information is included to assist the advanced VSE user. Many parameters can be changed via IPL parameters or run time commands. You are should alter such parameters rather than reassemble your supervisor.

In order to generate a supervisor, you must first install the "Generation Feature" of VSE. This is an optional part of the install of VSE, and may not have been done previously. The IBM manual *VSE/ESA Planning Guide* contains a discussion of what is required to install the Generation Feature. This manual also contains documentation for the supervisor generation macros that are covered in overview form here. IBM has been rapidly simplifying the supervisor generation process with the intention of eliminating the need for it in the future. At this time, most users do not need to assemble supervisors.

The three supervisor macros remaining and their parameters are:

```
SUPVR ID=
      MICR=
      MODE=
FOPT  DASDSHR=
      FASTTR=
      RPS=
      TRKHLD=
      TTIME=
      USERID=
IOTAB IODEV=
      NPGR=
```

18.1.1   SUPVR Macro

The old NPARTS= parameter has been eliminated in VSE/ESA. A value of 12 is forced in VSE/ESA for the number of static partitions. For older VSE releases this parameter was altered to save small amounts of storage, when all of the partitions were not required.

ID=1|c is used to specify a single character that is used to suffix the name of the supervisor as $$A$SUPc. Since one can rename a supervisor as desired, this parameter is not usually required. IBM supplied supervisors use this parameter to generate their various names.

MICR=NO|1419|1419D

The IBM supplied 370 supervisor includes MICR=1419, so it is not usually necessary to assemble a supervisor to include support for MICR. No significant benefit results from removal of this specification. MODE=VM|MODE=VMESA supervisors require MICR=NO.

MODE=370 | ESA | VM | VMESA

The MODE= parameter is used to specify the hardware (or simulated hardware) environment in which VSE will be run. The valid options are 370, ESA, VM, and VMESA. IBM provides supervisors for each possible option.

MODE=370 supports VAE mode execution on a real 370 mode processor, or in VAE mode for a virtual machine running under VM. Use this mode if you are running native on a 370 processor. If your system supports XA or ESA, you should not run in 370 mode. It is less efficient and you lose certain VSE/ESA benefits.

MODE=ESA supports execution on a 370-XA or ESA mode processor, or in VAE mode under VM/XA or VM/ESA. If you wish to run POWER in private, the processor must be run in ESA mode. If your processor supports this mode, you should run with an ESA mode supervisor for performance reasons.

MODE=VM supports execution under VM. A single 16MB address space is supported. Real mode execution is not supported. Dynamic partitions are not supported. There is little difference between a VSE/ESA MODE=VM system and a VSE/SP MODE=VM system. A MODE=VM system will run under any type of VM system (VM/SP, VM/HPO, VM/XA, or VM/ESA).

MODE=VMESA supports execution under VM on a 370-XA or ESA processor. A single 16MB address space is supported. Real mode execution is not supported. Dynamic partitions are not supported. The ESA I/O subsystem is used by the MODE=VMESA system, and requires either VM/XA or VM/ESA.

Both VM options are used to reduce VM overhead when running VSE/ESA in a VM environment. These options are only effective when your system will fit in the single 16MB address space. Note that MODE=370 and MODE=ESA execution under VM result in relatively high overhead (similar to that encountered for an MVS system). This overhead is due to a reduction in hand-shaking between VSE and VM in these modes. Running VSE/ESA as a preferred guest or V=R under VM can eliminate much of this cost. In general, it is preferable to run a single VSE in V=R or V=F mode under VM rather than running multiple MODE=VM VSE systems under VM. This is especially true when one can run a single VSE without DASD sharing, rather than multiple VSE machines with DASD sharing. Examples of the pregenerated supervisors may be seen in Figure 18.1.

```
SUPVR ID=3,      FOPT DASDSHR=YES,     IOTAB IODEV=254,
      MICR=1419,      FASTTR=YES,            NPGR=3050,
      MODE=370        RPS=YES,
                      TRKHLD=12,
                      TTIME=NO,
                      USERID=VSE.370.SUP3

SUPVR ID=X,      FOPT DASDSHR=YES,     IOTAB IODEV=254,
      MICR=NO,        FASTTR=YES,            NPGR=3050,
      MODE=ESA        RPS=YES,
                      TRKHLD=12,
                      TTIME=NO,
                      USERID=VSE.370.SUPX

SUPVR ID=M,      FOPT DASDSHR=YES,     IOTAB IODEV=254,
      MICR=NO,        FASTTR=NO,             NPGR=3050,
      MODE=VMESA      RPS=YES,
                      TRKHLD=12,
                      TTIME=NO,
                      USERID=VSE.370.SUPM
```

Figure 18.1 Pregenerated Supervisors

18.1.2   FOPT Macro

DASDSHR=NO | YES

The IBM provided supervisors all specify DASDSHR=YES.

Since DASDSHR support is disabled when a lock file is not defined, it is not required to assemble a VSE supervisor without this option. This option will be disabled if you are not sharing DASD. Refer to the chapter on DASD Sharing for additional information.

FASTTR=NO | YES

The provided supervisors include FASTTR=YES where it is valid. This option results in a supervisor with support to manage and reuse previously translated channel programs.

Since FASTTR may be disabled via STDOPT FASTTR=NO, it is not required to assemble a supervisor without this option. However, let us note that FASTTR is generally a poor option from a performance standpoint, and that it should often be disabled. Additional discussion of this option is done in the "I/O Scheduling" section.

RPS=NO | YES

The provided supervisors all include RPS=YES. This is a desirable option and should not be altered in any supervisor you assemble. RPS support enables DASD devices to disconnect from the channel while the arm is being positioned to the desired cylinder, head, and record.

TRKHLD=NO | n

The IBM provided supervisors all include TRKHLD=12. TRKHLD is an old option that is not generally used by current software. The provided value does not impact performance and is normally adequate.

TTIME=NO | BG | Fn

The IBM provided supervisors all specify TTIME=NO. You will need to assemble your own supervisor if you require this option. The task timer does not impact performance and is not generally used.

USERID=identifier

The 16-character identifier specified is displayed as part of the normal IPL COMPLETED message. This option has no effect upon performance. If you assemble your own supervisor, your should specify a unique and descriptive value for the operand.

18.1.3   IOTAB Macro

IODEV=25 | n

The IBM provided supervisors all specify IODEV=254, which is the maximum value for VSE/ESA Version 1.   User alteration is not typically required for these systems.   For VSE/ESA 1.2 the maximum value is 1024.   You may wish to increase the IOTAB specification when many devices are defined.

NPGR=n

Specify the total number of logical units for all static partitions combined.   The IBM supplied supervisors all specify NPGR=3060. This value is the maximum possible.   User alteration is not required.   The NPGR Job Control Command may be issued to alter the specific number of logical units for partitions once the system has been IPLed.   This is typically done as part of the ASI procedure for BG.

18.2   IPL Parameters

This section describes system parameters that may be altered at IPL time.   Refer to *VSE/ESA System Control Statements* for further details on these commands.   The IPL commands include:

ADD   Define I/O devices at IPL time
DEF   Define system logical units
DEL   Delete I/O devices previously ADDed
DLA   Define label area
DLF   Define lock file
DPD   Define page dataset(s)
SET   Set system date/time
SET   XPCC control for SQL/DS database sharing
SVA   Increase the default SVA size
SYS   Set/update the various system options at IPL time

All of these commands may be included in a VSE Automatic System Initialization (ASI) IPL procedure. This $IPLPROC procedure is illustrated by Figure 18.2 below. In addition to the above commands, a special command may be used within an ASI procedure to define the name of the supervisor, the location of the console, and machine characteristics. This is the supervisor parameters command and has the following form,

```
cuu SUP=name,N|P,VPOOL=vpoolv,VIO=viov,VSIZE=vsizev
```

The SUP= parameter identifies the name of the supervisor to be loaded.
The VPOOL value defines the size of the buffer used to manage the VIO area and is not valid for a MODE=VM system.
The VIO value defines the size of the VIO area (used by POWER, CICS, and temporary LINK).
The VSIZE value determines the maximum total virtual area size.

```
01F,$$A$SUP1
ADD  01F,3277
ADD  00E,PRT1
ADD  120:12F,3380
DEF  SYSCAT=DOSRES,SYSREC=SYSWK1
DLA  NAME=AREA1
DPD  VOLID=DOSRES
SYS  NPARTS=24,SPSIZE=1024K
SVA  SDL=300,PSIZE=400K,GETVIS=800K
```

Figure 18.2 $IPLPROC Procedure

18.2.1   ADD Command

The ADD command is used to define I/O devices at IPL time. The formats of the ADD command are:

```
ADD cuu,CONS
ADD cuu{:cuu}{(S)},type{,mode}{,SHR}{,EML}
```

The first form of the command is used only to define a dummy console device when VSE is IPLed with a disconnected console, and is to run without a real console.

The second form of the command is the one that interests us. The cuu field is limited to three characters even though VSE supports up to 256 channels in ESA mode. This is accomplished by using a pseudo device address in the ADD statement and defining the real device address to the processor. Likewise, the (S) parameter is used to specify channel switching which is limited to the old two channel switch support (the S option is not supported for MODE=ESA|VMESA). VSE/ESA actually supports up to four paths to a device. This is accomplished through the real hardware definition done to the processor (called the IOCP gen) making the (S) software option meaningless.

The ,SHR parameter is used to all DASD that are shared with other virtual or real VSE systems. If a DASD is shared, this parameter MUST be specified to avoid corruption of data. If a DASD is not shared, or is never shared at the same time, then you should omit the ,SHR parameter. The ,SHR parameter enables the VSE external lock manager and dramatically increases the overhead of operations like open and close.

18.2.2   DEF Command

The DEF command is used to assign SYSREC and SYSCAT. Its format is:

```
DEF  SYSREC=,SYSCAT=
```

SYSREC specifies the DASD device containing the recorder file, the hardcopy file, and the system history file. All of these files must reside on the same DASD. Because the hardcopy file and recorder file together may be relatively high use datasets, SYSREC should not be placed on a DASD that has high use. For example, it is a good idea to separate SYSREC from the lock file, page datasets, and the POWER files.

SYSCAT specifies the DASD containing the VSAM master catalog. The VSAM master catalog is also a high-use dataset, and should not be placed on a high-use DASD.

18.2.3 DLA Command

The DLA command defines the location and size of the system label area. The label area may be placed on any DASD, but the label area is a *busy* file and care should be taken to avoid other high-use DASD. The label area is relatively cheap if mostly system standard labels are used in your environment. If many temporary labels are defined, then the cost of the label area increases. A performance tool will indicate the use of the label area in your shop.

18.2.4 DLF Command

The DLF command is used to define the location and size of the external DASD lock file used by a DASDSHR=YES supervisor when one or more DASD are defined with the ,SHR parameter. If no DASD is added with the ,SHR parameter then the DLF command is invalid.

The lock file is frequently the highest used dataset in a shop, and should be carefully placed away from all other high usage or critical datasets. Files placed on the same volume as the VSE lock file can experience long delays in service time. Delays result from the lock file being serviced by a system task that receives the top I/O scheduling priority, and from the use of hardware reserve for the entire lock file volume.

The lock file must be defined on a DASD that is not defined as switchable. This can seriously impact performance for all other datasets on the same volume. Lastly, the supervisor employs DASD RESERVE/RELEASE commands on a frequent basis for the lockfile. This use can cripple the performance of all other users of the volume containing the lock file.

In an all VM environment, the lock file may be defined on a mini-disk using virtual reserve/release. This one step often results in a visible improvement in batch job throughput.

18.2.5 DPD Command

The DPD command is used to define the location and size of the page data set(s). Up to fifteen page dataset extents may be defined, with up to three extents defined upon a single volume. Multiple page datasets are used to improve the overall performance of paging, when paging use is significant in your environment.

You should specify a small number of low-usage DASD volumes rather than define page dataset space on a large number of volumes including high-use volumes. VSE distributes page space across the volumes provided, but one slow volume can impact unrelated paging performance. Only the fastest available volumes should be used.

18.2.6   SET Command

The SET command is used to define the DATE, CLOCK, and ZONE values. An alternate form of the SET command is used to enable VSE XPCC/APPC/VM support that is required for SQL/DS database sharing with VM. This command is specified within the ASI IPL procedure.

18.2.7   SVA Command

The SVA command defines the size of the SVA tables and must be the last command supplied during an IPL. The format of the SVA command is:

```
SVA SDL=n,PSIZE=n,GETVIS=n,SHARED=HIGH|LOW
```

SDL is used to specify the number of additional System Directory List (SDL) entries required by the user. This number is added to the number of entries computed by VSE, and the total must not exceed 1022. An SDL entry is required for every move mode phase, every SVA resident phase, and all SYSRES phases that have directory entries built via SET SDL commands.

PSIZE specifies the size of the SVA virtual library area reserved for user loaded phases. The number you specify is added to the system determined value. Do not include space for any phases automatically loaded by VSE, as these are already included in the VSE base value. You must provide some extra space in the SVA to allow for maintenance while your system is up. Failure to provide this space could result in the need for an IPL, when a new version of a phase cannot be loaded into your filled SVA.

GETVIS specifies the amount of additional system GETVIS area to reserve over the amount computed by VSE during the IPL. Again, you should provide additional system GETVIS area to allow for maintenance to your system. In general, running out of system GETVIS on a running VSE system will result in VSE failure. Best case, exhausting system GETVIS will result in unusual abends and error messages that are difficult to diagnose.

SHARED is used to specify the location of the SVA. The SVA may be placed in either the highest storage addresses via SHARED=HIGH, or adjacent to the supervisor in low storage via SHARED=LOW. SHARED=HIGH is the default for MODE=370 and MODE=VM supervisors. SHARED=LOW is the default for MODE=ESA and MODE=VMESA supervisors. Use SHARED=LOW for MODE=ESA systems to save up to an average of 512K in virtual storage. VSE/ESA uses 1MB segments. This means that your address spaces are defined on megabyte boundaries. Losses due to rounding can cause a net loss in available virtual storage when SHARED=HIGH is used. Since only a single boundary is rounded (the one following the combined supervisor and shared partition and SVA area) for SHARED=LOW, this is the preferred option.

18.2.8   SYS Command

The SYS command is optional. It is used to specify VSE system options during an IPL. Because some of the default values may not be good for performance, you should specify your own SYS command as part of your ASI procedure. The SYS parameters that pertain to performance are:

```
BUFSIZE=n
```

Use BUFSIZE=n to specify the number of supervisor buffers used for I/O CCW translation processing. The number entered may be increased by the system. The actual number is displayed by VSE during the IPL. If the number of buffers in your system is under 1500, especially if you are running with FASTTR enabled, you should consider increasing the number of supervisor buffers. Buffer waits are reported by a performance product, and may be used to judge the need in your environment.

Note that the default value of the BUFSIZE parameter was always too small for systems prior to VSE/ESA. Even if you are running on VSE/ESA, you should analyze the number of buffers provided.

CHANQ=n

Specify the number of channel queue entries.   The current maximum is 255, and should be the number specified in your system, unless you know (via a performance monitor) that you can run with less. The maximum number of channel queue entries and devices is increased by VSE/ESA 1.2 to 1024. When you upgrade to this level, you may wish to review your usage.

DASDFP=NO | YES

Specify YES to enable DASD file protection. If you do not have your own applications that include DTFDA or direct DASD I/O with channel programs, you should not specify DASD file protection.

   DASDFP is an option of little real value. Essentially all IBM software and OEM software that uses its own channel programs will disable DASD file protection. LIOCS, using sequential disk or VSAM, contains superior address error checking.   DASDFP increases operating system CPU overhead and can significantly increase paging in environments that are real storage constrained. However, the CPU cost of DASDFP is typically less than 3 percent and it may be left on with little impact.

SPSIZE=nM

Specify either nK or nM to reserve that amount of virtual storage for the shared partitions. The amount specified is the maximum area that may be allocated via the ALLOC command. Any storage reserved via SPSIZE, but not used, is not available for any other use. SPSIZE reduces the size of the private area, and thus reduces the size of each non-shared address space and of the largest dynamic partition.

   The amount specified is rounded up to the next segment boundary. For 370 mode systems, this is the next 64KB boundary. For an ESA mode system, this is the next megabyte boundary.

   Refer to the SCP chapter Address Space SIZE section for further information on the calculation of the size of the private area.

18.3 JCL Commands

Job Control Language (JCL) commands are usually issued from within a batch job. They may also be packaged into an Automatic System Initialization (ASI) JCL procedure. The ASI JCL procedure is used to define system and partition defaults at IPL time, or when a partition is started. See Figure 18.3 below for an example of a BG ASI JCL procedure.

```
STDOPT ACANCEL=NO,DECK=NO,DUMP=PART,SYSDMP=YES,SXREF (1)
ALLOC S,F1=1M      (3)
ALLOC 1,BG=2M,FA=512K,FB=512K
ALLOC 2,F2=1M,F3=1024K,F4=1024K
ALLOC 3,F5=896K,F6=1M,F7=1M,F8=1M
SIZE BG=512K,F1=512K,F2=512K        (4)
NPGR BG=100,F2=255
// JOB BG ASI JCL
SET SDL
$$BOCRTA,MOVE
/*
ASSGN SYSLST,UA
START F1 ,     Startup POWER
STOP       ,   Wait for POWER to initialize
PRTY BG,FB=FA=F9=F8=F7,S,F6,F5,F4,F3,T,F2,F1      (2)
ASSGN SYSLST,FEE
ASSGN SYSPCH,FED
ASSGN SYSIN,FEC,PERM
```

Figure 18.3 BG ASI JCL Procedure Example

The STDOPT statement (1) establishes the standard JCL options for all partitions. These options may be overridden within a single job via the // OPTION statement. In our example we have disabled the automatic cancel and the deck options, plus we have requested that partition dumps be taken to the SYSDMP dataset.

The PRTY statement (2) defines the relative priorities of the various partitions. In our example we have balanced a group of partitions by separating their partition IDs with equal signs.

The ALLOC statements (3) define the sizes of the various static partitions, and identify what address space each static partition belongs in. In our example "S" is the shared address space, and "R" is the real address space.

The JCC SIZE command (4) is used to define the default size parameter, and consequently the GETVIS area size, for each of the static partitions.

The NPGR statement defines the number of programmer logical units available in each partition.

18.3.1   ALLOC

The ALLOC Job Control Command (JCC) is used within a static partition to define the size of one or more static partitions. Dynamic partitions are not controlled via the ALLOC command. The format of this command is,

```
ALLOC [space,]part=size
```

The *space* parameter is optional and supplied to specify the address space ID. Provide 1 through 9 for a virtual address space, an "S" for the shared area, or an "R" for a real processor storage allocation.

The *part=size* parameter is coded one or more times to define the size of the designated partition in Kilobytes (nnK) or in Megabytes (nnM). Thus F6=128K defines a 128 Kilobyte partition, and F6=4M defines a 4-Megabyte partition.

The VSE BG partition has a default size of 1M at IPL time, all other partitions have no allocation. One or more ALLOC commands are normally included as part of the BG ASI IPL procedure to define the permanent sizes of all of the static partitions to be used in the VSE system. This is done at IPL time as altering the size of a partition after IPL can be complicated. To delete a foreground partition after IPL, you must first PSTOP the partition to POWER, then UNBATCH it to job control, and lastly ALLOC it 0K.

18.3.2   JCC SIZE

The Job Control Command (JCC) SIZE statement is used to define the default problem program area size value for a partition. When a program is executed in the designated partition without an

explicit SIZE= parameter, then the default size value is used. The
format of the SIZE command is,

```
SIZE part=size
```

The *part=size* parameter is coded one or more times to define the
default sizes of the named partitions. Thus SIZE
BG=200K,F4=512K,F5=1M defines BG to have a problem program
area size of 200 Kilobytes, F4 of 512 Kilobytes, and F5 of 1
Megabyte.

The current SIZE specification value is displayed in the MAP
command output. Note that the last JCC SIZE value is displayed,
and not any current EXEC command SIZE= override value.

The SIZE command may only be specified for static partitions.
Dynamic partitions are controlled via the POWER DTR$DYNC
table. Only inactive static partitions that are not using their
GETVIS area may have their size altered. In general, the best
place to issue this command is from within the BG ASI IPL
procedure.

18.3.3   EXEC SIZE=

The Job Control Statement EXEC has an optional SIZE=
parameter. The EXEC SIZE parameter is used to specify the
problem program area size for this single execution. When no
SIZE= parameter is provided then the JCC SIZE command value
is used. When the SIZE= parameter is provided, it supersedes any
default value provided to job control. The format of this parameter
is one of the following:

```
// EXEC  PGM=pname1,SIZE=pname2
// EXEC  PGM=pname1,SIZE=(pname2,nnK)
// EXEC  PGM=pname1,SIZE=AUTO
// EXEC  PGM=pname1,SIZE=(AUTO,nnK)
```

The four statements do the following:

1.   Execute program pname1 in an area exactly the size of
     program pname2. Programs pname1 and pname2 are
     normally the same name but pname2 may not be omitted.

Thus, `EXEC PGM=BILL,SIZE=BILL` would execute the program named BILL in an area the exact size of BILL.

2. Execute program pname1 in an area the size of program pname2 plus an additional nnK bytes. This is similar to number one except that an extra nnK bytes are added to the problem program area size.

3. Execute program pname1 in an area as large as the largest program with the same first four characters in its name as pname1. This is an old option, and one to be avoided because the size value can not be determined without looking at other unrelated programs.

4. Execute program pname1 in an area the size of the largest program with the same first four characters in its name as pname1 plus an additional nnK bytes. This is similar to number three except that we add an extra nnK bytes. It is an old option, and one to be avoided.

Only the first two examples are recommended. Why is this? Options three and four have one very serious, very negative characteristic. They both allow a program to work in one library, and fail when the exact same program is executed from another library. Very few shops follow a standard where the first four characters of a program name are unique. Any shop that does not follow this standard can encounter cases where the problem program area will be too large or too small depending on what programs, with what names, happen to be in the current library.

18.3.4 LIBDEFs

The Job Control Statement *LIBDEF* is used to define libraries to be processed by the fetch routine and various system utilities, except for the librarian. The LIBDEF statement is not used to define libraries to be processed by the Librarian utility LIBR.

Libraries can be defined as type PHASE, OBJ, PROC, SOURCE, and DUMP. The libraries may be defined to be searched, or catalogued to. The format of the LIBDEF statement is:

```
// LIBDEF type,SEARCH=chain,CATALOG=dest,duration
```

The *type* parameter is included to specify which of PHASE, OBJ, PROC, or SOURCE is being referenced for a SEARCH chain, or which of these four plus DUMP is being defined for a CATALOG destination. The type may also be specified as an asterisk to define the same search chain for all types of library (PHASE, OBJ, PROC, and SOURCE).

The *dest* parameter is coded to define a CATALOG destination. This is only valid for the DUMP and PHASE parameters. DUMP defines the target library for system dumps produced under control of OPTION SYSDUMP at abnormal termination. PHASE defines the target library for the linkage editor utility (LNKEDT).

18.3.5 PRTY (PBAL)

The *PRTY* Job Control Command is used to define the priorities of the static partitions, and the priorities of the classes of dynamic partitions. The format of this command is,

```
PRTY part|class
```

Specify one or more partition IDs or dynamic partition classes separated by commas. Specify the lowest priority partition first, followed by the next lowest priority partition, and ending with the highest priority partition. If all valid partition IDs and classes are not specified then any not named assume a priority less than the lowest specified, within the previous priority sequence. Thus, if the current priority had F6 below F7 and a new priority statement PRTY BG,F1 was encountered then the new priority sequence would be F6,F7,BG,F1.

The user may separate partition IDs and classes with commas or with equal signs. Commas indicate a strict priority sequence, while equal signs indicates partitions of equal priority, that are to be balanced partitions. Balanced partitions have their priority periodically switched such that each partition within a balanced group has an equal share of the system with all other partitions within that balanced group. Thus, PRTY BG=F6=F7,F1 specifies that F1 has the highest priority, and that BG, F6, and F7 have an equal priority below that of F1. These three partitions will have their priorities altered to ensure an equal share of the system. Only one balanced partition group is supported.

The keywords EQUAL and BELOW may be included at the end of a list of partition IDs or classes to place the partition IDs within an existing priority sequence. For example, PRTY F4,F5,BELOW,N would place F4 and F5 just below the dynamic class N within the current priority list.

No keyword ABOVE is needed since the default is to place all named partitions and classes above any previously listed. Thus, coding PRTY Q,F1 will ensure that partition F1 is the highest priority partition and that the dynamic partitions of class Q are immediately lower than F1.

18.3.6   PRTYIO

The PRTYIO parameter is used to favor the I/O requests of the designated partition. This parameter can be very effective for a production CICS, or for a production database partition (such as SQL/DS). The format of the PRTYIO command is:

```
PRTYIO partlist
```

Partlist can be a list of partitions in high-to-low priority sequence. (Note that this is the opposite of the PRTY command.) Any partitions with an equal I/O priority are separated with equal signs. Partitions to have a higher priority than those following are separated with commas.

The PRTYIO parameter is best used for performance critical partitions such as a production CICS, POWER, or VTAM. Performance improvements for these partitions typically benefit many users or improve the overall performance of the VSE system without substantially impacting other users.

18.4   POWER Parameters

The POWER parameters determine the characteristics of the POWER datasets in addition to specifying runtime information. In general, altering a POWER dataset's characteristics requires the coldstart of POWER and the reinitialization of the affected dataset. The POWER runtime parameters usually only require that POWER be restarted and do not affect it's datasets.

18.4.1 DBLK Group Size

The data file block group size is specified by the DBLKGP=
parameter of the POWER macro. Too large a value causes
fragmentation of DASD space. Too small a value causes overhead
in positioning printouts. The default value is 10 blocks to the block
group.

If you process large printouts frequently, you should consider
increasing the DBLKGP value. However, because this is the
smallest unit of allocation for the data file, a large value results in
wasted space for each small report or small input card file
processed by POWER. Also, because the DBLK group size is
associated with the DBLK block size, it is important to decrease the
DBLKGP value when the DBLK block size is increased. It is also
important to increase the DBLKGP value when the DBLK block
size is decreased.

No correct value exists for the DBLKGP parameter. The default
of 10 blocks is a good starting point. If you greatly increase the
DBLK block size, you should consider reducing the DBLKGP value.
Most environments do not need to increase the DBLKGP value.
Good results have been seen with values as large as 50 in
environments that process very large spool files.

18.4.2 DBLK Buffer Size

The data file block size is specified via the **DBLK=** parameter of
the POWER macro. Too large a value causes REAL and VIRTUAL
storage problems. Too small a value increases the I/O done by
POWER. Sadly, the default value (typically 2016 bytes) is not large
enough and most VSE users do a great deal of unnecessary POWER
I/O.

The minimum value for the DBLK parameter is 1000 bytes. The
maximum value is 12288 bytes. If you omit this parameter, or
specify a value of zero, then the default value is used. The DBLK
parameter value may only be changed with a POWER coldstart.
When you warmstart POWER, the current DBLK value defined
within the queue file is the value that is used.

A suggested starting value for the DBLK parameter is 4K. If
your environment includes many large spool files, you may wish to

consider increasing the DBLK value further. Values as high as 12K have been found to be effective in some cases.

18.4.3   DASD Sharing Parameters

If your system is running shared POWER then your major tuning option is the TIME= parameter of the POWER macro. The format of this command is,

```
TIME=(t1,t2,t3)
```

The three parameters each represent a time in seconds. The values specified do not have to be the same for all POWER systems. In fact, you are encouraged to specify different values for different POWER systems to improve the performance of key systems.

t1   The *active* time in seconds. This is the time that POWER is allowed to hold onto the queue file once it has been given access. The value must be between 1 and 99 seconds. The default value is five seconds. Too small a value can cause excessive overhead for long operations. Too large a value causes other systems to wait (on the average, a system will wait for one half of the t1 value of the system owning the queue file).

t2   The idle time in number of seconds. This is the amount of time POWER must wait after giving up control of the queue file before attempting to regain control of it. This value may be specified from 0 to 9 seconds. The default is zero seconds. The strongly suggested value is also 0 seconds. Specify a non-zero value to impose a performance penalty on a low priority VSE system and to ensure that the high priority systems have queue file access.

t3   The *polling time* as a number of seconds. This is the amount of time an inactive POWER waits before reading the shared queue file to see if another system has queued work to it. Specify a value from 1 to 999 seconds. The default value is 60 seconds. On the average, an idle system will wait for one-half of the t3 time before detecting a job. Note that this value only has an effect when the new job is added by another POWER.

Your POWER will immediately detect work placed in the queue by itself. It only waits for work queued by other POWER systems.

18.4.4 GETVIS Size

POWER makes extensive use of GETVIS space. When inadequate space is available, POWER waits. The GETVIS console command can be used to view the status of the GETVIS area in your POWER partition. The POWER PDISPLAY STATUS command may be used to determine the current amount of used and free GETVIS storage.

18.4.5 POWER Autostart Parameters

The execution of POWER may be followed by a series of commands used to automatically define and startup the static partitions, define real spooled devices, and initialize the dynamic partition environment. These are called the POWER *Autostart Parameters*. The available commands are listed in Figure 18.4. Refer to POWER manuals for additional information.

```
DEFINE     defines additional JECL output operands
FORMAT     determines if POWER DASD is to be formatted
PRINTERS   define virtual printers to be spooled
PUNCHES    defines virtual punches to be spooled
READER     defines virtual reader to be spooled
SET        determines control values
Commands   General POWER commands such as PSTART, PLOAD,
           PVARY, PACT may be placed in AUTOSTART deck.
```

Figure 18.4 POWER Autostart Parameters

18.5 AR commands

In this section we look at the console commands related to tuning. These are also called Attention Routine commands.

18.5.1   GETVIS

The *GETVIS partid* command is used to display the status of the
GETVIS area for the *partid* partition. Thus the GETVIS F7
command will display the status of the F7 GETVIS area.
Figure 18.5 below is an example of the output from this command.

```
GETVIS USAGE OF F7
   AREA SIZE : 2,012 K-BYTES    HIGH WATER MARK   :  1,580 K-BYTES
   ALLOCATED : 1,122 K-BYTES    LARGEST FREE AREA :    740 K-BYTES
```

Figure 18.5 GETVIS F7 Command Output

18.5.2   MAP

The AR MAP command displays a map of all partitions along with
the supervisor areas. An example of the output of the MAP
command is provided in Figure 18.6. V-SIZE is the current SIZE
value (the size of the problem program area). Note that the V-SIZE
shown is taken from the last JCC SIZE command and is not the
value currently in effect from an EXEC command SIZE= parameter.
The GETVIS size shown is the actual GETVIS area size. Add
V-SIZE and GETVIS together for the total partition allocation.

18.5.3   STATUS

The STATUS command is used to display the status of all VSE
tasks. The partition ID, task ID, and wait status code are
displayed. When a task is waiting on I/O, the device being waited
on is also displayed. An example of the output of the STATUS
command is provided in Figure 18.7. Additional forms of this
command include STATUS pp (display the status of partition pp),
STATUS cuu (status of a device), and STATUS SCHIB (status of a
subchannel).

```
SPACE  AREA PRTY  V-SIZE GETVIS V-ADDR R-SIZE R-ADDR NAME
  S    SUP          448K            0   352K      0  $$A$SUP3
  1    BG  V    7    256K  3840K 70000   32K  70000  NO NAME
  1    UNUSED        3840K        470000
  2    F2  V    5   5120K  1024K 70000   256K 98000  CICSMROA
  2    UNUSED        1792K        670000
  3    F6  V    7    512K  1536K 70000   128K 182000 SQLMON
  3    UNUSED        5888K        270000
  4    F5  V    6    512K  1536K 70000   128K 162000 EVSEI57
  4    UNUSED        5888K        270000
  5    F7  V    3    512K  1536K 70000   256K 1A2000 JCLSCHED
  5    F9  V    7    512K  1472K 270000    0K        EXPCDEV
  5    UNUSED        3904K        460000
  6    F8  V    7    512K   512K 70000   128K 1E2000 NO NAME
  6    UNUSED        6912K        170000
  7    F4  V    7    512K  5632K 70000   128K 142000 CICSMROB
  7    UNUSED        1792K        670000
  9    FA  V    7    512K  1472K 70000    0K         NO NAME
  9    FB  V    7    512K  3072K 260000  128K 202000 SQL310
  9    UNUSED        2368K        5E0000
  S    F3  V    2    300K  2772K 830000  424K D8000  VTAMSTRT
  S    F1  V    1    480K   544K B30000  128K 78000  IPWPOWER
  S    SVA          2068K  1836K C30000  8096K
       AVAIL        1408K                6200K
       TOTAL       40960K               16384K
```

Figure 18.6 MAP Command Output

18.5.4   TPBAL

The TPBAL command is used to change the status of the TP balancing function of VSE. This function is used to delay processing for designated low priority partitions. The format of the command is TPBAL n where "n" specifies the number of partitions that are to be delayed. The TPBAL value is initially zero.

The current TPBAL value may be displayed by issuing the TPBAL command with no argument. If TPBAL is not currently in effect, then the output of this command will be TPBAL NONE, else the current number of partitions that could be de-activated will be displayed.

The TPBAL command should be issued with care. Delayed partitions will experience a substantial reduction in throughput. The purpose of TPBAL is to favor the execution of a few preferred partitions, at the expense of batch processing. You should take care that the CICS partition and partitions needed to support CICS are not affected. For example, you do not wish to include VTAM nor SQL/DS partitions in the range affected by TPBAL, if these partitions are needed for CICS throughput. You should experiment with TPBAL, adding one batch partition at a time. Monitor the effect of each parameter change *under load* before attempting to

```
S01 -F1      WAITING FOR I/O, ECB, OR TECB
S03 -F1      WAITING FOR I/O, ECB, OR TECB
S02 -F1      WAITING FOR I/O, ECB, OR TECB
S04 -F1      WAITING FOR I/O, ECB, OR TECB
F1           WAITING FOR I/O, ECB, OR TECB
F2           WAITING FOR OPERATORS RESPONSE
F3           WAITING FOR I/O, ECB, OR TECB
F4           WAITING FOR I/O, ECB, OR TECB
S16 -F5      WAITING FOR I/O ON DEVICE=121
F5           WAITING FOR I/O, ECB, OR TECB
F6           WAITING FOR I/O, ECB, OR TECB
S11 -F7      WAITING FOR I/O ON DEVICE=550
S12 -F7      READY TO RUN
F7           WAITING FOR OPERATORS RESPONSE
F8           READY TO RUN                SEIZED SYSTEM
S06 -F9      WAITING FOR I/O, ECB, OR TECB
S07 -F9      WAITING FOR I/O, ECB, OR TECB
S08 -F9      WAITING FOR I/O, ECB, OR TECB
F9           WAITING FOR I/O, ECB, OR TECB
FA           WAITING FOR I/O, ECB, OR TECB
FB           WAITING FOR I/O, ECB, OR TECB
```

Figure 18.7 STATUS Command Output

add additional batch partitions to TPBAL. Again, TPBAL is used to deliberately impact batch performance to provide addition resources for an online partition.

Appendix A: VSE Performance Tools

This chapter briefly describes some of the performance tools that are available for VSE systems. Performance monitors and products that improve VSE performance are both described. Products are listed in alpha sequence. This is not intended to be a complete list, many other fine products are also available from a variety of suppliers.

A.1 BIM VIO

The BIM VIO product improves the performance of VSE disk I/O processing by using the VIO area for simulated DASD. It is marketed by B.I. Moyle.

A.2 VM Magic

VM Magic is a product that adds caching capabilities to VM. The product modifies VM to allow caching of selected DASD volumes. VM Magic can improve the performance of a VSE system in the same fashion as a hardware caching control unit. The savings can be larger than those for the hardware control unit because of the reduced elapsed time compared to the real hardware (assuming that the CPU resources needed by the product are available). VM Magic can also be used to emulate FBA DASD on CKD DASD. You must have sufficient available real memory to run VM Magic else VM (and VSE) performance can be impacted by increased paging.

355

A.3 Explore for VSE

Explore for VSE is a VSE performance monitor marketed by Goal Systems. It offers realtime displays, online historical flashback, and batch historical reporting. Explore will analyze performance, report on exceptions, and suggest areas for improvement. An extensive PC graphics presentation interface is also included with this product.

A.4 Extend for VSE

Extend for VSE is marketed by Goal Systems. It improves VSE performance by replacing the VSE lock manager, and by caching label information. It functions under VM with no additional hardware. It also will perform the same functions without VM, but it requires and uses a CTCA in the standalone environment.

A.5 TMON

TMON is a CICS performance monitor marketed by Landmark Systems. TMON offers realtime and batch reporting capabilities. Exception reporting is also implemented.

A.6 VSE/PT

VSE/PT is the IBM performance monitor. It is not available for VSE/ESA. IBM markets the Explore performance monitor for VSE/ESA systems.

Appendix B: Move Mode Recommendations

This appendix lists the transients that should be made resident within the SVA in move mode, plus additional phases that should be listed in the SDL so their directory entries are resident. The IBM supplied SET SDL procedure contains many of these transients, but you should verify that your system includes all of the following list. Most performance monitors and a number of other OEM products include a facility to track the number of times each transient is loaded in your environment. If you have access to such a tool, you should use it to adjust the following list.

Resident Directory Entries

$JOBCTLA
$JOBCTLD
$JOBCTLE
$JOBCTLG
$JOBCTLN
$JOBCTL5

CRT Transients

$$BOCRTA,MOVE
$$BOCRTC,MOVE
$$BOCRTG,MOVE
$$BOCRTH,MOVE
$$BOCRTK,MOVE
$$BOCRTZ,MOVE

Attention Routine

$$BATTNA,MOVE
$$BATTN2,MOVE

LIOCS Transients

$$BOCPMF,MOVE
$$BOESTV,MOVE
$$BOKUL1,MOVE
$$BOMLTA,MOVE
$$BOMSVA,MOVE
$$BOMSV2,MOVE
$$BOPEN,MOVE
$$BOPEN1,MOVE
$$BOPEN2,MOVE
$$BOPEN4,MOVE
$$BOPLBL,MOVE
$$BOPENR,MOVE
$$BOPNR2,MOVE
$$BOPNR3,MOVE
$$BOUR01,MOVE
$$BOSDC1,MOVE
$$BOSFBL,MOVE
$$BOSVLT,MOVE
$$BOCP03,MOVE
$$BCLOSE,MOVE
$$BCLOS2,MOVE
$$BCLOS5,MOVE
$$BCLRPS,MOVE
$$BSGMNT,MOVE

VSAM Transients

$$BCVS02,MOVE
$$BCVSAM,MOVE
$$BOVSAM,MOVE
$$BACLOS,MOVE
$$BOSV01,MOVE
$$BOSMMW,MOVE
$$BOSMXT,MOVE

Bibliography

In this bibliography we will list various books and IBM manuals that were used as technical sources, or that you may wish to consider for additional information. The manuals and books are listed under main subject areas used within this book. Where an IBM manual is referenced, the manual title is followed by the IBM order number (within parenthesis). The IBM manual numbers listed here are generally those applicable to VSE/ESA Version 1 systems. The manuals for the older VSE/SP systems have different order numbers and many have different titles. SC33-6177 VSE/SP Planning is a good guide to the manuals for these earlier releases.

All of the IBM manuals are available in hardcopy form, and many of them are supplied on a single CD ROM in BookManager Read format. The VSE/ESA CD ROM is an excellent delivery vehicle, and the IBM Book Manager Read product offers powerful search and retrieval capabilities. The search engine was instrumental in finding some of the more obscure items presented in this book. In several cases performance items that were not listed in any table of contents or index were located in a few seconds. Try the Book Manager Read product if you have not yet encountered it.

CICS

CICS: A Practical Guide to System Fine Tuning by S. Piggott (ISBN 0-07-050054-1).

CICS/VSE: CICS-Supplied Transactions (SC33-0710).

CICS/VSE: Performance Guide (SC33-0703).

CICS/VSE: System Programming Reference (SC33-0711).

Hardware

DASD: IBM's Direct Access Storage Devices by Robert Johnson and R. Daniel Johnson (ISBN 0-07-032674-6).

IBM Mainframes: Architecture and Design (ISBN 0-07-050686-8).

ICCF (VSE/ICCF)

VSE/ICCF: Administration and Operation (SC33-6562).

POWER (VSE/POWER)

IBM VSE/POWER: Administration and Operation (SC33-6571).

IBM VSE/POWER: Networking (SC33-6573).

SQL/DS

SQL/Data System: System Administration for VSE (GH09-8096).

SQL/DS Performance Analysis and Tuning Cookbook (GG24-3429).

DB2/SQL: A Professional Programmers Guide by Tim Martyn and Tim Hartley (ISBN 0-07-040666-9).

SQL/DS Performance: Techniques for Improvement by Dov Gilor.

VM

VM and CMS Performance and Fine Tuning by Jeffrey Savit (ISBN 0-07-054972-9).

VSAM (VSE/VSAM)

IBM VSE/VSAM: Programmer's Reference (SC33-6535).

VSAM: Concepts, Programming, and Design by J. Ranade and Hirday Ranade (ISBN 0-672-22546-8).

VSAM: Performance, Design, and Fine Tuning by J. Ranade (ISBN 0-07-051245-0).

VSE General

VSE/ESA: Evolution and Support of ESA/390 (GC33-6502).

VSE/ESA: Operation (SC33-6506).

VSE/ESA: System Utilities (SC33-6517).

VTAM (ACF/VTAM)

IBM VSE/ESA: Networking Support (SC33-6508).

Planning and Reference for Netview, NCP, and VTAM (SC31-6092).

SNA: Architecture, Protocols, and Implementation by A. Kapoor (ISBN 0-07-033727).

VTAM Network Implementation Guide (SC31-6404).

VTAM Resource Definition Reference (SC31-6412).

Glossary

This glossary defines the technical terms used in this book. The definitions are based on the IBM manual *Vocabulary for Data Processing, Telecommunications, and Office Systems, GC20-1699* and on additional information from a number of VSE specific manuals.

Address Space
An address space is a view of virtual storage. It is comprised of a shared and a private portion. The shared portion of an address space is common to all other address spaces. The private portion of an address space is unique to the one view of storage.

APPC Advanced Peer to Peer Communications
APPC implements the VTAM LU 6.2 protocol. It is commonly used for communications with PCs and LANs, and is becoming more frequently used for mainframe to mainframe communications.

AR Attention Routine
AR is the processor for all operator console commands. AR is the lowest priority VSE system task. The commands processed by AR include CANCEL, MAP, and PRTY.

ARISQLDS
The SQL/DS database services main program. ARISQLDS is executed within the SQL/DS partition.

ASI Automatic System Initialization
The term ASI is normally applied to the set of procedure library members used to automate the VSE IPL. The first procedure is named $ASIPROC, the subsequent procedures include the CPU ID and partition dependent procedures.

BG
The BG partition is the "background" partition of VSE. It is the first static partition, and is automatically started at IPL time. It is used to define the other static partitions plus start POWER.

CA Control Area
A control area is a unit of VSAM DASD space allocation. The maximum size of a CA is a cylinder. The minimum size of a CA on CKD DASD is a track.

CCB Channel Command Block
The CCB is the parameter block for the VSE start I/O (SVC 0) request. The CCB names the logical unit and addresses the channel program for an I/O request.

CCW Channel Control Word
CCWs are I/O instructions executed by the channels. A channel program is comprised of one or more CCWs and is used to direct I/O requests. In VSE, the CCB contains the address of the first CCW of the channel program.

CI Control Interval
A control interval is a unit of VSAM data transfer. It is a VSAM buffer. It is also a VSAM unit of virtual storage allocation. A CI is similar to a logical block for other access methods. A VSAM CI may comprise one or more physical blocks on disk.

CICS Customer Information Control System
CICS is a transaction processing system supported by VSE and MVS. It is part of the SAA support of VSE. Each CICS system occupies a single VSE partition. This may be a dynamic partition.

DSA Dynamic Storage Area
The CICS DSA is the area used to load programs, and maps, and to satisfy requests for transaction storage. It is the portion of the program area not required to initialize CICS.

Dynamic Partition
The new partitions added by VSE/ESA are called dynamic partitions. This term is used because these partitions are created "dynamically" as needed by POWER, and occupy no resources when they are no longer needed. The old partitions are termed static partitions because they are always present in the supervisor tables whether or not they are allocated.

ECB Event Control Block
ECBs are used by tasks to wait for event completion, usually in a multitasking environment. A task can wait on an ECB, a CCB, or an XECB.

ESA Enterprise System Architecture
The term ESA refers to Enterprise System Architecture. It is the new hardware support in VSE/ESA. VSE/ESA was delivered in late 1990. It extended real and virtual storage support for VSE, added support for XA/ESA mode execution of the operating system, and implemented the XA I/O subsystem. VSE/ESA replaces the older VSE/SP.

ESCON Enterprise System Connection
The term ESCON is new to the System/390 architecture. It is an acronym for Enterprise System Architecture and refers to the new I/O channels implemented on S/390 processors. It uses high-speed serial channels that exploit fiber-optic technology.

ESDS Entry Sequenced DataSet.
An ESDS is a type of VSAM file. Records within an ESDS are accessed via Relative Byte Address (RBA).

Foreground Partition
The foreground partitions are the static partitions F1-F9, FA, and FB that are defined via the ALLOC statement, and occupy one of the static address spaces.

GETVIS
GETVIS is VSE dynamically allocated storage, similar to MVS GETMAIN storage. GETVIS storage is available at the partition level (controlled via SIZE command or parameter) and at the system level (controlled via IPL SYS parameter).

IPL Initial Program Load
The IPL process initializes the VSE system by resetting memory, loading the VSE supervisor, and defining tables used to control the system. The ASI members control the IPL process.

JCC Job Control Command
A job control record with no "//" (slash slash) in column one is a job control command. The ALLOC and the SIZE commands are examples of JCC.

JCS Job Control Statement
A job control record with "//" (slash slash) in column one is a job control statement. The JOB statement and DLBL statement are JCS examples.

KSDS Key Sequenced DataSet
A KSDS is a type of VSAM file. Each record within a KSDS contains a key at a fixed offset, and for a fixed length within each record. The key is used for record retrieval. VSAM manages an index for a KSDS, which is used to translate the key into an RBA.

LAN Local Area Network
A Local Area Network is a group of PCs connected via a communications channel where direct data sharing is supported. Data present on a *file server* may be accessed as though it was on a local disk drive by specifying the correct drive letter.

LIBR
The librarian batch utility is named LIBR. This utility is used to defined, alter, and delete; libraries, sublibraries, and members.

LRU Least Recently Used
An algorithm used to manage buffers such that the oldest buffer is reused before recently used buffers are reused. VSE paging, CICS DSA storage, and VSAM LSR are examples of functions where LRU algorithms are employed.

LUW Logical Unit of Work
For SQL/DS, an LUW is used to track the status of a request as long as buffers and locks are associated with the request. A COMMIT WORK or a ROLLBACK WORK statement ends an LUW.

Maintask
In VSE, the maintask is the task created at the time a partition is allocated by the operating system. A program invoked via the EXEC statement runs as the VSE maintask.

NCP Network Control Program
The NCP is the VTAM software running within the communications controller. VTAM involves software running on the mainframe, and within the communications controller.

Partition
In VSE, a partition is an allocation of virtual storage. The static partitions are BG, F1-F9, plus FA and FB and are allocated via ALLOC statements. The dynamic partitions are managed by POWER and have names based upon their POWER class plus a number.

POWER
POWER is the VSE spooling system. It is an integral part of any VSE/ESA system as POWER manages the dynamic partitions.

Private Area
The Private Area is that part of an address space not addressable from other address spaces. It is that portion of the address range not included in the Shared Area.

Program Area
The program area is the portion of the partition where the EXEC statement program is loaded. It is specified via the SIZE statement or the SIZE option of the EXEC statement.

PRTY
The PRTY command is used to specify the priority of the VSE static and dynamic partitions.

RBA Relative Byte Address
AN RBA is a four-byte integer value used by VSAM to designate the offset in bytes into a file for a specific record. RBAs are used by VSAM for all file accesses.

Real Storage

The term Real Storage refers to physical processor memory. Real memory may be allocated via the ALLOCR statement, and is also automatically allocated as needed for virtual storage via the VSE page manager.

RRDS Relative Record DataSet

An RRDS is a type of VSAM file that is accessed using a relative record number. VSAM internally translates the record number into a Relative Byte Offset (RBA) used to access the record.

SCP Systems Control Program

SCP is an old term that applied when IBM provided basic operating systems at no charge. This term is often still used to refer to the operating system as a whole. The term SCP applies to the basic VSE system as ordered from IBM. It includes the supervisor and support software. The term SCP does not usually include software like CICS, POWER, or VTAM. Nor does it includes utilities such as LIBR and MSHP that are executed within partitions.

SDL Systems Directory List

The SDL contains storage resident directory entries. SDL entries exist for all SVA and MOVE mode phases, and may be optionally created for selected IJSYSRS.SYSLIB (SYSRES) members to eliminate the directory search and improve program fetch performance.

Shared Area

The Shared Area is the portion of an address space that is commonly accessible in all address spaces. In VSE/ESA, the supervisor and SVA are always in the Shared Area. Static partitions may optionally be defined within the Shared Area.

SPSIZE

This is an IPL time parameter used to specify the size of the shared partition area. The sum of the sizes of all allocated shared partitions must be less than or equal to the SPSIZE value.

SQL

The Structured Query Language used to access a SQL/DS database. SQL statements are issued by applications programs. They are processed by ARISQLDS (the SQL/DS main program).

SQL/DS
The VSE relational database. The ARISQLDS main program is executed to startup VSE SQL/DS.

SSCH Start SubCHannel
The hardware instruction used to schedule an XA mode I/O request. SSCH simply queues the I/O request for processing by the I/O subsystem.

Start I/O Fast (SIOF)
A feature of the I/O hardware where the operating system can start an I/O request without waiting for initiation status. If the device is busy, the request can be automatically queued within the channel without further software involvement.

Static Partition
A static partition is one of the twelve partitions that is defined via the ALLOC statement. The term "Static Partition" was created in VSE/ESA to differentiate the old fixed partitions from the new dynamic partitions. Static partitions occupy virtual storage address space for as long as they are allocated. The Job Control ALLOC command is used to manage static partitions, POWER tables and console commands are used to manage the dynamic partitions.

Subchannel
XA mode channels are subdivided into subchannels. Each addressable unit on an XA channel is referred to as a separate subchannel.

Subtask
A VSE subtask is any task attached by a partition's maintask, or by another subtask. Subtasks always have a higher priority than the maintask.

SVA Shared Virtual Area
The Shared Virtual Area in VSE contains read only programs. The SVA is similar to the MVS LPA. The SVA is allocated at IPL time via the SYS parameter. Programs are loaded into the SVA via your SET SDL phasename, SVA statements.

SVC Supervisor Call
An SVC is a special machine instruction used to communicate service requests from applications to the operating system. In VSE, SVCs are the only way applications communicate with the supervisor.

Task
A task is a logical unit of execution. In VSE, each partition contains a minimum of a main task that is created when the partition is defined. A program invoked via the EXEC statement runs as the main task of a partition. Tasks may attach other tasks. Tasks which are attached by other tasks are called subtasks.

TCB
A Task Control Block is used as supervisor workspace for each VSE task. The TCB is a control block of about 500 bytes assembled into the supervisor for the static partitions, and dynamically allocated from System GETVIS for dynamic partitions. The TCB is in fetch protected key 0 storage.

TIB
A Task Information Block is used to track the dispatching status of each VSE task. The TIB is a small control block assembled into the supervisor for the static partitions, and dynamically allocated from System GETVIS for dynamic partitions. The TIB is in fetch protected key 0 storage.

VIO
The Virtual I/O area is page dataset space used for storage of the POWER Queue file and for linkage editor work. In a MODE=VM system, the entire VIO area occupies VSE storage addresses. In a non-VM system, only a buffer area occupies VSE virtual addresses. This area is buffered in real storage by the VSE page manager.

Virtual Storage
The term Virtual Storage is used to describe the memory of a simulated computer system. This virtual memory can exceed the amount of real storage available on the computer. The architectural limitation for virtual memory is determined by the size of the processor's address register. Thus, 370 systems in 24-bit mode support up to 16 megabytes of virtual storage. And ESA

systems in 31 bit mode support up to two billion bytes of virtual storage.

VPOOL
VPOOL refers to buffer space reserved for VIO area accesses. Under VM, the VPOOL area is actually the same as the VIO area.

VSIZE
An IPL time parameter used to specify the total amount of virtual storage required by a VSE system. This value includes the System GETVIS area, SVA, supervisor area, and all partition space.

VSAM Virtual Storage Access Method
VSAM is a file management system used by MVS and VSE. In VSE, VSAM is also the basis for SAM managed VSAM, which is a basic disk space manager provided by IBM. VSE libraries are often allocated within VSAM space. VSAM file tuning is a major component of tuning any VSE application.

VSE Virtual Storage Extended
The term *VSE* has been used to refer to the DOS operating system for over ten years. In this book, it is used to refer generically to either VSE/SP or VSE/ESA.

VTAM Virtual Telecommunication Access Method
VTAM is the standard remote and local terminal manager for VSE. VTAM requires a partition. (It may not be run in a dynamic partition.) A few VSE customers still use the old BTAM (Basic Telecommunications Access Method).

Wait
A VSE task is in a *wait* state when it is not able to run until an event is completed, or cannot run because a needed resource is occupied by other tasks. The VSE dispatcher determines what tasks can run, and what tasks are waiting. WAIT is also a VSE supervisor request (SVC 7) used to wait for event completion.

XA Extended Architecture
The term XA was used for the original 31 bit and enhanced I/O support originally added for MVS use in the early 1980s. ESA further extended the flexibility of accessing the 31-bit address space. VSE/ESA supports XA and ESA hardware.

Index

ABOUT THE AUTHOR

Bill Merrow has more than 25 years of computer experience, particularly in the DOS and VSE environments. He is responsible for research and development of VSE advanced projects for Legent, a major producer of operating systems software. Bill has taught classes on VSE to over 2000 people. He is also an active GUIDE member in the VSE group.